Overcoming Obsessive Compulsive
Disorder

The aim of the **Overcoming** series is to enable people with a range of common problems and disorders to take control of their own recovery program. Each title, with its specially tailored program, is devised by a practising clinician using the latest techniques of cognitive behavioral therapy – techniques which have been shown to be highly effective in changing the way people think about themselves and their problems.

The series was initiated in 1993 by Peter Cooper, Professor of Psychology at Reading University and Research Fellow at the University of Cambridge in the UK whose original volume on overcoming Bulimia nervosa and binge-eating continues to help many people in the USA, the UK, and Europe.

All titles in the series are available by mail order.
Please see the order form at the back of this book.

OVERCOMING
OBSESSIVE
COMPULSIVE
DISORDER

A *self-help guide using*
Cognitive Behavioral Techniques

David Veale and Rob Willson

ROBINSON
London

Constable & Robinson Ltd
3 The Lanchesters
162 Fulham Palace Road
London W6 9ER
www.constablerobinson.com

First published in the UK by Robinson,
an imprint of Constable & Robinson Ltd 2005

A copy of the British Library Cataloguing in Publication
Data for this title is available from the British Library.

ISBN 978-1-84529-936-8

4 6 8 10 9 7 5

Important Note
This book is not intended as a substitute for medical advice or treatment.
Any person with a condition requiring medical attention should consult
a qualified medical practitioner or suitable therapist.

Printed and bound in the EU.

Contents

Contents

Acknowledgments

We would like to acknowledge a host of individuals who have inspired or taught us and who have done most of the psychological research into obsessive compulsive disorder. This book is not referenced, but most of the research findings are taken from the publications of Professors Paul Salkovskis, Isaac Marks, Jack Rachman, Mark Freeston, Randy Frost, Edna Foa, Gail Steketee, Padmal de Silva, as well as the work of other researchers too numerous to mention. We would especially like to thank Cynthia Turner, who co-authored the chapters on children and adolescents, and on families; Isobel Heyman and Lynn Jones, for their helpful comments on children and adolescents; and Elizabeth Nicholson, for her pre-editing. Finally, we thank all our patients with obsessive compulsive disorder from whom we have learned and whose everyday struggle we recognize.

Foreword

Obsessive Compulsive Disorder is a solvable problem, and the solution is in your hands.

As someone working on a daily basis with Obsessive-Compulsive Disorder (OCD), I know that sufferers, caregivers, and professionals need all the help that they can get, and here it is! This is the book which I have long hoped someone would write to help all of us. It presents an approach closely based on Cognitive Behavior Therapy (CBT), which is the only psychological treatment that has been shown to be effective in OCD. You will find this book clear, practical, focused, and helpful. It will be extremely useful both for those who suffer from OCD and those who care for them. How will it help? At the very least, it will help to improve understanding of this seemingly complicated problem by helping you to understand what OCD is and how it works. As the reader will find out, OCD has its roots in normal thinking. The sufferer is not crazy, bad, or dangerous to know, but is someone who has been trapped by a particular pattern of thinking and reacting. The book will help you identify the vicious circles which form the basis of the persistence of OCD. For many, a better understanding of how OCD works will allow them to progress to a better understanding of how to deal with it. In this book they will find detailed help with how to begin to do that. For some this book may even show the way to recovery and take them down that path. If it doesn't take you that far, it will at least provide you with a useful map for that journey. And it will help you understand your enemy; your enemy is OCD.

Surely people know that OCD is the problem? Often not. We now know from research that it takes on average seven years from the point where obsessional problems start to interfere with the person's life to the diagnosis being made. And that is just the beginning of trying to get the right treatment. Surely then it is clear what the problem is? Again, often not. It is in the nature of the problem that OCD makes you think that the problem is something else. You feel dirty, unsure, or responsible for harm, and it seems like these feelings reflect the reality. These feelings are not true. If you are a washer, your problem is not dirt. If you are a checker, your problem is not uncertainty. If you fear that you will harm others, your problem is not loss of control. And so on. The problem is *worry* about being contaminated, causing harm, of not being careful enough. In fact, the person suffering from OCD cares so much that they try to deal with the worry about slight risks in ways which are counter-productive and damaging, and which increase and exaggerate their perception of the risk itself. The fears triggered by OCD make the sufferer try too hard to be clean, to be sure, to keep in control and so on. The solution *becomes* the problem as the person feels unable to ignore their thoughts and doubts because it seems to them to be too risky. It seems paradoxical (but isn't) that OCD is a problem particularly likely to be suffered by people who are especially sensitive or caring. The loving mother has thoughts of harming her children, the person who values cleanliness is tortured by the idea that they are spreading contamination, the careful person fears that they are being careless, the religious person is tortured by apparently blasphemous thoughts and so on. The harder the person with OCD tries to deal with the obsessional ideas the more distressed they become.

How can the solution become the problem and the sufferer not be aware of it? The answer lies in the nature of OCD. Obsessive Compulsive Disorder is many things, none of them good. But it does not always seem that way from the inside.

Foreword

When it starts, it often masquerades as a friend or helper; 'if only you can do a little more, then everything will be fine'; 'it helps me stop worrying'. These ideas are true only in the short term and early in the problem. As time goes on, it begins to be clear that the promises offered by OCD concealed a trap. A quick check becomes several checks, then becomes hours of checking and finally endless checking.

The reality is that OCD is best thought of as being like a bully or blackmailer, progressively demanding and taking more and more, finally forcing the sufferer to obey its every whim, often to the point of total humiliation and subjugation. For some, it can take them to the point of total desperation where life no longer seems worth living. Whilst most sufferers know how distressing it can be, what is less obvious is the way in which OCD acts like the worst kind of manipulative compulsive liar and cheat. It promises relief if you do things 'just one more time', avoid the next situation and so on. It seems as if resistance is futile, and that only by giving in does the person have any hope of peace of mind or happiness. Nothing could be further from the truth; no one, however hard they tried, has ever become happy through obsessional behavior.

It is very hard indeed for sufferers to gain the perspective they need to break out of the vicious circle of obsessional worry leading to compulsive behaviors (trying too hard to combat their worries through washing, checking, and neutralizing). An outside perspective is vital if the person is to be able to choose to change. In this book, David and Rob have provided some of the insights which can help the person begin to see OCD for what it really is. So will it be enough? Probably not for some, maybe a little for others, but it is a really good start. OCD is allergic to being understood. It seems likely that there are many people in the community who deal with their OCD without professional help. I hope that this book will increase the number of people seeking the advice of professionals.

The fact that some find ways of helping themselves does not mean that everyone can. People suffering from OCD are used to being told that they should 'pull themselves together'. Good advice, but pretty pointless by itself. There is nothing that a sufferer wants to do more than pull themselves together, and they would have done it a long time ago *if only they had known how to*. This book provides both the background and some of the tools which will help the sufferer begin the process of pulling themselves together, and should also help their caregivers to support them in this task.

How about the caregivers? They don't suffer from OCD, but have to cope with it on a daily basis. Which means that the caregiver in fact also suffers from OCD in an indirect way. Rather like that which happens for the OCD sufferer, their involvement can begin in small ways. They can check things for their loved one (the door, the gas, the electric . . .). They can avoid touching the 'contaminated' object or saying particular things. In this way they are gradually recruited into rituals and can end up behaving as if they were obsessional themselves. Caregivers and sufferers need a different way of thinking about (and talking about) the problems they face together. This book should provide the basis for helping them communicate and focus on what really needs to be done. Both need support in this enterprise, and to find ways of supporting each other in the process of change.

Surely a book can't deal with all these problems? Not on its own of course. But every little helps, and this book provides more than a little. We now know that problems such as OCD are so common that it would still not be nearly enough if all those offering psychological treatment were offering cognitive behavior therapy. The reality is that most psychological therapists do not offer CBT and there is not enough expert help to go round. To try to deal with this shortfall, professionals are moving towards what is called 'stepped care'. This means that help can be offered at different levels of intensity and expertise, from self-help groups and books at one end through to specialist units with highly skilled CBT professionals at the other. If the less intensive options don't help or don't help enough, then the next step needs to be taken. This book is a marvellous first step, providing the sufferer and their caregivers with a solid foundation for the work which they need to do on their own or with professional help. If it doesn't 'cure' OCD, that's no surprise, because everybody needs something a little bit different. However, the book will also help you work with a CBT therapist if you are able to find a good one.

In my view, cure is possible and if you have OCD your aim should be to free yourself of your problem, using the strategies described in this book. However, remember that achieving that aim doesn't just involve fighting the OCD. It also involves reclaiming your life and taking up your hopes, goals, and dreams rather than being swamped by your fears. You need to be in touch with and working towards what you are fighting for as well as understanding and dealing with what you have to fight against.

In summary I particularly like this book because it offers people suffering from OCD a fighting chance, and that is good news to me for two reasons. First, I detest OCD and what it does to people who suffer from it and their loved ones. Second, I like and admire the people we try to help fight against OCD, and think that they need and deserve the best possible help in their struggle to overcome this destructive and all-consuming problem. This book will help in that struggle.

Paul Salkovskis
Professor of Clinical Psychology and Applied Science,
Institute of Psychiatry, King's College, London,
and Clinical Director, Maudsley Hospital Centre for Anxiety
Disorder and Trauma.
London, November 2004.

Introduction: Why Cognitive Behavior Therapy?

Over the past two or three decades there has been something of a revolution in the field of psychological treatment. Freud and his followers had a major impact on the way in which psychological therapy was conceptualized, and psychoanalysis and psychodynamic psychotherapy dominated the field for the first half of the twentieth century. So, long-term treatments were offered that were designed to uncover the childhood roots of personal problems – offered, that is, to those who could afford it. There was some attempt by a few health service practitioners with a public conscience to modify this form of treatment (e.g. by offering short-term treatment or group therapy), but the demand for help was so great that this had little impact. Also, although numerous case histories can be found of people who are convinced that psychotherapy did help them, practitioners of this form of therapy showed remarkably little interest in demonstrating that what they were offering their patients was, in fact, helpful.

As a reaction to the exclusivity of psychodynamic therapies and the slender evidence for its usefulness, in the 1950s and 1960s a set of techniques was developed, broadly termed 'behavior therapy'. These techniques shared two basic features. First, they aimed to remove symptoms (such as anxiety) by dealing with those symptoms themselves, rather than their deep-seated underlying historical causes. Second, they were loosely related to what laboratory psychologists were finding out about the mechanisms of learning, and formulated in testable terms. Indeed, practitioners of behavior therapy were committed to using techniques of proven value or, at worst, of a form which could potentially be put to the test. The area where these techniques proved of most value was in the treatment of anxiety disorders, especially specific phobias (such as fear of animals or heights) and agoraphobia, both notoriously difficult to treat using conventional psychotherapies.

After an initial flush of enthusiasm, discontent with behavior therapy grew. There were a number of reasons for this, an important one of which was the fact that behavior therapy did not deal with the internal thoughts that were so obviously central to the distress that patients were experiencing. In this context, the fact that behavior therapy proved so inadequate when it came to the treatment of depression highlighted the need for major revision. In the late 1960s and early 1970s a treatment called 'cognitive therapy' was developed specifically for depression. The pioneer in this enterprise was an American psychiatrist, Professor Aaron T. Beck, who developed a theory of depression that emphasized the importance of people's depressed styles of thinking. He also specified a new form of therapy. It would not be an exaggeration to say that Beck's work changed the nature of psychotherapy, not only for depression, but also for a range of psychological problems.

In recent years, the cognitive techniques introduced by Beck have been merged with techniques developed earlier by behavior therapists to produce a body of theory and practice that has come to be known as 'cognitive behavior therapy'. There are two main reasons why this form of treatment has come to be so important within the field of psychotherapy. First, cognitive therapy for depression, as originally described by Beck and developed by his successors, has been subjected to the strictest scientific testing, and has been found to be a highly successful treatment for a significant proportion of cases of depression. Not only has it proved to be as effective as the best alternative treatments (except in the most severe cases, where medication is required), but some studies suggest that people treated successfully with cognitive behavior therapy are less likely to experience a later recurrence of their depression than people treated successfully with other forms of therapy (such as anti-depressant medication). Second, it has become clear that specific patterns of thinking are associated with a range of psychological problems, and that treatments which deal with these styles of thinking are highly effective. So, specific cognitive behavioral treatments have been developed for anxiety disorders, such as panic disorder, generalized anxiety disorder, specific phobias and social phobia, obsessive compulsive disorder, and hypochondriasis (health anxiety), as well as for other conditions such as compulsive gambling, alcohol and drug addiction, and eating disorders such as bulimia nervosa and binge-eating disorder. Indeed, cognitive behavioral techniques have a wide application beyond the narrow categories of psychological disorders: they have been applied effectively, for example, to help people with low self-esteem and those with marital difficulties.

At any one time, almost 10 per cent of the general population is suffering from depression, and more than 10 per cent has one or other of the anxiety disorders. Many others have a range of psychological problems and personal difficulties. It is of the greatest importance that treatments of proven effectiveness are developed. However, even when the armory of therapies is, as it were, full, there remains a very great problem – namely, that the delivery of treatment is expensive and resources are not infinite or guaranteed to be indefinitely available. Although this shortfall could be met by lots of people helping themselves, commonly the natural inclination to make oneself feel better in the present is to do precisely those things that perpetuate or even exacerbate one's problems. For example, the person with agoraphobia will stay at home to prevent the possibility of an anxiety attack; and the person with bulimia nervosa will avoid eating all potentially fattening foods. Although such strategies might resolve some immediate crisis, they leave the underlying problem intact and provide no real help in dealing with future difficulties.

Introduction

So, there is a twin problem here: although effective treatments have been developed, they are not widely available; and when people try to help themselves they often make matters worse. In recent years the community of cognitive behavior therapists has responded to this situation. What they have done is to take the principles and techniques of specific cognitive behavior therapies for particular problems and represent them in self-help manuals. These manuals specify a systematic program of treatment that the individual sufferer is advised to work through to overcome their difficulties. In this way, cognitive behavioral therapeutic techniques of proven value are being made available on the widest possible basis.

Self-help manuals are never going to replace therapists. Many people will need individual treatment from a qualified therapist. It is also the case that, despite the widespread success of cognitive behavioral therapy, some people will not respond to it and will need one of the other treatments available. Nevertheless, although research on the use of cognitive behavioral self-help manuals is at an early stage, the work done to date indicates that for a very great many people such a manual will prove sufficient for them to overcome their problems without professional help.

Many people suffer silently and secretly for years. Sometimes appropriate help is not forthcoming despite their efforts to find it. Sometimes they feel too ashamed or guilty to reveal their problems to anyone. For many of these people the cognitive behavioral self-help manual will provide a lifeline to recovery and a better future.

Professor Peter Cooper
The University of Reading

PART ONE

Understanding Obsessive Compulsive Disorder

What Is Obsessive Compulsive Disorder?

A Day in the Life of Maureen

My day starts at 6 a.m. I am very tired as I have been obsessing during the night. I get up because if, for some reason, I am delayed by a ritual, I will start to panic that I will be late. I am filled with dread waiting for a trigger to set my mind off. After I have showered, I step out and carefully switch off the tap. I stare at the showerhead with a deep concentration to ensure it is switched off. I repeat the words 'check, check, check'. I brush my teeth at the sink. Once finished, I turn off the cold tap so hard it could snap any day. I now turn both taps in the off direction just to make sure and follow this by placing my hands under both taps to feel there is no water running: 'check, check, check'. I stare at the sink with the utmost concentration until I am convinced the water is absolutely, 100 per cent switched off. I then get a roll of kitchen towel (I go through a pack of four a day). I start by wiping over the shower door to remove any drops of water. I wipe the shower door over and over; I know it looks perfectly clean but I do it just in case I have missed one little mark. I wipe the window-sill, the toothbrush mug (which is never used: I am too frightened of making a mess). I then clean the soap dish holder. I try to put the liquid soap bottle back on the dish so it is straight. No matter how I do it, it just doesn't look straight. Five minutes go by and I still can't do it and I start to panic. I know I am going to be late and then my whole day will be messed up. I finally get the soap into a position which, although it doesn't look quite right, is OK because I have counted to ten. By counting to ten I get comfortable with it in my mind and so can move on to the next thing. I make sure the towels are aligned and check that the floor mats are straight. I then completely clean the sink and taps so that there's not a drop of water or a single mark anywhere.

Before leaving the bathroom I repeat the checking of the shower and sink – both with my hands and with long, concentrated stares – chanting my mantra 'check, check, check', until I feel safe to move out of the door backwards, not turning away until the 'moment feels right'. I now move out of the bathroom backwards; everything is still OK. Then I switch off lights – pausing to check they are all off: 'check, check, check' – until it's safe. If there is any interruption, I have to start again.

I again resort to counting to ten as I slowly shut the door. I must not bang the door as I am sure the vibration will knock something out of place. I am not completely happy with the bathroom, but move on to the bedroom. I then check the curtains, bed, wardrobe, and drawers to see if they are symmetrical, with everything in the right order. All my clothes are hung in groups: long-sleeved tops, dresses, jeans, skirts, T-shirts, more jeans, belts. My clothes are also colour-coordinated from the lightest shade to the darkest shade. I spend hours straightening the clothes before I feel comfortable; I actually wear the same thing nearly every day and wash it each night so I don't mess anything up. My jewellery is arranged and grouped in boxes but I don't even open the boxes any more, let alone take any jewellery out, as I am frightened of moving anything. I have to force myself to leave the room. I really want to go back in and check everything again, but it is getting late, so I don't – but I feel very anxious.

I then go into the kitchen. I avoid using the sink as it is so clean and perfect. I am frightened that if I do use it, I will never get it looking as perfect as it does now. If I have any dirty dishes, I wash them with the tap in the garden. I check the tea, coffee, and sugar jars for any marks. I always touch them using a kitchen towel as my fingers would make marks. I then check the kettle, toaster, bin, hob, oven, and coffee machine. I then wipe the cupboard doors in case there are any marks. I then check inside the cupboards, although no one touches them except me as I don't allow anyone in the kitchen. I have cans of food perfectly arranged with the labels facing outward. I avoid using any of this food. I prefer to take food out of the refrigerator, which is easier as it is all microwaveable. I gave up cooking a long time ago as it was far too messy. I generally don't eat or drink too much anyway, as I could need to use the bathroom when I am out of the house and would not want to use any public toilets. I always travel with a roll of toilet paper just in case.

I then check the table and chairs, which have not been used for over a year. The place mats, salt and pepper pots, and flower vase are all perfectly symmetrically arranged, as are the table and chairs. I have even drawn around the chair legs just in case I knock a chair. The marks are very reassuring. It is just not worth the trouble of using the table and chairs as it would take me hours to get them all back perfectly in place. I scan the table and chairs for five minutes trying to find anything out of place. When I feel they are just right in my mind, I feel a bit less panicky.

Get ready to go out. I put things in my handbag in a precise order: 'phone, cigarettes, lighter, keys, money, credit card'. Repeat these words over and over until I feel comfortable. I call my husband to lock the door and check the stove and kitchen taps – THIS I HATE DOING. However, if I checked these, it would hold me up for another thirty minutes until I felt comfortable. I tell my husband what I have switched on, or opened, and ask him to recheck after I have left. I repeat my 'six-item handbag mantra' in front of him and then leave. Now I am at the front gate. I make sure it is closed behind me, several times. 'Check, check, check.'

At last I am in the car. Have I got my handbag? Look hard and concentrate. 'Check, check, check.' I briefly check the six items in my bag and then drive off. At the end of the street I recheck my bag, while driving – so this check takes a while. I turn off the radio, as otherwise I can't concentrate. 'Check, check, check' until I feel comfortable. Then I recheck my six handbag items while driving – all must be spoken out loud in the right order and right rhythm until I feel comfortable.

I eventually reach the shopping centre and park the car. I then start my car-locking ritual. There are eight things to be checked in precise order and rhythm. 'Passenger window closed, my window closed, handbrake on, car in gear, lights off, ashtray closed, radio off, inside light off'. I may need to repeat this ritual several times until I feel comfortable. I must also touch all the different things as I check them. I am especially hard on the hand-brake, pulling it up further each time I check it. Hence my brake cable frequently gets replaced. I can now get out of the car. I close and lock the door. Begin my five-item 'outside car' ritual. 'My door locked, my window closed, trunk locked, passenger door locked, passenger window closed.' I repeat the words 'check, check, check' at each stage until I feel comfortable. I pray that no one I know arrives in the supermarket parking lot while I am in the midst of these rituals – otherwise I have to smile, pretend to go into the supermarket, and then return when all is clear to start all over again. I flinch when I see some small girls walking across the supermarket parking lot. I get that awful thought inside my head, and anxiety and fear fill my body with dread. I freeze. 'What if I get turned on?' Horrible images bombard my head and uncontrollable feelings fill my body. I think I must be disgusting to have such things go through my head and try really hard to push them out of my mind but I can't make them go away. Eventually I leave to make sure I don't do any-thing awful. I go over and over again about what having these thoughts and feelings must mean. All I can come up with is that I'm sick and disgusting. I can never be sexual, I can never be normal. I am evil and horrible . . .

Maureen has *some* of the symptoms of obsessive compulsive dis-order (OCD), which is a condition characterized by the pres-ence of either obsessions or compulsions (but commonly both). We shall define obsessions and compulsions shortly, but first want to emphasize that if you have OCD *you are not alone*. It is estimated that about 1 in 100 people has the condition to some degree. OCD can be a serious problem, and if left untreated can lead an individual to be isolated and significantly handicapped.

Because of this, the World Health Organization has listed OCD *in the top ten most disabling illnesses in the world.*

Is This Book for You?

Despite its many chapters, this book has a simple central message; OCD is a common problem, individuals with OCD are not crazy, and OCD *can* be overcome. The book is aimed at individuals with OCD and their families or partners. We are both clinicians and researchers with, between us, over twenty-five years' experience in helping patients with OCD. The book will guide you through some tried and tested steps in overcoming OCD.

Our experience is that individuals with OCD may struggle with self-help books for three common reasons. If you do have any of these concerns, please do read on as there is every chance that these fears will be allayed.

The first reason is that they fear that thinking about their problem will make it worse. In fact, the opposite is true. When individuals try to avoid thinking about their OCD and what they can do about it, then the problems persist and over time become more difficult to solve. We shall try to help you develop a good psychological understanding of what is keeping your problem going and therefore of what you can do to stop OCD ruining your life.

Second, they fear that if they learn about other obsessions or compulsions, they will 'pick up' another worry. There is no evidence that you can 'catch' or exacerbate OCD from reading about other obsessions. If you develop a new obsession, then unfortunately it or a different one would probably have arisen in any case. The content of an obsession may fluctuate, but the form remains the same. This book will help you to reach a better understanding of OCD, which you can then apply to your own problems, with or without the help of a therapist.

Third, individuals with OCD believe that because obsessions can vary enormously, no one book will be able to cover all of the different types of obsessions and compulsions. Maureen has just some of the common obsessions and compulsions, but later on we will introduce several other individuals with different types of OCD. Even so, a reader may fear that a book will not directly mention their particular obsession and for that reason will not be directly relevant to them. A related fear is that if one's own obsession is not precisely described, then the information that intrusive thoughts are safe may not apply, because 'mine is different'. This can quickly lead people to conclude that their particular obsession really *does* have a meaning, for example that it will influence the chance of bad events happening, or that it reveals something sinister about them.

OCD can have many features, and it is true that every person with OCD is unique. Every person with OCD whom we have treated has at least one feature that we have not seen before. However, there are overwhelmingly more common features than there are differences among individuals with OCD. When you read the descriptions in this book, whether of OCD itself or of treatment, try to focus on the similarities in the form rather than the differences in the content. Ultimately, one of the most helpful tools in overcoming OCD is to understand the way in which your OCD works – what is maintaining the symptoms and what the *real* problem is. If, as you work through the book, you are not sure whether certain principles apply to you, try to see if there is a way you can find out for yourself by testing that principle out.

What Is an Obsession?

Obsessive, but not OCD

The everyday use of the word 'obsession' often differs from what is meant by obsession in OCD. For example, the media might describe a person who stalks a celebrity as obsessed. Someone who seems to talk non-stop about the new love in their life might be described as 'obsessed' by their friends. A person who spends most of their spare time on a hobby like plane-spotting might be described as having an 'obsession'.

Table 1.1 **Common obsessions in OCD**

Obsession	Prevalence among those with OCD (%)
Fear of contamination from dirt, germs, viruses (e.g. HIV), bodily fluids or excrement, chemicals, sticky substances, or dangerous materials (e.g. asbestos)	38
Doubts about harm occurring (e.g. door locks are not secure)	24
Excessive concern with exactness, order, or symmetry	10
Obsessions with the body or physical symptoms	7
Religious, sacrilegious, or blasphemous thoughts	6
Sexual thoughts or images (e.g. being a pedophile or a homosexual)	6
Urge to hoard useless or worn out possessions (although not always regarded as such by the hoarder)	5
Thoughts or images of violence or aggression (e.g. stabbing your baby)	4
Intrusive thoughts or music	1

However, these 'obsessions' are very different from obsessions in OCD; in fact, it would be preferable, and more accurate, to use the term 'preoccupation' to describe them.

Obsessions in OCD

An obsession, in the world of OCD, is defined as a persistent thought, image, or urge that just pops into your mind and triggers distress. These obsessions are frequent, unwanted, and difficult to control or get rid of. An example of an obsession might be an intrusive thought or image about stabbing your baby. You experience this thought as very upsetting and try to push it out of your mind.

Examples of the most common obsessions are listed in Table 1.1. The percentages refer to one of the largest surveys of OCD, which was carried out by researchers in the USA. A more detailed checklist of obsessions is given in the 'Obsessive

Compulsive Inventory' at the beginning of Appendix 4. Commonly, individuals with OCD have multiple obsessions, although one or two are the more dominant. (Certain 'obsessions' are excluded from OCD, including those about food – e.g. in someone with an eating disorder, who may have a number of rituals around eating – and the excessive dwelling on feelings of guilt that can occur in depression.)

Obsessions in OCD are not, however, simply worries about real-life problems or distressing images, but are associated in the person's mind with the power to prevent harm occurring. Almost everybody experiences some of the intrusive thoughts or urges that people with OCD have (e.g. having the urge to push someone on to a railway track, or worrying that the gas tap on the cooker might still be on). People with OCD, however, not only cannot ignore such thoughts but ascribe a different meaning to them. They believe that they have the pivotal power to cause harm or prevent bad things from happening (e.g., they believe they are dangerous when they think about pushing someone onto a railway track). Consequently, they try too hard to prevent the bad events from happening; and this in turn means that the thoughts become more frequent and distressing so that, over time, they affect all areas of the person's life.

In OCD, then, *obsessions have a special meaning, namely, that harm might occur to oneself, a loved one, or another vulnerable person through what the person with OCD might do or fail to do.* 'Harm' here is interpreted in the broadest sense and includes mental suffering – for example, some people with OCD find it difficult to articulate the meaning of their obsession; they just feel very anxious and may believe that they will go crazy, or that the anxiety will go on for ever and ever and endanger their mental or physical health. Individuals with OCD believe *they can and should prevent harm from occurring,* and this leads to trying too hard in the form of *compulsions* and *avoidance behaviors*. This exaggerated sense of responsibility and the consequent excessive attempts to avoid causing harm are the very essence of OCD; we will explore this in more detail in Chapter 2.

Most people with OCD recognize their obsessions to be senseless or absurd. However, about 5 per cent of individuals with OCD are more convinced by their obsessions. They are said to hold their beliefs as 'over-valued ideas': that is, convictions that are deeply entrenched and based on values that are idealized and impossible to reach. For example, some people value perfectionism in this way; or the importance of possessions, which may be important in the development of obsessional hoarding. This small proportion of people with OCD are more difficult to help, and may require professional treatment.

What Are Compulsions?

Like an obsession, a compulsion also has an everyday meaning. It is defined in the dictionary as an irresistible impulse to act, regardless of the motivation. However, this includes all sorts of behaviors such as shoplifting, binge-eating, sex addiction, or gambling, which are done for immediate gratification, and are different from the compulsions of OCD.

We saw a dramatic example of the inappropriate use of the terms 'obsessive' and 'compulsive' when one of our patients brought in a newspaper article following the death of the British serial killer Dr Harold Shipman. We read the article with mounting concern. Shipman was described as being 'obsessive' over inducing death and controlling the moment of death, and as having a 'compulsive urge to kill repeatedly'. Anyone who read the article would have concluded – as did our alarmed patient – that OCD was extremely dangerous. However, Dr Shipman was a psychopath. He was extremely callous, and enjoyed his control over others and the prospect of harming them. Such a person could not be further removed from an individual with OCD, who is a member of one of the safest groups in the world. Secure hospitals for mental disorders house hundreds of psychopaths like Dr Shipman, but have never admitted anyone with OCD. If you have intrusive thoughts about killing children, you will learn that it is extremely normal to have such thoughts, and that individuals with OCD are trying too hard to stop themselves from harming others. We would be the first to ask a person with OCD to babysit for our children and to concentrate very hard on having thoughts about killing them . . . but more about this shortly.

Another word often used to describe compulsions in OCD is 'ritual'. The two are often synonymous, although rituals usually refer to actions rather than mental acts, whereas compulsions refer to both. However, the term 'ritual' also has a popular meaning. Many people describe themselves as carrying out a 'morning ritual' to help themselves get ready for the day, but this might only mean jogging, showering, coffee, and breakfast. Religious ceremonies often involve rituals, but these are rarely as idiosyncratic as the rituals in OCD. None of these activities is part of OCD because they are not aimed at reducing anxiety and threat in the same way that compulsions are in OCD. More similar, up to a point, is the use of ritual by sportspeople, many of whom try to reduce stress by carrying out little rituals before a big match or shot. However, the sportsperson is not likely to experience extreme anxiety or guilt if they resist carrying out the behavior.

Compulsions in OCD

In OCD, compulsions are acts that you repeat over and over again in response to an obsession. The aim of a compulsion is to reduce the likelihood of harm, so that you can feel 'just right' or 'comfortable', although as we shall see, over time they sometimes stop 'working'. A compulsion can be an act that may be observed by others (e.g. checking that a door is locked until you feel 'just right') or a mental act that cannot be observed by others (e.g. saying a certain phrase in your mind). Mental compulsions are often complex, and may not be repeated over and over again. An example in OCD is saying a special phrase to prevent one's partner from dying. This is referred to as 'neutralizing'. Just as with obsessions, there are many types of compulsion; some of the most common are listed in Table 1.2, which is based on the same survey as Table 1.1. Do not worry

Table 1.2   **Common compulsions in OCD**

Compulsion	Prevalence among those with OCD (%)
Checking (e.g. gas taps)	29
Repeating acts	11
Mental rituals (e.g. special words or prayers repeated in a set manner or counting	11
Ordering or arranging acts	6
Hoarding/collecting	3.5
Counting	2

if yours is not listed in the table, as it contains only a few of the most widespread forms. (A more detailed checklist is given in the 'Obsessive Compulsive Inventory' in Appendix 4.) We never cease to be amazed that in every new patient we are asked to see there is always one symptom or variation on a theme that we have not seen before. Most people with OCD have more than one compulsion, but one or two predominate.

Certain compulsions tend to go with certain obsessions. For example, the most common combination is an obsession about contamination from germs or a bodily fluid that is linked with compulsive washing and cleaning. Another common combination is an obsession about causing harm leading to frequent checking (e.g. of door locks, gas taps, electrical appliances).

Compulsions like washing and checking persist because they seem to 'work' by reducing distress or preventing anxiety. However, over time compulsions do not always go on 'working'. Carrying out a compulsion may briefly reduce anxiety, but in the long term it increases the frequency of the obsession and the urge to perform the compulsion again. A vicious circle is thus maintained (Figure 1.1).

One of the main differences between compulsions and the same actions performed normally by individuals without OCD is the reason for finishing a compulsion. Someone without OCD finishes washing their hands when they can see that their

Figure 1.1   The vicious circle of OCD

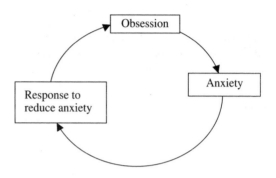

hands are clean. However, someone with an obsessive fear of contamination finishes not when they can see that their hands are clean, but only when they feel 'comfortable' or 'just right'. This same principle can be equally applied to other compulsions. We will look at this in more detail in Chapter 2, as it is one of the main factors that maintain a compulsion and keep the person feeling dirty or unsafe. Successful therapy will involve giving up these criteria, and ending a ritual even when you feel uncomfortable or not right. Once you can do this, over time the feelings of discomfort or jarring will fade.

Not Just Obsessions and Compulsions: Avoidance Behavior

Although avoidance is not part of the definition of OCD, it is an integral part of the disorder. You may be avoiding situations to prevent yourself feeling anxious and having to carry out a compulsion. Thus, when avoidance is high, the frequency of compulsions may be low, and vice versa, like a seesaw.

An example of avoidance behavior is Christine – a woman with a fear of contamination from dirt. If she felt contaminated, she would not want to touch her body or her possessions around her home. So she would not touch toilet seats, door handles, or a wash tap used by others. She would hover over the toilet seat, open doors with her feet or elbows, use her elbow to turn on wash taps. Christine would use rubber gloves to put waste in the bin; she would avoid touching her genitals without a large amount of toilet paper; she would avoid picking items up from the floor, shaking hands with other people, or touching any substance that looked dangerous to her.

As you can see from this example, the content of obsessions, compulsions, and avoidance behavior are closely related. When Christine has to touch something that she normally avoids, then the compulsive washing starts to reduce the potential for harm and discomfort.

Another example of avoidance in OCD is Karina who has an obsessional fear of stabbing her baby. She might *avoid* being alone with her baby and put all knives or sharp objects out of sight, 'just in case' she has the urge to harm her baby. Karina tries to *avoid* thinking about it by distracting herself or suppressing the thought. When this does not work, she may perform various mental compulsions to check and confirm her memory that she has not stabbed her baby; this, in turn, increases her anxiety and the vicious circle continues.

Another form of avoidance occurs when an individual avoids or restricts normal activities like washing or self-care because once they begin they will have to go through a lengthy compulsion. Alternatively, they may avoid or give up responsibility for checking a lock or tap because a relative has agreed to check for them.

Safety-Seeking Behaviors

Another term that we shall be using throughout this book is 'safety-seeking behavior'. This is defined as an action within a feared situation that is performed with the aim of preventing harm and reducing anxiety. So all types of escape from a particular situation, as well as neutralizing and performing compulsions, are forms of safety-seeking behavior. They are all ways of *responding* to an obsession.

A message we will return to over and over again is that *safety-seeking behaviors maintain obsessions*. They prevent you from testing out your fears, allow the obsession to persist, and make the problem worse in the long term. Safety-seeking behaviors are a way of 'trying too hard' to prevent bad things happening; but they don't work, because the solutions then become the problem. We will look at this pattern more closely in Chapter 2, when we go into a psychological understanding of OCD. Needless to say, if you are to overcome your OCD successfully you will need to find a way to give up all your safety-seeking behaviors. This book will help you to do this.

Pure Obsessions

Some people have so called 'pure' obsessions, which are recurrent intrusive thoughts, images, or doubts without any of the compulsions shown in Table 1.2. Examples might be obsessions along the following lines: 'Why do I exist?', 'Am I studying hard enough?', 'What will happen after I die?' If this applies to you, you might be spending hours trying to resolve unanswerable questions. Although you may not be responding by performing a mental compulsion which is repeated over and over again, you probably still *respond* in ways that will be unhelpful, and which can be broadly classified as 'safety-seeking behaviors'. For example, trying to solve a problem that either does not exist or cannot be solved or analyzing a question from different angles. Inevitably this will lead to an increase in doubts and further 'But what if . . .?' type questions. What marks these out as obsessions, rather than just interesting ideas for which there are no definitive answers, is the meaning you apply to such thoughts: for example, 'I have to know the complete answer and feel comfortable before I can do anything else.'

Emotions in OCD

Some individuals with OCD find the emotional consequences of an obsession difficult to articulate. These emotions are often described in terms of 'discomfort' or 'distress'. For most people with OCD who believe that they might be responsible for preventing harm or a catastrophe in the future, the main emotion is of anxiety. This may be severe and sudden, like a panic attack, or may be continuous worry in anticipation of harm in the future. Many also experience an emotion of disgust: either a physical disgust, for example when they think they may have been in touch with a contaminant, such as dog excrement, or a moral disgust for having intrusive thoughts. Others feel extremely ashamed and condemn themselves for having intrusive thoughts of, for example, a sexual or aggressive nature, which they believe they should not have and that others would condemn. Occasionally, a person with OCD believes that he may be responsible for a catastrophic event in the past, and feels intense guilt as a result. Many individuals are also depressed by the consequences of having OCD, for example if it occupies many hours of the day and causes other problems. Others become intensely frustrated and irritable, and OCD seriously affects their relationships with their families and friends. Thus, although in this book we concentrate mainly on the principles of overcoming anxiety and OCD, there are often other secondary symptoms such as shame, guilt, or depression that may also need attention, which we discuss in Chapter 5.

How Much Can OCD Affect a Person's Life?

The severity of OCD differs markedly from one person to another, but each person's distress is very real. A person with OCD can appear to function perfectly normally despite being greatly distressed. This makes it possible for some individuals to hide their OCD – often even from their own family. OCD generally tends to have an impact on all areas of your life – relationships, family life, social life, hobbies, and the ability to work. You can measure the degree to which OCD handicaps your life by completing the Disability Scales in Appendix 4 and then doing the same thing again during and after working through the self-help program set out in this book.

OCD often causes havoc in intimate relationships, and a large number of those with the condition are celibate. For those who do marry or enter long-term partnerships, discord, separation, and divorce are disproportionately common. There are many examples of how OCD might impact on family life. A person with OCD might try to ensure that other family members avoid touching 'contaminated' objects around the house, wash excessively when they have touched something 'contaminated', or leave certain clothes or shoes outside. Another might want other family members to check the door-lock repeatedly, or may constantly be seeking reassurance that nothing bad has happened. There are frequent difficulties taking trips or holidays. Not surprisingly, these kinds of restriction may lead to bursts of anger and growing irritation on the part of other members of the family. Sometimes individuals with OCD may be housebound, eat a very restricted diet, or be unable to prepare their food, change their clothes, or care for themselves. We look at what the caregivers and families of people with OCD can do to help in Chapter 9.

OCD tends to interfere with your ability to follow a hobby or interest or to make normal friendships. It interferes with your ability to study or work, sometimes making it impossible, and at the least putting you at a disadvantage. Statistically, you are more likely to be unemployed if you have OCD. Lost productivity is responsible for about three-quarters of the economic cost of OCD.

It's worth repeating here that OCD is in the *top ten* most handicapping illnesses as calculated by the World Health Organization in terms of lost income and decreased quality of life. Indeed, it is worth pointing this out over and over again, almost chanting it as a mantra, to politicians, health purchasers, doctors, and psychologists until OCD is taken seriously, and more resources are made available for research, treatment, and specialist services. People with OCD do not generally tend to commit suicide or be violent, and this may be one reason why OCD is regarded as a low priority for research and clinical work; and yet someone with OCD can be just as handicapped and distressed as someone with schizophrenia or severe depression. We are certainly *not* suggesting that individuals with OCD should make attempts on their life or be violent; we are just trying to understand why so little attention, relatively speaking, is paid to OCD.

Getting treatment to overcome OCD will improve the quality of your life and give you the opportunity to improve your relationships, your social life, and your ability to study or work. We hope that reading and using this book may take you some way along that path.

How Common Is OCD?

OCD is more common than was once thought. In fact, it is the fourth most common mental disorder after depression, alcohol and substance abuse, and social phobia. A team of researchers working in the late 1980s, who interviewed large numbers of people in their homes, estimated that about 2 in every 100 of the world's population have OCD at some time in their life. However, it is possible that many of these people have a mild form of the disorder that is not too disabling or that the interview technique used may have led to over-diagnosis of OCD. The true frequency of OCD in the community is therefore not known. At the core, however, are at least 1 in every 100 of the adult population who are significantly distressed and handicapped by their OCD, along with about 1 in every 200 children and adolescents.

This frequency is much the same all over the world, although the form of OCD may differ from one culture to another. This is because the content of an obsession is usually what a person does not want to think, or a kind of harm they particularly want to prevent. We are all influenced by current trends in what we see as important. For example, religious obsessions used to be very common but are now less frequent in western cultures. By contrast, contemporary concerns with health and social problems, such as AIDS and child abuse, are increasingly reflected in the obsessions described by individuals with OCD. However, while the content of obsessions and compulsions may vary across individuals, cultures, and periods, the form remains the same.

OCD is generally equally common in men and women, although there are some interesting differences in the symptoms. For example, more women than men have aggressive obsessions and compulsions to do with washing, while men are more likely to have obsessions about numbers, symmetry, or exactness, or sexual obsessions, or to suffer from obsessional slowness. Women are especially at risk during pregnancy and in the postnatal period, probably because of the increased sense of responsibility. Young children with OCD are twice as likely to be boys as to be girls.

At What Age Does OCD Begin?

Different individuals develop OCD at different ages. There is a group who develop OCD from the age of about six years onwards (these are more often boys than girls; we discuss these children more in Chapter 8), and there is another group that starts to develop OCD during adolescence, but the average age of onset is the early twenties. It is slightly earlier for men, who tend to develop OCD in the late teens, than for women, in whom it tends to emerge in the mid-twenties. There is, however, wide variation in the age of onset of OCD: it can occur for the first time in children as young as three and also in the elderly.

In many ways, OCD in children is much the same as in adults, although children often find it difficult to articulate the meaning of their obsession or the feared consequences of not carrying out their compulsion.

Interestingly, it is far less common to develop OCD for the first time at an advanced age. However, there are elderly individuals who have had OCD throughout their lives, but have not yet sought or received effective treatment. Some have had mild OCD for years, finding it possible to contain within a relatively normal life, but have then experienced something significant, such as the death of a spouse or partner, which has led to their OCD becoming much worse and getting beyond their control.

One reason why the level of OCD has been underestimated in the past is that people with OCD are often too afraid or too ashamed to seek help. Often individuals with OCD struggle on by themselves for 10–15 years before they seek professional help. There is a variety of reasons for this reluctance: many individuals with OCD worry that other people will think they are crazy, do not know that their disorder is a recognized condition, or think that they should just be able to pull themselves together. We look at ways of overcoming shame at having OCD in more detail in Chapter 5.

The more OCD is acknowledged, discussed, and treated, the better it will be for all those people with the disorder, who will be able to see that many of their fears and anxieties about it are unfounded. For this reason, it is worth repeating that it is very important to raise the profile of OCD with the general public, politicians, and mental health professionals, so that OCD will not continue indefinitely to be a hidden disorder that is not taken seriously enough. Support your national OCD charities (details of which are found in Appendix 3). We all need to put OCD on the political agenda in order to improve services and raise money for research.

Can Religion Cause OCD?

Most religions contain 'rituals' – prescribed forms of speech, gesture, and action – as part of the normal rites and prayers. OCD occurs in people from all religious backgrounds, and in those who have had no involvement in organized religion. Religion by itself does not cause OCD, but for some individuals, religion may play a role in the content of OCD. In a culture where religion is a dominant part of the usual upbringing, a religious theme may dominate the content of OCD. In other words, if you had been brought up in a different culture, you would probably have developed a different form of OCD. Research has found, too, that more severe OCD tends to be associated with more religiosity and guilt.

Examples of religious obsessions include doubts about the existence of God or religious figures, images of a sexual act with a religious figure, having to have totally 'pure' thoughts during prayer, or blasphemy. Examples of religious compulsions include repetitive praying, making the sign of a cross, or repeatedly apologizing to God. They also often overlap with other obsessions and compulsions such as contamination, checking, or repetition. Sometimes it is difficult to separate normal religious practice from OCD rituals, but the key difference is the function of the behavior.

For example, a young Jewish boy was taught to follow various commandments in his Jewish studies. Although the boy was carrying out a normal religious practice, it was done excessively (taking several hours a day) to the point where it had become disabling and dominated his life. The crucial point was that he believed – contrary to normal practice in his faith – that he was performing the ritual to prevent something bad happening to his family. The practice was excessive because the ritual had to be repeated until he felt comfortable and was certain that he had done it perfectly and shown enough effort to demonstrate that religion was an important part of his life. In short, in his OCD the boy was distorting and exaggerating normal religious practice. He had almost developed a belief in his own God-like power to stop bad things happening to his family. In such circumstances, we usually recommend that the person temporarily drops their religious observance until they have overcome their OCD and can then choose to return to a normal religious practice.

How Does Superstitious Behavior Relate to OCD?

Superstitions are common in various cultures, often linked to magic and astrology. When taken to an extreme, they are an alternative to science or religion, attempting to provide an 'explanation' to establish chains of cause and effect and predict future events. Simple superstition is a very common feature of normal childhood thinking, when we believe that we can make things happen by making a wish, or prevent bad things from happening by a simple action. However, when superstition persists in adults it is generally driven by fear and insecurity; it reduces the feeling of uncertainty in the world and makes us feel more in control of our destiny.

Superstitious rituals in OCD are similar to 'normal' superstitions but tend to be more complex and lengthier; like other compulsions, they become disabling, and can be finished only when the person feels comfortable. A person with OCD will want to repeat the ritual if it is not done in a precise way or at the 'right' time, or if they are not feeling completely comfortable or right. Superstitious rituals are believed to have the function of eliminating or neutralizing bad events that have come to mind. Examples include counting up to a magic number or multiples thereof, repeating specific words or images, stepping in special ways when walking, washing off bad ideas or memories, and touching certain things in a special way or a particular number of times. Superstitions can also lead to the avoidance of certain numbers (e.g. 13, 666, odd numbers), colours, ideas, or words (e.g. the devil) which are associated with bad events.

How Is Hoarding Part of OCD?

Compulsive hoarding is a significant feature of some people with OCD, but in many ways it is different from other more common symptoms such as checking and washing. Some researchers have argued that hoarding represents a separate subtype of OCD or even a separate diagnosis. However, we follow convention in including it in our general survey of OCD. What follows here is a brief overview of what is known about hoarding and the implications for overcoming it.

Hoarding refers to the stockpiling of possessions, which can be useful or helpful in certain situations, for example where one is likely to be cut off from supplies by weather, war, or transport problems. Compulsive hoarding has been defined as the acquisition of and failure to discard a large number of possessions (or, in rare cases, animals), that appear to be either useless or of limited value. These objects may be acquired by excessive or impulsive shopping, or by collecting free items such as newspapers or promotional giveaways, or objects that have been discarded by others. Some individuals may acquire objects by shoplifting. Hoarders develop an emotional attachment to their possessions, so that they become part of the 'self', like a limb. Where a person is suffering from compulsive hoarding, the clutter resulting from this accumulation of objects also causes significant distress or a reduced ability to function. When severe, clutter may prevent cooking, cleaning, moving freely through the house, or even sleeping. It may give rise to poor sanitation and pose a risk for fire or falls, especially in elderly people.

The definition distinguishes compulsive hoarding from the organized collection of objects that are considered interesting or valuable, where the individual collecting them can still function normally. Sometimes there is no clear boundary between compulsive hoarding and having a collection of valuable objects, but usually the distinction is fairly clear-cut.

Hoarding can also be a feature of a person with an obsessive compulsive personality (see the section later in this chapter, 'What Is an Obsessive Compulsive Personality?'). Such individuals may be extremely conscientious, meticulous, and over-attentive to detail, perfectionists, or constantly striving for control. They are often unemotional and find it difficult to be playful. They may have a rigid approach to decision-making and think in very black-and-white terms. They believe in correct solutions and want to eliminate all mistakes and failures. They often have low self-esteem and might compensate by being overachievers. If the perfect course of action cannot be taken, they may procrastinate and avoid making a decision. For such individuals, hoarding may be a way of procrastinating, reflecting a reluctance to throw away clutter 'just in case' the items may be useful. Hoarding can also occur in the context of other psychiatric disorders such as anorexia nervosa and depression.

Hoarding, like OCD, usually starts during the early twenties and increases in severity with age. Extreme problems do not usually occur for another 10–15 years, when the individual is in their mid-thirties or older and the clutter has accumulated. Individuals who hoard tend not to marry, and to live alone. We do not know if this is because no one else can bear the same lifestyle, or if a desire for solitude is characteristic of someone who hoards.

The most important difference between hoarding and other symptoms of OCD is that it responds the least well to treatment, either by medication or through cognitive behavior therapy (CBT: the system underlying this book). As professionals, we are struck by how rare it is for individuals who hoard compulsively to seek help. The most common reason for this is that the person does not view their hoarding as a problem. Although others might see them as unable to function, the individual concerned believes that the inconvenience caused by the clutter is a reasonable sacrifice to be made and that they can adapt their lifestyle. One person's 'clutter' is another person's valued possession, and if the clutter means that it is impossible to invite a friend around for a meal or to stay the night, then this is not viewed as a major problem. Conversely, when the clutter *is* regarded as a problem, it might be viewed as being too big a problem to tackle, and is therefore avoided until a bigger goal arises (e.g. wanting to sell one's home).

For these and other reasons, it is more often outside agencies, such as social services or an environmental health officer who is concerned about a fire hazard, that encourage compulsive hoarders to seek help. Or a partner or family member, unable to tolerate the conditions and perhaps threatening separation, may force their relative to seek help. As a result of being pressured into treatment, motivation to change is often poor, and individuals may drop out from treatment early. Even where they have sought help for themselves, they may do less well in treatment compared with other individuals with OCD receiving CBT. Hoarding does not usually respond to serotonergic medication, which is usually helpful in other individuals with OCD (see Appendix 1). However, they may do better with a dopamine blocker in addition to serotonergic drugs. You can monitor your progress in overcoming hoarding by using the Savings Inventory, which is reproduced by permission of Randy Frost, in Appendix 4. We also describe in Chapter 4, an example of someone who overcame their hoarding.

What Is Obsessional Slowness?

A person for whom obsessional slowness is part of OCD carries out simple everyday tasks, such as washing and dressing, very meticulously and in a precise and ordered manner or sequence. As a result, it may take many hours to get ready in the morning, and such individuals rarely reach an appointment on time! This was originally termed 'primary obsessional slowness' because it was not secondary to other compulsions, such as checking, which have taken an inordinate amount of time. Some controversy exists as to the cause of primary obsessional slowness. It could be secondary to severe compulsions of order and exactness, or there could be more biological factors involved (like a neurological disorder). Fortunately it is rare, as it is very difficult to treat. Although an individual can often 'speed up' with prompting and pacing by a therapist, the problem is helping the person to maintain any gains on their own. Expert help is often required to carry out a detailed functional analysis of the behavior and to work out a program that involves exposure to tasks done unmeticulously, imprecisely, and in a disordered manner.

Can OCD Change Over Time?

The course of OCD can vary enormously from one person to another. The symptoms may also change, so that you may be a washer at one time and checker later in life. At one extreme,

OCD can be relatively mild, consisting of one or two episodes and never returning. At the other extreme, usually when the onset is earlier, it is unremitting, constant, and more severely disabling. In between these two extremes are people for whom OCD comes and goes in episodes, usually at times of stress.

One study, carried out before effective treatments were available, found that if left untreated the majority of individuals with OCD generally make minor improvements over the 10–20 years after onset but do continue to experience significant symptoms. About 10 per cent made no improvement and 10 per cent became worse. Fortunately, things have improved since then, and the message we want to get across is that *OCD is treatable*: it is possible either to banish it or at least diminish it so that you will get more enjoyment out of life and find it easier to function.

Extra Problems with OCD

OCD often coexists with other problems, which may make it harder to treat. The most common additional problem is depression, which occurs in about one-third of individuals with OCD. Depression nearly always occurs after the onset of OCD, suggesting that it is a response to the OCD. More often, individuals with OCD do not necessarily have full-blown clinical depression but rather experience fluctuating mood, a sense of frustration and irritability with their OCD. We have included a screening questionnaire for depression in Appendix 4 (where we discuss overcoming depression in more detail). If you suffer from depression then you may find some help in Chapter 3 of this book, and also another book in this series – *Overcoming Depression* by Paul Gilbert. After years of social isolation and underachievement, individuals with OCD often have low self-esteem. If this is a problem, then we would recommend the book *Overcoming Low Self-Esteem* by Melanie Fennell (also in this series).

Another common condition that coexists with OCD is *social phobia* or *social anxiety disorder*. This consists of extreme self-consciousness caused by a fear of being judged negatively in social situations. It usually leads to avoidance of situations, for example talking to a group, that make the person anxious. If you have social anxiety, then you may find it helpful to read the book *Overcoming Social Anxiety and Shyness* by Gillian Butler (in this series).

OCD is also often found alongside anorexia or bulimia nervosa, and alcohol or drug misuse. For eating disorders, we recommend, *Overcoming Anorexia Nervosa* by Christopher Freeman and *Overcoming Bulimia Nervosa and Binge-Eating* by Peter J. Cooper.

There are also conditions such as body dysmorphic disorder (BDD), health anxiety, morbid jealousy, trichotillomania, tics, and Tourette's syndrome that are related to OCD and regarded by some as being on the spectrum of obsessive compulsive symptoms. We will take a brief look at each of these.

Body Dysmorphic Disorder

BDD consists of a preoccupation with one or more aspects of one's appearance that is not noticeable to others, usually causing individuals to feel that they are ugly or very unattractive and to be very self-conscious. About 10 per cent of individuals with OCD also have BDD. Individuals with BDD usually perform time-consuming rituals such as mirror-checking and may resort to needless cosmetic and dermatological procedures. They are usually significantly depressed and their lives severely restricted. Individuals with BDD may find it helpful to read the book *The Broken Mirror* by Katherine Phillips (Oxford University Press). We will shortly be publishing a self-help book on overcoming body image problems and body dysmorphic disorder as part of this series.

Health Anxiety or Hypochondriasis

This consists of a preoccupation with a fear that one has a serious disease. A large group of individuals have health anxiety that overlaps with OCD, and the two are barely distinguishable. These individuals have usually misinterpreted normal bodily sensations as evidence of impending illness and compulsively check their body and seek repeated reassurance. They have a lasting belief about being ill despite medical investigations and reassurance. The same principles we describe in this book for the purposes of overcoming OCD can also be used to overcome health anxiety; indeed, in Chapter 4 we describe an individual who had a particular fear of AIDS.

Morbid Jealousy

This is characterized by a preoccupation with a fear or suspicion that one's partner is being unfaithful. It is treated like OCD as it consists of intrusive worries with compulsive checking and reassurance-seeking that the partner is remaining faithful. There is also a more severe form of morbid jealousy, associated with alcoholism or psychoses, that can lead to violence or even murder of one's partner. However, it is important to recognize that this is a quite different condition, and that in OCD intrusive thoughts of harming others are not the prelude to actual violence.

Trichotillomania

This condition often coexists with OCD. It consists of impulsive pulling at one's hair, often resulting in noticeable hair loss. Individuals experience a sense of tension immediately before pulling or when attempting to resist the urge. They then experience a sense of relief and gratification when the hair is pulled out. Trichotillomania can be helped by behavior therapy, and we would recommend the book *The Hair Pulling Problem: A Complete Guide to Trichotillomania* by Fred Penzel (Oxford University Press).

Tics

Tics are sudden, rapid, recurrent movements or vocalizations, which are involuntary, but may be suppressed temporarily. They are a common accompaniment of OCD, especially in young people. Tics have some similarities with compulsions, as seemingly driven, but purposeless, behavior. You may be able to suppress a tic for a long time or cover it up with socially acceptable behaviors – like spitting into a Kleenex or coughing following a vocal tic. Tics are classified by clinicians as being: (a) motor (movements) or vocal, and (b) simple or complex.

Simple motor tics are sudden, brief, meaningless behaviors (e.g. blinking, face grimacing, lip pouting, head jerks, tapping, nose-twitching). Complex motor tics are slower, longer, more purposeful behaviors (e.g. sustained looks, facial gestures, touching objects or self, cracking knuckles, finger-sniffing, some types of skin-picking, hair twirling, obscene gestures, biting, tapping, or jumping).

Simple vocal tics are sudden meaningless sounds (e.g. throat-clearing, coughing, sniffling, screeching, humming, barking, or grunting). Complex vocal tics are sudden sounds but are more meaningful than the simple tics (e.g. syllables, words, phrases, or statements such as 'Shut up', 'You know', 'Okay honey', 'How about it?'). Complex vocal tics can include obscene words: this is called coprolalia. Making obscene gestures is called copropraxia.

Tourette's Syndrome

This is the name given to the condition of someone who has both complex motor and vocal tics, with or without coprolalia or copropraxia. Tourette's syndrome and simple tics are probably largely genetically determined. At least half of the people with Tourette's syndrome have OCD symptoms. However, OCD symptoms are more often characterized by order and counting.

Distinguishing between a tic and a compulsion can sometimes be difficult. The main differences are:

- you usually know when a tic is coming;
- you usually have a physical sensation before a tic;
- tics can generally be suppressed temporarily, but compulsions can be resisted permanently;
- tics are done without a reason, but compulsions usually have an aim of reducing anxiety or preventing harm;
- tics involve a build-up of tension which is released when you perform the action.

Tics can be helped by behavior therapy, in particular a technique called self-monitoring and habit reversal. This involves learning to perform a movement that is incompatible with the original behavior and can be tricky to do. If you need help with tics and other habits such as nail-biting and skin-picking then we would recommend the relevant chapters in *Obsessive-Compulsive Disorders* by Fred Penzel (Oxford, Oxford University Press, 2000). Tourette's syndrome can also be helped by medication that blocks dopamine receptors (for more on this, see Appendix 1).

What Is an Obsessive Compulsive Personality?

Despite the similarity in the name, obsessive compulsive personality disorder (OCPD) has only a superficial resemblance to OCD. It is sometimes referred to as anankastic personality or, after Freud, as being 'anal retentive'. It is possible for someone with OCD to have OCPD as well, although other personality traits are more common. Individuals with OCPD may be perfectionist, excessively tidy, excessively concerned with rules, and constantly making lists. They may be somewhat inflexible, unemotional, and overly devoted to work. Such traits are difficult to change, but if you do have OCD with OCPD then small shifts usually occur when you overcome OCD.

Famous People with OCD

Individuals with OCD are in good company. There are many famous people who are known or thought to have had OCD. The lesson from this is that OCD can affect people from all walks of life. Intelligence, money, success, adoration, and fame are no protection from the problem. For obvious ethical reasons, we cannot mention here well-known individuals with OCD who are alive today! There are, however, several examples from earlier years.

Howard Hughes (1905–1976)

Howard Hughes is one of the most famous individuals known to have had OCD. He led an extraordinary life, which illustrates perfectly what happens if you have the means to capitulate completely to your OCD and insist that others accommodate it. Hughes had a fortune, and generously paid a small group of aides to follow his extensive avoidance and safety behaviors. This fatally fueled his obsessions.

At the age of eighteen, Hughes started a career in Hollywood as a producer and director after he had inherited an engineering business from his father. He also became an accomplished pilot, and set an aviation record in 1938 for the first round-the-world flight, after which he became a public figure. He was able to take enormous risks in some areas, such as test-flying new planes, and was involved in two air accidents from which he was lucky to emerge alive. One of his businesses, in the military industry (which he left others to run), was extremely successful and made his fortune. However, most of the other enterprises in which he was directly involved were abject failures, at least in part as a result of his OCD and his personality. He was too preoccupied with detail and unable to delegate or make decisions until he felt totally comfortable.

Hughes' main obsession was a fear of contamination. Early in his Hollywood career he had private investigators monitor actresses, including Ava Gardner, for signs of illness. If one of them fell ill, he insisted that she was seen by his personal physician so that he could obtain, without her knowledge, a full medical report – presumably to determine if he might have been infected.

The severity of his OCD fluctuated over the years, but, with the help of his aides, he continued to avoid contact with any 'contaminants' by minutely monitoring his environment. Eventually, he began to keep himself to a single room, seeing only his small group of aides. When he discovered that the wife of one of his aides was ill, the man was ordered to work at home and Hughes did not see him again for fifteen years.

Even while he was alive Hughes' public image was that of a reclusive eccentric; however, the true picture emerged only after his death. Hughes was especially preoccupied with the transfer of germs. He lived in a hotel room whose windows and doors were sealed with masking tape to prevent the ingress of 'germs'. The windows were also heavily draped to keep out sunlight, which he believed would encourage the proliferation of bacteria. Everything had to be handed to him covered in 'handles' of paper tissues so that it did not come into contact with germs.

On one occasion he was invited to the funeral of a business associate who had died from cancer. He could not attend, of course, because he avoided contact with everybody except his aides. However, he became convinced that the colleague had in fact died from hepatitis. He sent a courier to the funeral with flowers and condolences, and then went to great lengths to ensure that his aides did not use that courier company again. He took steps to prevent the company from sending him any literature, or a bill, in case it had become infected following the delivery. He also gave detailed instructions on how to prevent any 'backflow' of germs, that is, to prevent any incoming messages of thanks or mail from the grieving family or the associate's business. The belief that 'contaminants' can transfer from an infected source to another person or to an inanimate object, which can then infect you, is a common one in OCD and totally without medical foundation. What is being transferred is the *idea* of contamination.

Hughes' aides were instructed to follow numerous detailed rituals that could take hours to perform. For example, in order to remove his hearing-aid from the bathroom cabinet, his aides were instructed:

- to use six to eight tissues to open the bathroom door;
- to use six to eight new tissues to open the bathroom cabinet, remove an unused bar of soap, and clean their hands with the soap;
- to use at least 15 tissues to open the door to another cabinet containing the hearing aid; and
- to remove the sealed envelope containing the hearing aid with two hands using another 15 tissues in each hand.

Tissues were spread everywhere on the bed, chair, and bathroom floor to prevent contact with contaminants. Later he discarded his clothes and went about naked in his room in front of his aides. We presume he thought that his clothing could be contaminated and that there was less risk if he was naked. At one time, he would spend most of the day sitting naked in a leather chair in the middle of his room, in an area he called a 'germ-free zone', watching old movies. He kicked open the bathroom door to avoid touching the handle, and then banned his aides from using his bathroom.

Paradoxically, despite Hughes' fear of contamination, in later life he paid no attention to his personal hygiene. When his symptoms were severe he would urinate on the floor or against the bathroom door (presumably because he regarded opening the door or going into the bathroom as too anxiety-provoking) and refuse to allow anyone to clean it up, preferring instead for paper towels to be spread around. He did not brush his teeth and stopped cutting the nails on his hands and feet, letting them grow to a grotesque length. He did not cut his hair and rarely bathed.

Retaining his hair and nails may have been an aspect of

hoarding, as he kept large vaults of memorabilia, including all the negatives and prints of his movies and thousands of feet of unused film, hundreds of scrapbooks containing photographs, newsreel, pilot logs of every minute in the air, aviation trophies, and airplane models. He spent millions storing aircraft he never visited or flew. Within his room, he was surrounded by piles of magazines, newspapers, old film cans, memoranda, and contracts. By the end of his life, he was hoarding his urine in jars.

When he was more lucid, he became preoccupied with atomic testing deep in the rocks of the Nevada desert. He tried to bribe President Johnson with $1 million to stop the testing and gave donations of $100,000 to Democrat and Republican presidential candidates to prevent future testing. He was not opposed to atomic weapons; he just did not want the testing done near him, probably because of his fears of contamination. In a similar vein, he besought the mayor of Nevada to improve the water-purification system as he was worried that the water had not been adequately cleansed from effluent. He drank only bottled water and ate a very restricted diet that had to be handed to him ritualistically to prevent contamination from 'germs'.

In effect, Hughes paid his aides and doctors to capitulate to all his avoidance and safety behaviors. He was initially prescribed codeine as a painkiller after one of the plane accidents, but became addicted to it and later injected it and increasing doses of Valium (a tranquillizer). Both drugs were probably used in an attempt to reduce anxiety, but they are addictive, and the withdrawal symptoms associated with codeine would have led to more anxiety. They are ineffective for OCD and create other problems such as constipation – although this is something he may have wanted if he thought it reduced his risk of contamination.

When Hughes died at the age of seventy-two in 1976, he was totally emaciated and an extremely sad figure. During his lifetime he had set up the Howard Hughes Medical Institute, partly as a means of reducing his tax burden. It is probable that his OCD would have influenced his expressed wish for the institute to prevent disease whether caused by 'bacteria, malignant growth or otherwise'. It has a current endowment of $11 billion and now conducts research into genes and molecular biology. This is undoubtedly important work, but it would have been fitting if it could have financed some research of relevance to OCD, in view of the terrible effects the disorder had on his life. If only Howard Hughes had been born slightly later, or his OCD had been diagnosed and treated, he might have had a much happier and productive life and his inheritance might have been devoted to research into OCD!

Samuel Johnson (1709–1784)

Samuel Johnson had both OCD and Tourette's syndrome. He was a brilliantly creative man, a greatly respected intellectual and author, and compiler of the first English dictionary. Johnson would perform highly ritualized movements when passing over the threshold of a door, as described by his biographer, James Boswell: 'I have, upon innumerable occasions, observed him suddenly stop, and then seem to count his steps with a deep earnestness, and when he had neglected or gone wrong in this sort of magical movement, I have seen him go back again, put himself in a proper posture to begin the ceremony, and having gone through it, break from his abstraction, walk briskly on, and join his companion.' At that time there was no understanding of OCD; such practices were simply referred to as 'bad habit' and ridiculed. Johnson appears also to have had obsessions involving moral standards with compulsions that probably involved prayers. He wrote in his book *Prayers and Meditations* in 1766: 'O God, grant me repentance, grant me reformation. Grant that I may be no longer disturbed with doubts and harassed with vain terrors,' and Boswell wrote of him: 'Talking to himself was, indeed one of his singularities ever since I knew him. I was certain that he was frequently uttering pious ejaculations; for fragments of the Lord's Prayer have been distinctly overheard.'

Charles Dickens (1812–1870)

Charles Dickens may have had OCD. He had high levels of anxiety and was universally described as 'highly strung'. Biographers have described him as being preoccupied with his hair and combing it in a mirror hundreds of times a day, which suggests a diagnosis of BDD. He had a compulsion for ordering the furniture in any room in which he stayed or worked, to try to achieve its exactly 'correct' position. Certain objects had to be touched three times for luck. Dickens compulsively tidied up after others and was angered by sloppiness. If he did have OCD or BDD, however, the disorder was probably mild, certainly not severe enough to interfere with his creativity.

Hans Christian Andersen (1805–1875)

Hans Christian Andersen was a famous Danish writer of fairy tales who it is thought had OCD and depression. According to Andersen, he 'had plagued himself to the most exquisite degree'. He would become obsessed with the idea that something he had just eaten would poison him, or that some trivial event would be exaggerated and would lead to his death. Most nights, he repeatedly rose from his bed in order to check that he had extinguished the candle by his bed, though he had never failed to do so when he retired to bed. Andersen would often worry that he had paid the wrong amount in a shop or that he had mixed up the envelopes of the letters he had sent. He would have been unable to check this, and probably have spent many hours reviewing his actions in his mind.

John Bunyan (1628–1688)

The English author John Bunyan had OCD. In his autobiography, *Grace Abounding to the Chief of Sinners*, Bunyan vividly describes intrusive thoughts, most of which were blasphemous in nature. 'A very great storm came down upon me . . . whole floods of blasphemies, both against God, Christ, and the

Scriptures, were poured upon my spirit, to my great confusion and astonishment . . . I felt as if there were nothing else but these from morning to night.' Bunyan obsessed about his urges to scream out obscenities in public and would physically restrain himself to prevent himself from acting on his impulses. 'The temper would provoke me to desire to sin . . . if it were to be committed by speaking of such a word, then in so strong a measure was this temptation upon me, that often I have been ready to clap my hand under my chin, to hold my mouth from opening.'

According to Bunyan in *Pilgrim's Progress*, 'There was a castle called Doubting Castle, the owner whereof was Giant Despair.' Bunyan's obsession that a church bell would fall on him illustrates his torturing doubt: 'I began to think, what if one of the bells should fall? I chose to stand under a main beam . . . thinking there I might stand safely. But then I thought again, what if the bell fell with a swing, it might first hit the wall, and then rebounding upon me, might kill me, despite the beam. This made me stand in the steeple-door; and now, thought I, I am safe enough. But then it came into my head. What if the steeple itself should fall? And this thought did continually so shake my mind, that I dared not stand at the steeple-door any longer, but was forced to flee, for fear the steeple should fall upon my head.'

Martin Luther (1483–1546)

The great Reformation priest and theologian Luther was also a tortured soul who had OCD relating to religious doubts and blasphemy. In his *Commentary on Galatians* he wrote: 'When I was a monk I thought that I was utterly cast away. If at any time I felt fleshy lust, wrath, hatred, or envy against my brother, I assayed many ways to quiet my conscience, but it would not be; for the lust did always return, so that I could not rest, but was continually vexed with these thoughts: This or that sin thou last committed: thou are infected with envy; with impatience; and such other sins.' Like John Bunyan, Luther also experienced blasphemous thoughts: 'For more than a week I have been thrown back and forth in death and Hell; my whole body feels beaten, my limbs are still trembling. I almost lost Christ completely, driven about on waves and storms of despair and blasphemy against God.'

Have I Got OCD?

Only a trained health professional can diagnose you as having OCD. However, there are questionnaires and checklists that may help you assess yourself.

The following is a screening questionnaire from the International Council on OCD:

1 Do you wash or clean a lot?
2 Do you check things a lot?
3 Is there any thought that keeps bothering you that you would like to get rid of but can't?
4 Do your activities take a long time to finish?
5 Are you concerned with orderliness or symmetry?

If you answered yes to one or more of these questions *and* it causes either significant distress *or* it interferes with your ability to work or study, your role as a homemaker, your social or family life, or your relationships, then there is a significant chance that you have OCD. The test is not perfect, however, and can be a bit over-sensitive at diagnosing OCD, so it may be a good idea to try another questionnaire as well.

Another good screening test is the Obsessive Compulsive Inventory devised by Professors Foa and Salkovskis (included in Appendix 4). If you score 21 or above then you are likely to be suffering from OCD. Finally, read the checklist of symptoms from the Yale Brown Obsessive Compulsive Scale (YBOCS), also reproduced in Appendix 4. If you tick any of these, then you probably have OCD. The checklist can be useful to define your most troublesome obsessions and compulsions, and these can then be rated on the YBOCS as a measure of severity. This is widely used by professionals as a measure of severity of OCD for treatment trials to determine whether a therapy is effective or not. In summary, OCD is a complex problem with many different faces. However, as we shall describe there are some core principles of self-help that can be used to overcome this distressing problem.

2

What Caused Your Obsessive Compulsive Disorder?

Know Your Enemy – Understanding is Part of the Cure

When considering the cause of your OCD, it is usually helpful to think of factors that:

- have made you vulnerable to developing OCD;
- have triggered your OCD;
- maintain your symptoms of OCD.

In this book, we emphasize the factors maintaining your OCD, as it is these factors that you can change and that form the cornerstone of self-help and cognitive behavior therapy (CBT). However, a good understanding of how your OCD has developed can help you to take a more sympathetic, compassionate view of yourself, and this will make you more effective in your attempts to overcome OCD.

Scientists do not fully understand what causes OCD, and – as with most other mental disorders – a massive amount of research is still needed. The causes of OCD may be particularly difficult to understand because there are different types of the disorder – for example, the cause in someone whose chief symptom is hoarding may not be the same as the cause for someone with fears of contamination; and fears of contamination in two different people may have different causes.

OCD, like all mental disorders, results from a combination

of biological (or genetic), psychological, and social or 'life experience' factors. However, people with the same symptoms may have different combinations of these 'risk factors', which makes OCD complicated to unravel. It is often difficult to say which risk factors are relevant in a given person and, at the moment, the treatment does not differ according to which seem to be most prominent. One person's OCD may be caused mainly by biological factors, whereas in another person it may arise from mainly psychological or social factors. For example, at one extreme, a young boy may have a rare immune response to a throat infection, which has triggered symptoms of OCD: he is biologically vulnerable. At the other extreme, a woman may have developed OCD after a trauma like rape: she is psychologically vulnerable as the result of her life experience. One way of thinking about the different contributions made by these different factors is to imagine that having OCD is like having a glass full of a cocktail. The ingredients and quantities that make up the cocktail in the glass will be different for each unique individual, and they also mix in different ways. This is illustrated in Figure 2.1.

One day there will be an adequate model of OCD that integrates biological, psychological, and social factors, but a lot more research needs to be done before we arrive at it. For the present, when anyone tells you '*the* cause' of your OCD, don't believe them; the combination of causes for each person is likely to be unique, with different factors all interacting in a complex manner. In some people, especially young children

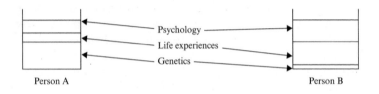

Person A   Person B

Figure 2.1   What causes OCD? The 'cocktail' of factors

with OCD, biological factors are likely to loom larger; for others, psychological factors will be more prominent. Many people with OCD would like more certainty on the cause, but at present our knowledge is very limited and there are many uncertainties, and often disagreements, among scientists!

Can OCD Be Inherited or Passed On?

Factors that can make you vulnerable to OCD include your genes or an anxious temperament. OCD can sometimes run in families. Studies have found that 5 per cent of the close family of someone with OCD are likely also to have OCD at some time in their lives. Remember, though, that OCD occurs naturally in up to 1–2 per cent of the population, so this is only a little higher than normal risk. Casting the net more widely, obsessive compulsive symptoms (but not OCD) are seen in another 10–15 per cent of the close family members of those with OCD. It is likely that the influence here is genetic rather than social, although the genetic factors involved have not yet been identified, because individuals with OCD often keep their symptoms secret, so close family members will not necessarily know what another member of the family is up to behind closed doors. In addition, the symptoms may be mild, or may have ceased many years ago. Sometimes, too, one member of the family may be a washer and another a checker, suggesting that neither has learned the behavior from the other.

Even those individuals who are genetically disposed to OCD usually develop the disorder itself only after life experiences 'switch on' their OCD: in different or better circumstances the person might have never developed OCD. Life experiences that may 'trigger' OCD include serious events during childhood or adolescence such as emotional neglect or sexual abuse; however, less extreme events such as changing job or school could be important as a trigger.

Adults with OCD often worry about passing OCD on to their children. However, as noted above, the chances of your child developing full OCD are as low as 5 per cent; furthermore, if your child is unlucky and this does happen, you will be more aware of the problem and the signs to look for so that you can obtain help at an early stage. We are also likely to learn more about OCD over time, and newer types of medication or psychological therapies to treat or prevent OCD may be developed. The possibility of a child of yours developing OCD should not, therefore, influence your decision about whether to have a family too much. A more important consideration, if you have severe OCD, is whether you think you can care for a child adequately.

It is interesting to speculate why there may be a genetic predisposition for OCD. Some researchers have proposed evolutionary theories, suggesting that the behavior might have had an advantage for survival or breeding. For example, by washing and grooming regularly, early man would have been less likely to suffer from infections and more likely to find a better mate. Checking for danger from predators would have improved his chances of survival. Hoarding would be an instinctive nesting behavior and an advantage in times of shortage. (However, while this is easy to relate to animals, which tend to hoard only foodstuffs, humans hoard a wide variety of objects.) Because of the advantages they conferred, the genes for this behavior would have been 'selected' and transferred to the next generation. Such theories sound plausible, but are impossible to prove. Even if correct, they are only one tiny part of the jigsaw puzzle of what causes OCD today.

Triggers for OCD

OCD usually begins gradually, and this makes it harder to pinpoint the factors that might trigger it or 'switch it on'. You may be one of the 50 per cent of individuals with OCD in whom there are no specific triggers. People who have OCD are, however, more likely than others to have had one or more major event in their life in the six months prior to the onset of their OCD. Some report a specific event, such as having a child, which led to their developing OCD: as we shall see later in the book, an increased sense of responsibility is an important issue for many people who have OCD. For others, a trauma, such as rape or an accident, or some other kind of bad experience, such as bullying or conflict, may 'switch on' or aggravate OCD. Occasionally, use of stimulant drugs such as cocaine or amphetamines may trigger or aggravate OCD. In such cases, OCD usually – but not necessarily – improves when the person stops taking the drug.

OCD and the Brain: Some Biological Explanations

Do I Have OCD because There's Something Wrong with My Brain?

Some scientists describe OCD as having a 'neurobiological' cause. The possible advantage of a biological explanation that links OCD, for example, with a neurological illness like migraine is that it may reduce stigma in the face of ignorant people who think that individuals with OCD should just 'pull themselves together'. However, there is no evidence that stigma is in fact reduced, and neurobiological explanations alone do not fully explain the symptoms of OCD or the psychological factors that maintain the disorder.

Biological explanations of OCD often start with the observation that animals show innate or fixed patterns of behavior, such as nest-building or grooming rituals. For example, cats will lick the face or paws; a bird will systematically collect suitable material for a nest and weave it together at particular times in a mating cycle. These behaviors occur whether an animal is raised in the wild or in complete isolation in captivity. Furthermore, fixed patterns of behavior often occur inappropriately at times of stress. For example, a dog under stress may compulsively lick its paws excessively so that they become raw and painful, a condition called 'acral lick dermatitis'. Humans also have innate and fixed patterns of behavior like washing and grooming that are 'hard-wired' in a primitive area of the brain called the basal ganglia. The theory is that these primitive fixed patterns of behavior are inappropriately activated at times of stress. The thinking part of the brain (in the frontal lobes) usually knows that the behavior is irrational and desperately tries to stop the fixed patterns of behavior driven by the basal ganglia.

Biological explanations of OCD are supported by research using brain scans that show increased activity in the frontal lobes of the brain of individuals with OCD, compared with people who do not have OCD. In some studies, the scans suggest a reduction in the size of the basal ganglia. However, theses changes are not consistent in all studies and may be unrelated to OCD. Furthermore, the increased activity in the brain returns to normal following behavior therapy or medication. This suggests that the abnormal brain activity and changes in size of parts of the brain are *consequences* rather than *causes* of OCD. (To draw an analogy: a fast heart rate occurs in a panic attack; but this is not a cause of the attack, it's a consequence of anxiety.) It also means that, for the overwhelming majority of individuals with OCD, there is no permanent damage or disease in the brain. In *extremely rare* cases, it has been known for a stroke in an elderly person to affect the blood supply to the basal ganglia in the brain and cause OCD.

It is also difficult to link the experience of someone with OCD with the findings on brain scans in a coherent and scientific manner. In summary, studies suggest that one part of the brain (the 'frontal lobes') is trying too hard to get a message through to another part of the brain (the 'basal ganglia') in order to switch off behavior patterns like washing or checking. The frontal lobes are, among other things, responsible for being aware of novelty or danger, whereas the basal ganglia store automatic behaviors like washing and grooming. In OCD, the frontal lobes are desperately trying to switch off the basal ganglia and to finish the routine. As a result, it is suggested, routines such as washing or checking that can normally be done 'without thinking', in OCD become compulsions which, if not resisted, may continue for several minutes or even hours until the anxiety has decreased.

Although the findings on brain scans are interesting and offer a valid biological *description* of the problem in OCD, they have not led to any new treatments. We believe that the findings on abnormal brain scans and animal models are best interpreted as a *consequence* of OCD rather than a cause. The picture is of a brain that is desperately trying to calm a system which is under pressure from too much anxiety. Also, biological explanations do not explain the content of the obsession or compulsion – for example, they do not focus on why someone checks rather than cleans; and they have little to say about the psychological aspects of OCD, such as excessive responsibility or magical thinking. Much research is still required, therefore, to bring together biological and psychological theories of OCD.

Do I Have OCD because I've Got a Chemical Deficiency in My Brain?

Other biological explanations focus on the role of serotonin in OCD. Serotonin, a chemical occurring in the nervous system, has a role in many aspects of normal human functioning including appetite, sexual desire, and moods such as depression and anxiety; so it is not unique to OCD, and its role in OCD is only one small part of the story. Medication that helps to increase activity in nerves that use serotonin can help OCD, and we look at such drugs in detail in Appendix 1. However, because drugs that help in treating OCD act on nerves that contain serotonin, this is not to say that there is a deficiency of serotonin in OCD. This would be like saying that if aspirin helps in cases of headache, then headaches are caused by a deficiency of aspirin.

We acknowledge that there is other evidence that points to changes in the nerve cells that contain serotonin in OCD. However, these changes are likely to occur *as a result of the brain trying to dampen the system down* – in other words, as a *consequence* of the OCD and associated anxiety. Drugs that act on the brain's use of serotonin may help in OCD (and depression, and other anxiety disorders) by *enhancing* the function of nerve cells in the brain that help to inhibit anxiety. If you are less anxious, you may be able to cope better in resisting rituals and to make a more realistic estimate of the degree of harm likely to result from your not performing your compulsions. Because of the way they work, serotonin-acting drugs are not usually effective in individuals with low levels of anxiety.

Do I Need to Check So Much because My Memory Doesn't Work Properly?

Other researchers have suggested that individuals with OCD have a deficit in their general memory, in an attempt to explain the doubting and checking features of OCD. Investigation has shown that this is not the case; in fact, OCD individuals tend to have an enhanced memory for information that is specifically related to their obsessions. However, they lack confidence in their memory for checking. We return to this 'lack of confidence' theme later.

An Alternative Model for OCD

In summary, trying to unravel the biology of OCD is a very complex enterprise, and statements that OCD is 'caused by' a deficiency of serotonin in the brain or a block in the basal ganglia are too simplistic. Remember that any biological changes observed in the brain with OCD can be reversed by using either psychological or physical therapy. If a person overcomes their OCD (by whatever method), then the brain will switch off the biological changes that have come about *in response to* the excessive anxiety, and the system will return to normal. There is *no* permanent structural damage in someone who recovers from OCD, and the use of medication does not tell us much about the cause of the disorder.

An alternative, psychological model for OCD (and other mental disorders) states that the normal mind consists of a large number of modules, each crafted to do a certain job. For example, there is a module for fear, another for memory, and so on. In some mental disorders there may be damage to a module. For example, in conditions like dementia there may be damage to the module for memory. In other disorders, certain modules are trying too hard because there is an excessive load on the system. According to this model, OCD can be regarded as *a failure in a system because it is overloaded*. It is overloaded because you think that you have the power to prevent awful events from occurring and as a result are extremely anxious about all the catastrophes that could occur if you don't make sure this power is used. Thus the brain is coping the best way it can to restabilize itself and reduce anxiety. This effort, which is a *normal* process, will be manifested in *abnormal* brain scans and changes in serotonin activity, which can be regarded as consequences of the mind desperately trying to restabilize itself.

A Cognitive Behavioral Model for the Maintenance of OCD

The key to overcoming your OCD is to understand what's keeping it going. The more you can understand the psychological mechanisms behind your OCD, the better equipped you will be to conquer it. Think of yourself as a scientist trying to cure a disease. You would need to learn a lot about the nature of the disease to find an effective cure, and then to stop it coming back. The problem for so many people suffering from OCD is that their ideas about the nature of the problem, and the solutions that follow from these ideas, are largely different from those of individuals without OCD. This is a critical point: the way you have understood your OCD so far, and the solutions you have applied, may well be a *cause* of your problem, actually be keeping it going.

Look at it this way. If you view the intrusive thoughts and urges that you have as the heart of the problem, it is logical for you to try to solve the problem by making efforts to respond to the intrusion and to stop or neutralize it until you feel comfortable. But intrusive thoughts, doubts, images, and urges are entirely normal; so trying to blot them out is something like trying to cure a physical illness by removing a healthy organ – a drastic 'remedy' that is highly likely to make the person less rather than more well.

The rest of this chapter is therefore about developing a good psychological understanding of how your symptoms of OCD are *maintained*, and then of the implications for treatment. Note the word 'maintained': we are *not* saying that OCD is *caused* by these processes, but rather that the processes are what keeps your OCD going in a series of vicious circles. As we have noted earlier in this chapter, there is a lot of controversy in medical circles about what predisposes individuals to OCD and about biological models of the disorder; but, conversely, there is a lot of agreement among researchers on the maintaining factors, and that is what we are concentrating on in this section. Breaking out of these cycles is crucial to overcoming OCD.

The first step is to understand why the self-help program being offered in this book, and the treatment model on which it is based, can help to overcome OCD, and why your solutions of avoidance, safety-seeking, and compulsions, and the meaning you attach to your intrusive thoughts, are not solving your problem, but maintaining it.

We would like to thank Steve Hayes for a good metaphor for OCD. Imagine you are placed in a field, blindfolded, and given a toolbox to carry. You are told your job is to run around this field, blindfolded. Now, unbeknown to you, in this field are a large number of deep holes. You don't know that at first. So you start running around and sooner or later you fall into a large hole. You cannot climb out and there are no escape routes you can find. Not surprisingly, you feel inside the toolbox you were given to see what is in there; maybe you can find something you can use to get you out. The only tool is a spade, and so you dutifully start to dig your hole further. Soon you notice you are not out of your hole, so you try digging faster and faster; but you are still in the hole. So you try big spadefuls; you try throwing the dirt far away from you; and so on – but still you are in the hole.

Does this relate to your experience of OCD? You might be seeking help from this book or going to a therapist in the hope that you can find a bigger or better spade, perhaps a golden spade, to get rid of your intrusive thoughts or anxiety. Well, you cannot dig your way out; all the digging you can do just digs you in further. However, there may be another way out, as we are about to show you a ladder. However, you won't be able to find the ladder (remember, you are blindfolded) until you drop the spade . . .

Avoidance and Safety-Seeking

Our earliest understanding about OCD was based on learning theory, and the effect of avoidance and compulsions on fear. Put simply, each time you avoid a situation or activity the behavior is reinforced because you have prevented yourself from experiencing anxiety and the harm that you think might have occurred if you hadn't avoided the situation. This 'reinforcing' means that you are more likely to act in the same way when you next have the opportunity of avoiding a situation. For example, if you avoid using public toilets because of the fear of contamination, you will have prevented yourself from feeling anxious and so you will go on avoiding public toilets because then you won't feel anxious. If you escape from a situation where you feel anxious because you think you will see blood, then you will do the same thing the next time. In both cases the avoidance behavior is reinforced.

A second key issue is the way you respond to anxiety and the belief that you can prevent harm. In OCD, a common response to anxiety is a ritual or a safety-seeking behavior. Rituals are also reinforced, so that when, for example, you check that a light switch is off and then feel less anxious, you are more likely to act in the same way in the future.

In short, avoidance and compulsions seem at first to 'work'! They work in the sense that you *think* that you have prevented harm (e.g. your electrics do not catch fire) and this usually either reduces your anxiety or stops you feeling anxious. Unfortunately, avoidance and compulsions have a high cost, and in the long term they make you *more* anxious and fearful. They feed the obsession. Thus trying too hard to get rid of your intrusive thoughts and feelings by avoidance and compulsions actually *becomes* the problem.

Our understanding of the function of avoidance led to the principles of 'exposure' therapy, in which a person with OCD repeatedly confronts the situations or activities that he or she has hitherto avoided without doing a compulsion (this is technically called 'response prevention' or sometimes 'ritual prevention') until the anxiety has subsided. This is known as 'habituation' and is the cornerstone of psychological treatment for OCD. Practicing alternative behaviors (or returning to old ones that you used before you had OCD) makes them automatic or routine, in just the same way as when you learn any new skill, like driving. This is the essence of the behavioral component of therapy, which is discussed in Chapter 3.

Exposure also allows you to find out whether what you expect to happen does in fact happen, and to learn new ways of behaving by acting against the way you feel. You can do a kind of formal 'behavioral experiment', in which you test out some of your feared consequences (e.g. the belief that when you are very anxious you will lose control and go crazy). During the experiment, you will see if there is another way of looking at being anxious that would allow you to act differently. In some situations, of course, you cannot test whether a belief is actually true, because the experiment could last for many years. For example, we had a patient who had a doubt about whether you can die of cancer brought on by 'radiation' stemming from a smoke detector. You would have to wait thirty or forty years before the end of any practical experiment (although the scientific evidence is that smoke detectors are very safe). In such situations, you will need to decide whether what you learn in an experiment fits best with one or the other of two *competing* theories:

- Theory A: You are at high risk of dying of cancer from being close to a smoke detector. Your solution is to take every possible step to avoid smoke detectors and keep checking for their presence.
- Theory B: You have an excessive worry about dying of cancer from being close to smoke detectors; your 'solutions' to this worry have become your problem and feed your anxiety.

Testing whether your symptoms best match Theory A or Theory B is the cornerstone of the cognitive component of therapy. Normally, someone with OCD has been pursuing Theory A for many years and as a result is significantly handicapped. However, in order to determine whether Theory B might be the correct explanation for your problems, you will have to act *as if it were* correct, at least for a limited time while you collect the evidence. If, after, say, three months, you remain unconvinced, you can always go back to Theory A and carry on with your current solutions and look for that bigger or better spade to get you out of your hole. You might believe it's an act of faith to drop your spade and think that the risk of getting cancer from smoke detectors through testing out Theory B is too high. However, if you do not let go of the spade, then you won't know if there is anything else there to take hold of. In the metaphor, after all, you are blindfolded; you will only know what else there is by touch, and you can only touch something else when you have let go of the spade. If you don't test out the alternative theory, all you will have is your spade, and all you will do is dig yourself further into the hole, causing yourself more distress and limiting your life yet further.

The next step in getting to grips with the factors that maintain OCD is understanding the *meaning* (that is, the 'cognitive' component) that you attach to normal experiences. We will discuss this with reference to a number of different ways of thinking in OCD.

Inflated Responsibility and Magical Thinking

Individuals with OCD have an inflated sense of responsibility. By this, we mean a type of thinking whereby you believe that you have an especially powerful influence that can either cause or prevent bad events which are personally important to you. For example, a person with OCD who is especially fearful of theft might believe that he has a particular influence in being able to prevent a burglary from occurring. This, in turn, leads to trying too hard to ensure that his doors and windows are locked. Another person with OCD who has a fear of contamination believes that her anxiety will go on forever and she will lose control and that she can prevent this by washing repeatedly.

As you improve, you will learn that you have a limited influence over whether bad events happen. If your child is going to get leukemia, it was probably largely determined by his genetic makeup when he was born. If a burglar really wants to break into your house, then it doesn't matter whether all the doors and windows are locked – the burglar can use a crowbar or break the window and ignore the alarm, which is all that is required if an intruder is really determined to find the valuables he wants. We know this because it has happened to one of us with the door locked and the alarm switched on. It would have made no difference how many times we had checked our locks or alarm! Many bad events occur simply because someone is in the wrong place at the wrong time; we all have very limited foreknowledge and very limited ability to prevent a bad event from occurring. OCD sufferers *think* they can prevent bad events that are relevant to them from occurring, and then try too hard to stop them.

Another aspect of OCD closely related to the inflated sense of responsibility is 'magical' or superstitious thinking that is taken to the extreme. Alas, many people without OCD act superstitiously (e.g. they touch wood or light a candle to prevent something bad from happening) as it makes them feel more comfortable and *as if* they had more influence and control over events. The cost of such behavior is usually low for most people without OCD: they treat superstitions as bit of a joke and, as bad things do not happen very often, the behavior is reinforced. Magical thinking and superstitious behavior, then, are somewhere on the same spectrum as OCD but for most people not distressing or frequent enough to be a problem. We personally go out of our way with our patients to act *anti-superstitiously*, for example, by using number 13 or 666, going under ladders, not touching wood, and so on. We hope to persuade you also to act rationally and anti-superstitiously to rid yourself of your OCD.

The Over-Importance of Thoughts

This overinflated sense of responsibility can be applied to intrusive thoughts or images and the belief that such thoughts are extremely important. Indeed, many people with OCD believe that the mere presence of a bad thought can produce a bad action, or that it is immoral to have such thoughts. (This has been termed 'thought–action fusion'.) Unfortunately, some religions have encouraged this belief. If you believe that it is immoral to have bad thoughts or that they will lead to bad actions then, not surprisingly, you will also believe that it is extremely desirable to *control* 'bad' thoughts and images, and that this is possible.

To understand these ideas in more detail, we need to know that all human beings experience intrusive thoughts, images, and doubts which are usually absurd and run counter to what the person wants to do or think. In experiments carried out in the 1970s, researchers asked some people with OCD and some people without OCD to list their intrusive thoughts. Researchers could find no difference in the types of thought reported by those with and those without OCD. Below is a list of the thoughts, images, and impulses used in the experiment:

1 *Impulse* to hurt or harm someone.
2 *Impulse* to say something nasty and damning to someone.

3 *Thought* of causing harm to, or the death of, close friend or family member.

4 *Thought* of acts of violence in sex.

5 *Impulse* to crash car, when driving.

6 *Thought* 'Why should they do that? They shouldn't do that,' in relation to people 'misbehaving'.

7 *Impulse* to attack or strangle cats or kittens.

8 *Thought* 'I wish he/she were dead,' with reference to persons close and dear.

9 *Thought* of harming partner with physical violence.

10 *Impulse* to attack or violently punish someone: for example, to throw a child out of a bus.

11 *Impulse* to engage in certain sexual practices that involve pain to the partner.

12 *Thought* 'Did I commit this crime?', when reading reports of crime.

13 *Thought* that one might go berserk all of a sudden.

14 *Thought*: wishing and imagining that someone close to you was hurt or harmed.

15 *Impulse* to violently attack and kill a dog that one loved.

16 *Thought* 'These boys when they were young' – a mechanically repeated phrase.

17 *Impulse* to attack or harm someone, especially own child, with bat, knife, or heavy object.

18 *Thought* of unnatural sexual acts.

19 *Thought* of hurting someone by doing something nasty, not physical violence: 'Would I or would I not do it?'

20 *Impulse* to be rude and say something nasty to people.

21 *Thought* of putting obscene words in print.

22 *Mental image* of stabbing a passer-by.

23 *Mental image* of stripping in church.

For the record, items 1, 2, 3, 6, 10, 11, 14, 15, 18, 19, 20 and 23 are intrusive thoughts provided by people without OCD and the remainder are taken from people with OCD. All humans, therefore, have intrusive thoughts, images, and urges that are absurd. Those who have OCD have more frequent and complex thoughts than others, and are more distressed by them, because of the meaning they attach to the thoughts and the way in which they have responded to them. OCD is maintained when you misinterpret intrusive thoughts as a sign not only that is there a serious risk of harm occurring to yourself or others (the overimportance of thoughts), but that you can prevent harm through what you do or what you fail to do (the overinflated responsibility). The problem is, therefore, *not* the intrusive thoughts but the *meaning* you attach to them: for example, 'Having thoughts about a bad action means I might actually do that action impulsively at some time. I might do something I couldn't bear to even think about.'

Some people with OCD believe that having such thoughts means that they *could have already* acted in that way, even though they can't remember it: for example, 'I could have attacked and hit a small child that I passed in the street.' This may then lead to a mixture of anxiety, doubt, excessive checking, mental reviews, and reassurance-seeking about whether they had in fact acted impulsively in a way that would be abhorrent to them.

There may be a moral dimension to the response, for example: 'I am bad for having such thoughts and urges which I shouldn't be having.' Interpreting thoughts in this way has the effect of increasing the feelings of threat and responsibility as you then try too hard to prevent yourself from having these 'harmful' thoughts. Needless to say, it is not that you shouldn't be having such thoughts. On the contrary, as a human being you *should* be having such thoughts. You would be abnormal if you didn't have intrusive thoughts. The difference between you and others who do not have OCD is the meaning you attach to the intrusive thoughts, the frequency and distress associated with the thoughts, and the way in which you respond to them.

Sometimes the development over several years of attitudes and beliefs that, in combination with normal thoughts or urges, cause anxiety and distress, can lead to OCD. A particular life experience may be the 'trigger'. For example, Toni had a 'premonition' that her grandmother was going to die; then her grandmother did die, of natural causes, which led her to conclude that she could have done more to prevent her death. Attitudes that may make you vulnerable to OCD include:

- If I think bad things, this is as bad as doing bad things.
- One can and should exercise control over one's thoughts.
- If I know harm is possible, I should always try to prevent it, however unlikely it seems.

To identify some of the attitudes that may make you vulnerable to developing OCD, you can complete the Responsibility Interpretations Questionnaire developed by Paul Salkovskis and his colleagues (see Appendix 4). We discuss ways of overcoming an excessive sense of responsibility in the next few chapters.

The Unique Content of Your Obsessions

Although obsessions tend to relate to one of the main themes (contamination, harm, aggression, sex, religion, order, or symmetry), the *exact* content usually depends upon the values of the individual, by which we mean which people or things he or she regards as most important to protect from harm. Hence a mother has an obsession about stabbing her baby son because he is the most precious thing that she can imagine and she cares deeply for him. Interestingly, such thoughts also occur in men and women without children, because children are important to their life in some other way: for example, they might want to work with children or wish they had a family. The intrusive thoughts represent their deepest fears – that they could be responsible for harming a vulnerable child, or that they will have their liberty taken away and be shamed. Intrusive thoughts and images therefore represent particular worries. Couple these thoughts/worries with the belief that you are able to prevent bad events from happening and suddenly, as if by magic, you have an obsession.

Similarly, Anthony – a man who has intrusive images of masturbating over his mother is revealing his deepest fears and disgust. His mother is dying from cancer; he loves her enormously and it's very important to him that he cares for her in her last days; and yet he avoids being in her company because he fears having the image with his mother because it would mean he was a bad and disgusting person. The content of obsessions, therefore, frequently represents the specific values and interests of the individual. They fear that if their thoughts became reality then their life would be devastated, and therefore all their energy is directed at preventing the harm from occurring.

Most of the examples above are obsessions to do with preventing harm in others. Obsessions are also commonly focused on preventing harm to yourself – for example, becoming ill or dying from a contaminant, or just feeling anxious about losing control and going crazy.

Sometimes it is difficult to work out how the content of your obsession relates to what is important in your life. It may just be self-preservation and not losing control or going crazy. Do not worry if you cannot work it out – sometimes it is very hard to articulate the meaning, and it may be helpful to talk it through with a therapist. If you avoid a great deal and have hardly *ever* resisted a compulsion (especially ordering and repeating), you will have become so good at OCD that you never get sufficiently anxious to acknowledge explicitly what it is you fear. Here, it will be important for you to do an experiment to confront your fears, just to find out what is going through your mind and what your obsession is or means to you.

Overestimation of Danger

Another aspect of meaning is the way you are more likely to overestimate the degree of threat to yourself and underestimate your ability to cope or seek help.

Thus, if you have a fear of contamination from HIV and see something red, then you immediately think it must be blood that contains HIV and that you could not protect yourself from the risk of infection. If you are a motorist and believe yourself to be at risk of knocking over cyclists, every cyclist you pass will be regarded as potentially run over and lying in the gutter. If you are an accountant with OCD, then every column of figures may be added wrongly, with disastrous and irremediable consequences that you should be responsible for preventing.

The habit of overestimating danger is not specific to OCD; it also occurs in other anxiety disorders. For example, someone with social phobia may overestimate the likelihood of the other members of a group being critical and rejecting. When it comes to helping yourself to face your fears, you will need to be aware of this bias in overestimating danger or threats and underestimating your ability to cope or seek help, and correct it by *acting as if* it is a false signal.

Intolerance of Uncertainty

Many people with OCD believe that they need to know for certain that something bad will not happen. Others believe that they are unable to cope with unpredictable change or ambiguous situations, and want a guarantee that nothing will change for the worse. An example is a man who wanted to know for certain that he would not be harmed if he touched a dirty overall, and that he would not get cancer from asbestos.

For these people, OCD is the ultimate insurance policy and usually means thinking that if you try hard enough and do more rituals and get more reassurance then you can be more certain. The reality is that trying harder usually increases doubts and the feeling of uncertainty. Indeed, it is often said that there are only two guarantees in life – death and taxes! We know of one further guarantee. It is that when you demand certainty in your life you will be distressed, and find it impossible to overcome your OCD.

A good analogy is the amount you are prepared to spend on an insurance policy to give yourself 'peace of mind'. All insurance policies have exclusions – for example, what are termed 'acts of God'. By taking out a policy that purported to guarantee you against such events, you might *feel* that you were giving yourself certain protection from danger; however, it is more likely that you would be paying an extremely high premium to cover acts that no one could actually prevent, with the insurers laughing all the way to the bank. Reducing risk and performing compulsions to make you feel more certain has a cost (e.g. the time involved and lost productivity) and often also has the paradoxical effect of increasing doubt.

Perfectionism

In some types of OCD there is a belief that there exists a perfect solution to everything; that doing something perfectly is possible and necessary; and that even minor mistakes have serious consequences. This leads to such beliefs as 'Failing partly is as bad as failing completely.' This may then lead to changes in behavior that are counterproductive. An example is spending hours correcting a document so you can feel it is 'just right' rather than 'good enough', and losing sight of the actual goal to be achieved, in this case the instruction or message to be communicated by the document. Perfectionism is a common feature of OCD in individuals with a desire for control and order, and is especially prevalent in those who also have anorexia nervosa.

The big issue in perfectionism is thinking in terms of black and white rather than shades of gray. The problem is the demand for a perfect solution: that is, you absolutely must reach the highest standard all the time or you are an utter failure. A healthy goal will be to strive for high standards and at the same time to accept that if you do not succeed 100 per cent you are not a failure; just a fallible human being, as we all are.

Hoarding

We discuss hoarding separately because the psychological characteristics are slightly different from other types of OCD. The first characteristic of hoarding is the emotional attachment to possessions. Another way of describing this is the degree of importance a person attaches to their possessions. You might say that people who hoard compulsively identify themselves through their possessions. Normally, at the centre of our identity are aspects of our personality, physical attributes, and values. Clustered around this core are the people, animals, and inanimate objects in which we have an investment, such as our family, friends, pets, and possessions. In compulsive hoarding, your possessions can develop such overriding importance that they become the centre of your identity, and you merely their custodian. Hence, losing your possessions feels like losing part of your self – like a snail losing its shell. Is it any wonder, then, that if you are a compulsive hoarder you want to hang on to your possessions for dear life? Avoiding throwing away possessions prevents marked anxiety and distress.

Another feature in hoarding is the excessive clutter, which prevents much being done as living space becomes crowded with objects. The reason the space gets so cluttered is that someone with hoarding tends to remember items visually (rather than knowing that they are hidden away according to a category, such as bank statements). Therapy must, therefore, be directed at learning to categorize possessions and trusting that you will be able to find them again without seeing them in front of you.

Individuals with OCD often express an excessive sense of responsibility towards their possessions, or believe they must protect them from harm. This echoes the general characteristic of all OCD thinking that we discussed earlier: belief in the influence and ability to prevent harm from occurring to yourself or to others. In relation to hoarding, when the possession is threatened, protecting the object from harm is the same as defending your 'self'. If you are a hoarder, this means that you will want to control your possessions entirely and will become very anxious if objects are moved or even touched without your permission. One aspect of the sense of responsibility is a wish to be fully and completely prepared for future needs: so you may buy more objects to avoid any possibility of being caught out with 'not enough' of something. Furthermore, you are likely to overestimate the potential value and inherent worth of an object you have the chance to acquire and view it as an opportunity not to be missed: hence more items are accumulated. At the same time, you can probably always think of more reasons to save an item than to discard one.

Another characteristic of idealized values about the importance of one's possessions is the *rigidity* with which the values are held. Such individuals are unable to adapt to changing circumstances and ignore the consequences of acting on their distorted value judgments. Cynthia had a severe hoarding problem and was virtually housebound because she felt she had to guard her possessions against being stolen. The possessions themselves were virtually worthless, but she would not allow anyone into her house and spent most of the day checking her possessions to determine whether anything was lost. The house had become a fire hazard; and yet she said that if her flat were to catch fire, she would rather stay with her possessions and die than escape and be left with nothing of her 'self'.

Another type of emotional attachment in hoarding is the sense of comfort and safety that possessions might provide. For example, when under stress, you may wish to return home and gather your possessions around you. This has the effect of reducing anxiety (like going back to a bunker) and giving a sense of protection from the outside world.

Attention

If you have OCD, then you are likely to focus your attention on situations that you think may be dangerous. This has the effect of magnifying the situation and making you more aware of it. This phenomenon is a normal one that happens in everyday life – for example, when a woman becomes pregnant, she starts to notice other pregnant women and babies everywhere. It is not that there are more pregnant women and babies; just that she is just more aware of them. Similarly, if you were to concentrate now on the sensations in your big toe for the next minute or so, you might start to feel a sensation of throbbing which you were not aware of before. So, if you have normal thoughts of stabbing your baby and then believe that this makes you a danger to your baby, then you are more likely to monitor the thoughts and they will appear to increase. Another vicious circle has been set up: the more you pay attention to your intrusive thoughts, the more you are aware of them, and the more they magnify; so you pay yet more attention to them, and so on and on.

In the same way, when you feel anxious and panicky, and experience the physical sensations of anxiety (e.g. sweaty, shaky, heart racing), you may focus your attention on these feelings and physical sensations, which will tend to make you more aware of them and further reinforce the belief that there is a danger or threat that must be avoided. Another vicious circle has been set up.

Being excessively focused on threats is likely to make you look out more closely for situations that might be dangerous. More of your attention is taken up by scanning for danger, and it becomes impossible to relax or concentrate on normal activities.

Excessive vigilance and the constant anticipation of danger are not specific to OCD and will occur in other anxiety disorders. For example, if you have had a car crash and suffer from Post Traumatic Stress Disorder, you are more likely to drive very cautiously and be constantly checking other road users.

Attention is bit like bandwidth: so, the more attention you direct at what you think may be dangerous and at how you feel, the less attention there is for normal tasks and your environment. When you come to help yourself, you will need to practice refocusing attention away from your intrusions and feelings of anxiety and towards living in the moment of the real world, acting against the way you feel. It will be important to stop scanning for danger and to take in the whole situation, not just one small part of it. You will need to direct your attention more at external objects or activities around you, or at other tasks, such as listening to someone with total concentration on what they are saying.

Interpreting Ambiguous Information

Someone with OCD is more likely to interpret ambiguous information as dangerous. For example, if you have an obsession with AIDS, and see a red mark on the pavement, you might be more likely than someone without OCD to think that it is blood and to avoid it at all costs. This tendency to categorize events as either dangerous or not (called 'black-and-white thinking') will lead to frequent false alarms.

Again, the tendency to interpret ambiguous information as dangerous is not specific to OCD, and occurs in all anxiety problems. If you have OCD, however, it means that you will frequently feel anxious in anticipation of dangers that you think may occur. In helping yourself, you will need to try to accept ambiguous information and uncertainty, and acknowledge that you can be in an area that is either totally safe or unsafe.

Anxiety

When we feel anxious, we are usually all too aware that we are in the unpleasant state of anxiety. For example, you might start to feel a whole range of sensations like being sweaty and shaky; your heart races and you feel sick, dizzy, or short of breath. Not everyone has all these feelings, but they are a normal response to believing that a catastrophe is about to occur which will threaten you or others, and that you can prevent the harm from occurring, whether by action or by escaping.

Nevertheless, the way we think about this experience can have an effect on just how bad it feels and how long it lasts. Like so many things about human emotions, this seems to work upside down: that is, the harder we resist the experience, the more unpleasant it feels and the longer it lasts. In almost all cases, the more we accept the feeling of anxiety in the moment it comes upon us, the faster it will pass.

Conversely, there are some ways of thinking about anxiety commonly understood to make the experience worse. These are termed 'awfulizing', 'catastrophizing', and having a 'low frustration tolerance'.

Awfulizing

Awfulizing means tending to describe something as 'awful', 'horrible', or 'terrible'; it's 'the end of the world', 'things couldn't be worse'. The problem is that such an extreme way of thinking about anxiety only serves to make it seem more frightening. The consequence? More anxiety. Instead, it is more helpful to try and keep this – certainly unpleasant – experience in perspective: for example, with the thought 'feeling anxious is very unpleasant, but not the worst thing in the world'. As with intrusive thoughts and images, try just to accept, and not to control. The aim here is not to minimize how disturbing and upsetting anxiety is, but to find a way of thinking about it that does not make it worse. However, we won't want you to develop this approach into a compulsion and giving yourself frequent reassurance!

Catastrophizing

Common examples in OCD of catastrophizing about feeling anxious are the beliefs that you are going crazy or losing control, and that it will go on for ever and ever. Others have more specific beliefs, for example: 'I'll get AIDS and then I'll pass it on to my partner and children,' or: 'If I feel a bit excited when I look at a child, that must mean I am a pedophile.' Then negative feedback occurs: if as a result of these thoughts you feel more anxious, this is then used as evidence that something catastrophic will happen unless you do something to stop it; or, if you misinterpret the signs of anxiety, such as feeling unreal, as evidence that you are losing control or will be physically ill, this further increases your anxiety. This, in turn, feeds the obsession and anxiety, and you have set up another vicious circle.

Low Frustration Tolerance

Low frustration tolerance (LFT) is another attitude that can add to the uncomfortable and distressing experience of anxiety. LFT refers to regarding anxiety as 'intolerable' or 'unbearable'. This again can make it seem more frightening, and has the unfortunate effect of increasing the likelihood that you will use short-term ways of getting rid of the 'intolerable' anxiety. This usually means avoidance, compulsions, or reassurance-seeking and thus entrenches your OCD. To combat this, and in order to resist being pushed around by your OCD as it tries to bully you using anxiety, try to think of anxiety as 'hard to bear, but not unbearable'.

The vicious circle related to anxiety also means that in situations that increase stress (e.g. a conflict with someone) your symptoms of OCD will tend to increase. Remember, managing to tolerate some anxiety now will be a big step towards overcoming your OCD, and that means much less anxiety and distress in the long run.

It's Not Just What You Do, It's the Way that You Do It

The next step in this story is the role of what therapists call 'safety-seeking behaviors' in anxiety-provoking situations. This is what you do to try to prevent harm from occurring and to prevent yourself feeling anxious. When we think we are in danger and anxiety is severe, then our natural response is to escape. This is a normal human process in anxiety. If I were being followed by a killer with a gun who was targeting me, I would feel extreme terror and my natural response would be to escape. If I could not escape, then I might freeze so that I was not noticed or try to seek help.

Safety-seeking behaviors, then, are rational actions that you perform to try to prevent harm from occurring and to reduce anxiety. For example, a mother with OCD may try to suppress or neutralize intrusive thoughts about stabbing her baby. However, we shall see that in fact intrusive thoughts are not the problem, and so dealing with them by the safety-seeking behavior of trying to suppress the thoughts will actually increase their frequency.

To see for yourself how trying not to think of something increases rather than decreases its intrusiveness, try the following exercise:

- Close your eyes and imagine a pink elephant.
- Try really hard not to think of pink elephants for a minute; try to push any images of pink elephants out of your mind.

What did you notice was the effect of trying not to think of pink elephants? Most people find that all they can think of is pink elephants. In research this effect is called the 'white bear effect', from studies showing that when participants were asked to not think of white bears, they had more thoughts about them.

Understanding the apparently upside-down way in which the human mind works is a key to understanding and overcoming OCD. Very many people with this problem are caught in the trap of trying too hard to rid themselves of thoughts and doubts, and as a result bringing about the very opposite of what they want.

Still not convinced that trying to get rid of intrusive thoughts, images, or doubts makes them worse? Try a more 'real-life' behavioral experiment.

(a) Spend one day dealing with your intrusive thoughts or doubts in the usual way, and record the frequency of them and the distress they cause you.
(b) Spend the next day trying even harder to get rid of your intrusive thoughts and record their frequency and the distress they cause you. Try as hard as you can to suppress them.
(c) The following day, go back to your usual way of dealing with your obsessions.
(d) The next day, repeat step (b).

Take a look at the results of your four-day experiment. What do you make of them? Most people discover that the harder they try to get rid of their obsessions, the more frequent and disturbing they become.

The implication for overcoming OCD is an obvious one: conduct experiments on your solutions for OCD. Observe whether carrying out a safety behavior increases or decreases your worrying about the harm that could occur. Then stop trying so hard not to have the doubt, thought, image, or impulse that's bothering you – you'll find that it will bother you much less! After all, a thought or urge is only *intrusive* if you don't let it in and recognize it for what it is. Stop trying to exclude it and it's just a thought or urge.

Criteria for Terminating Compulsions

We mentioned in Chapter 1 that one of the main differences between virtually all compulsions and normal actions in individuals without OCD is the reason for finishing a compulsion. Someone without OCD finishes checking the lights are off when they can see that the lights are off. However, someone with a fear of causing a fire finishes not when they can see that the lights are off, but when they also feel 'comfortable', 'certain', or 'just right'. This is the main reason why compulsions can take so long and why they do not always work.

Interestingly, individuals without OCD might use emotional criteria such as feeling comfortable when they make a major decision in their life such as buying a new home or whether they will marry someone. For example, when buying a new home, you might take into account whether you feel 'just right' when you are in the property as well as objective criteria such as whether you are close to shops or your place of work. For someone with OCD, it is as if they are making a major decision of momentous importance many times a day. Not surprisingly, this becomes extremely stressful and exhausting.

You may sometimes halt a compulsion if you have an important appointment or if you are interrupted by someone.

You may then feel you have to put the compulsion 'on hold' and return to it at a later time; but you still feel that isn't finished until you have fulfilled the same emotional criteria.

Using criteria such as feeling 'just right' or 'comfortable' is, therefore, a problem; indeed, it is a major factor in maintaining OCD and keeping you feeling anxious. Overcoming compulsions has to involve:

- giving up these emotional criteria and ending a ritual when you feel uncomfortable, uncertain, not right, or anxious;
- using only objective criteria (e.g. *seeing* that the light is turned off; *realizing* that you did not accidentally hurt a child because the child *looks* happy; *accepting* that some questions such as what will happen when you die are unanswerable).

Overcoming OCD

Whatever the cause of your OCD, it is worth restating that, for most people, OCD can be effectively overcome. Future research may reveal that different types of OCD improve with different types of treatments or techniques, but for the moment there is very little research to guide such questions.

When it comes to change, the 'cognitive' in cognitive behavior therapy refers to changing the *meaning* of intrusive thoughts and urges; 'behavior' means altering the way you *respond* to the obsessions. CBT will also try to help the person overcome other attitudes, such as the need for certainty that nothing bad will happen, and to alter the criteria they may use to terminate a compulsion (e.g. 'when I feel comfortable' or 'when it's just right') standards that will tend to maintain a compulsion.

You can learn to apply many of these principles by working through this book. If you are unsuccessful on your own, then don't give up: you can always seek professional help and use the book in addition to the therapy. If CBT is done formally then at least three-quarters of people can be helped substantially. If this does not work either, then you can always try adding medication, which can help the same proportion of people with OCD. So at the present the prospects are good; and in the future, if the necessary funding is devoted to research, there is every chance that further progress will be made in the psychological understanding of OCD, and that further improvements in therapy will follow.

PART TWO

Overcoming Obsessive Compulsive Disorder

3

Cognitive Behavior Therapy and Self-Help for Obsessive Compulsive Disorder

Now here comes the really important part – the techniques you can use to overcome your OCD. This chapter is a guide to the principles that are used in self-help and cognitive behavior therapy (CBT). There is good research to show the benefit to be gained if you apply these principles consistently and regularly. If you find the techniques difficult to apply, you might want to seek help from a therapist or consider recruiting an ally in overcoming your OCD (sometimes called a 'co-therapist').

As you strive to overcome your OCD it is inevitable that from time to time you will run into an obstacle or setback. This is an entirely natural part of therapy, and the more you expect this, the better you'll be able to reduce its impact. In Chapter 5 we talk about some common obstacles in applying these principles. It would be better to read right through Chapters 3, 4, and 5 before you start trying to overcome your OCD, because even the best laid plans do not always run smoothly, and if you have a good idea of both how the principles work and the difficulties you might face, you will have a better chance of staying the course.

Contemporary treatment of OCD has developed over time, and now has several strands, some of which overlap with others. To give the clearest picture we can, in this chapter we first outline the different elements of treatment and the way they have developed historically, and then show how they might be used to get the best results.

Exposure and Response Prevention

Exposure and response prevention was the first effective psychological treatment for OCD. It has been refined and developed over several years, and remains the foundation for an effective self-help approach to overcoming OCD.

Exposure

You may already be familiar with the principles of exposure. You may have heard of 'facing your fears' as the main treatment for phobias, such as fear of spiders, birds, or snakes. However, in many cases of OCD, the 'fear' is not just of an object or activity, but the thoughts, images, doubts, and impulses that it triggers. So *exposure* means facing your fears in a prolonged period of contact until the anxiety reduces naturally. *Response prevention* means not responding to your urges to ritualize or use one of your safety-seeking behaviors (which are just another way of avoiding fear and thinking that you can prevent harm). The theory behind exposure is that by deliberately and repeatedly facing your fears or obsessions, and not responding to them, you will become used to them, and your fear will subside.

The process of exposure and response prevention, and the gradual reduction in anxiety that follows, is called *habituation*. This is just a scientific word for getting used to something so that the strength of our reaction reduces. When you first get into a swimming pool, for example, the water can seem very cold, but you soon discover that the temperature is comfortable.

For someone with fears of contamination who is avoiding touching the floor, following this principle might mean touching the floor and not washing. For another person with intrusive thoughts of being a pedophile, it might mean experiencing the intrusive thoughts without responding to them, and being with children alone with the thought. In both these examples the anxiety will gradually fade if you are not doing something (such as responding to the thought) to maintain it.

Response Prevention

The term 'response prevention' (sometimes called 'ritual prevention') refers to stopping yourself responding to your intrusive thoughts or images by any form of engagement with the obsession. The usual response is a ritual or a safety-seeking behavior, which has the aim of reducing anxiety or harm. To overcome OCD, you'll need to resist the rituals and safety-seeking behaviors in order for the exposure to be effective and to allow the anxiety to fade. Response prevention is less effective if it is done without deliberate and repeated exposure. In general, it's important to tackle the rituals first before you start an exposure program. This is because there will be little benefit from doing exposure, for example, by touching a toilet seat, if you then compulsively wash your hands and 'decontaminate' yourself.

Figure 3.1 shows first what happens when your obsession is triggered and you do a ritual, and then what happens when you confront your fear *without* a ritual or safety behavior. Over time, the anxiety gradually fades and the urge to ritualize will fade too. When you then repeat the exposure (preferably as soon after the first exposure as possible), the anxiety will decrease further – and so on each time you do the exposure. This is illustrated in Figure 3.2.

Review your criteria for finishing a compulsion

An important development in response prevention stems from the observation that individuals with OCD use emotional criteria to finish their compulsions. Individuals without OCD finish a routine such as washing or checking when they have objective evidence that it has been adequately performed – for example, when they can see that their hands are clean. However, someone with OCD uses additional, subjective criteria to finish a ritual: they finish only when they feel 'comfortable', or 'just right', or 'certain', so the process usually takes much longer.

Using this basis for a decision, such as whether you're going

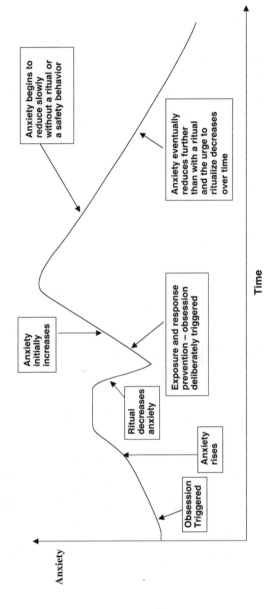

The boxes in the figure read:

Anxiety begins to reduce slowly without a ritual or a safety behavior

Anxiety eventually reduces further than with a ritual and the urge to ritualize decreases over time

Anxiety initially increases

Exposure and response prevention – obsession deliberately triggered

Ritual decreases anxiety

Anxiety rises

Obsession Triggered

Time

Anxiety

Figure 3.1 Effect of exposure and response prevention on anxiety within a session

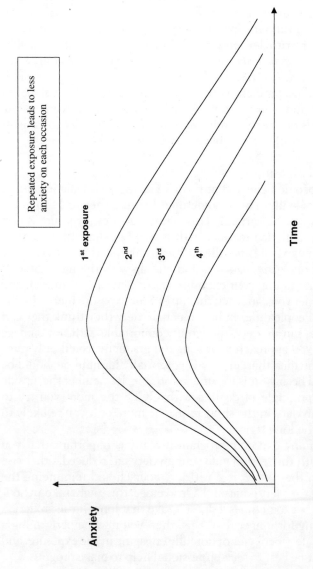

Repeated exposure leads to less
anxiety on each occasion

1st exposure

2nd

3rd

4th

Anxiety

Time

Figure 3.2   Effect of repeated exposure and response prevention

79

to stop washing or checking, will inevitably cause problems. Therefore, when finishing a ritual, do not go by how you 'feel'. Refocus your attention and concentrate on the environment around you and the external evidence. This means finishing an action or a ritual when you still feel anxious, so that you will be *acting against the way you feel.* This goes against the grain when you believe you have to be guided by your feelings or 'sixth sense'. The problem is that you're receiving a false signal of danger and you're now trying too hard to prevent harm. Compulsions become reinforced because they work (or at least used to work) and you have now become used to them.

Graded exposure

Many people believe that if you're facing your fears it must be done gradually. This is sometimes because they feel too much anxiety can be harmful. This is not true. Yes, exposure is best done in a graded manner with a series of steps (the planned steps for exposure are called a 'hierarchy'), so that you face your less intimidating fears first and end up with the most difficult last. But grading your exposure is just a means to an end, and the sooner you can reach the top of your exposure hierarchy the better. People differ in how much anxiety they think they can tolerate, but anxiety, though uncomfortable, will not damage you. If you approach your fears too gradually, you'll only reinforce the idea that anxiety is potentially harmful or should be avoided because it is too uncomfortable. Remember the 'upside down' principle of dealing with OCD: the more you try to avoid anxiety in the short term, the more of it you're likely to get in the long term.

With any exposure program it really is important that you stick with the session *until* your anxiety has reduced, otherwise you run the risk of 'resensitizing' yourself and reinforcing the idea that anxiety is harmful. On average, this might take an hour or two, but sometimes it doesn't take that long. If the anxiety is persisting for longer than this, then you may be performing a subtle safety behavior or not fully engaging in the exposure, and it might be best to seek professional help to make progress.

One way of remembering what exposure and response prevention means is the 'FEAR' acronym:

Face
Everything
And
Recover

The basic steps of exposure and response prevention are given below.

1 Develop a Hierarchy of Triggers

As noted above, a 'hierarchy' is the basis of a step by step plan of exposure that you carry out in order to face your fears and reduce your anxiety. Make a list of the triggers that you tend to fear or avoid because they activate your obsession. These may be activities, situations, substances, people, words, sounds, objects, or ideas – the range of forms will depend on your particular obsession. We have included a table for you to complete in Appendix 5. An example of some of Maureen's hierarchy is shown in Table 3.1.

Try to group the activities you avoid into different themes (e.g. contamination, aggression, order) and, within the themes, try to put them in order of how much distress would occur. You can measure the amount of distress by using a rating scale of 'SUDs'. SUD is an acronym for Standard Units of Distress, whereby 0 is no distress at all and 100 is the most distressing. Rate each activity according to how much distress you expect if you experience that trigger and don't perform a compulsion. For example, you may think that creating disorder in your wardrobe might be rated as 70 out of 100. Another individual with OCD might rate watching a videotape about the devil 99 out of 100, and so on.

People who have fears of contamination usually have no difficulty in finding lots of objects or activities that are contaminating, such as touching toilet seats or door handles. Once your

Table 3.1   **Maureen's hierarchy of exposure to feared triggers**

Trigger (object, word, place, person, situation, substance)	Estimated anxiety or distress (0–100)	Actual anxiety at end (0–100)
Theme – Order		
Leave drops of water on my shower door	100	
Make soap-dish holder in bathroom not straight	90	
Mess up towels in bathroom so not aligned	90	
Mess up floor mats in bathroom so not straight	80	
Put pillow to the side of the bed	80	
Rearrange shirts without being grouped by colour	70	
Make sleeves on tops and dresses look crooked	60	
Theme – Checking		
Deliberately leave the shower dripping	90	
Leave the house without checking my handbag	80	
Park the car without pulling the handbrake up too hard	80	
Park the car without checking it	70	

hands feel contaminated, exposure will often need to involve touching your face or your hair or possessions around your home.

The nature of an exposure task will depend upon your problem and whether you're someone who is avoiding lots of situations or activities (where it's easier to come up with suitable exposure) or a person who is avoiding fewer things but has lots of compulsions (where you may need to be a little more creative). Here it's not just a matter of resisting the compulsion: it's important to combine it wherever possible with exposure. For example, an exposure task for a checker might involve leaving a tap deliberately dripping. Some exposures are not possible – for example, we can't ask you to leave your front door unlocked unless you live in a very remote area! Here the exposure is to the *idea* of the door being unlocked, resisting the ritual to check and finishing when you feel uncomfortable or uncertain.

Exposure for someone who is worried about being aggressive to children might involve babysitting. Exposure for someone who is concerned with order might be deliberately creating disorder. Exposure for someone who has an obsession with correctly carrying out a religious ritual may be to do it incorrectly until they have recovered from OCD; then they can revert to performing the religious observance in the way it was intended. We hope you'll get ideas about suitable exposure tasks as you read this book.

Always plan your exposure in a series of steps that lead up to your final goals. Set a particular time frame, which you then attempt to keep to, like a set of instructions. The hierarchy should include things that you wouldn't normally do, or that seem bizarre – for example, one person had first to imagine and then try to transfer himself to a parallel world, as this was his obsession and was associated with enormous anxiety. Sometimes imagining your worst fears can be an important step or the most appropriate exposure. However, imagined exposure is, in general, not as potent as doing exposure in real life, and so wherever possible it is best to follow it up with actual situations or activities that are associated with the fear.

2 Face Your Fear: 'Just Do It'

Decide which targets you will take from the hierarchy and, for each, deliberately face your fear. Choose targets that are challenging but not overwhelming. Do not spend too much time on the easier targets if they are not sufficiently challenging and anxiety-provoking. You may need to ask a friend to come up with suitable tasks which are more anxiety-provoking.

3 Make Exposure Long Enough

Always ensure that your exposure is challenging and potent not only in terms of the target, but in terms of the time you expose yourself to it. Face your fear long enough for your anxiety to subside of its own accord, ideally by at least half. For example, when you touch a toilet seat, you might feel 95 SUDs; but within say 15 minutes, this will probably decrease to 60

SUDs, and within half an hour or an hour to 30 SUDs. At that point the best thing would be to rub your face and possessions with your 'contaminant' and spread it around as much as you can. This makes the exposure more potent.

4 Make Exposure Frequent Enough

Repeat the exposure as often as possible. Daily exposure is an absolute minimum until the anxiety has subsided between the sessions. Remember, you can never do too much exposure: aim for several times a day. Always think about how you can incorporate exposure into your everyday life so that it is easier to carry it out on a daily basis. More complex and severe OCD may require almost constant exposure.

5 No Anxiety-Reducing Strategies

Do the exposure without using distraction, drugs, alcohol, compulsions, or other safety-seeking behaviors such as saying a phrase to yourself or obtaining reassurance. It's important to 'engage fully' with the exposure, which means focusing on the trigger, allowing the obsession to enter your mind, and allowing your anxiety to increase and fall naturally. Ensure that you do the exposure without condemning, judging, ruminating, pitying, or blaming yourself. This is especially important if your exposure is reactivating an old memory which has been traumatic for you. The goal is to just accept the memory with the anxiety: don't engage with any of the intrusive ideas and wait for the anxiety to fade by itself. The key issue here is *acceptance*; we'll be discussing this in more detail shortly.

If you're not sure about whether what you're doing is a safety-seeking behavior, ask yourself what the aim is before you carry it out. If the aim is to reduce the risk of harm, or to make you feel less anxious, then it is a safety-seeking behavior and will reinforce your beliefs about being able to prevent harm.

6 If You Do a Ritual, Repeat the Exposure

If you cannot resist carrying out a ritual or safety behavior, you must redo the exposure so that you always finish with exposure. For example, if you wash ritualistically after you feel contaminated from touching a toilet handle, then touch it again; then touch your face and other possessions so that they are all 'contaminated'. If you checked that the tap or electrical appliance was switched off, then you may need to leave the tap dripping or the appliance switched on.

7 Monitor Your Exposure Tasks

Always monitor your exposure so you learn from it and watch your progress. This is also essential when you're seeing a therapist so he or she can monitor whether you're doing exposure that you negotiated in the previous session. You should also monitor the frequency of your rituals and how you coped with them. A suitable form is given in Appendix 5 (entitled 'Obsessions and Compulsions Record Sheet') and a completed sheet is shown in Table 3.2.

Complex Covert (Mental) Rituals

If you have complex intrusive thoughts and rituals in your head, you need to be clear exactly what thoughts or images are anxiety-provoking (which will be used for exposure) and how you normally respond to reduce anxiety (which may also be thoughts or images that you will need to resist). Intrusive thoughts and ruminations are generally more difficult to overcome than overt compulsions, and we discuss later in this book other strategies that you can use to tackle them. If you have severe problems here, it might be worth getting the assistance of a professional experienced in helping people overcome OCD.

Table 3.2 Obsessions and compulsions record sheet – an example

Trigger	Intrusive thought (words, image, doubt, impulse)	Interpretation: What the intrusive thought meant to me	Response: What I wanted to do (urges, compulsions, or safety behaviors)	Alternative response or behavioral experiment
Seeing a piece of broken glass on the path	The image of a child tripping and falling on the glass, leaving a piece of glass sticking out of her leg	Pictures in my mind are a portent for the future. If I don't do something to prevent this it will be my fault	I wanted to pick the glass up and throw it away and look carefully for glass on the path as I went home	This is just a picture in my mind. I'm not responsible for keeping the world safe. Just let the image happen
Touching my shoes as I took them off as I came in the front door	I might have trodden in dog excrement as I walked from the car without noticing and pass germs on to my children	The thought of treading in dog excrement is the same as it happening. It's irresponsible to take risks with my children's health. They could go blind	I wanted to place my shoes on some newspaper, wash my hands three times with anti-bacterial soap, change my clothes, and wash my hands again	It's just a thought that I'm contaminated. Not taking risks is making me ill. Next time I'll use the exposure and tolerate the doubts to make life better for myself and my kids
The children playing in the back garden	The things they are touching outside might not be clean, and the germs they have on them might make them ill	Thinking that the children are contaminated is the same as them being contaminated. I must make certain that they don't get ill. It's my responsibility as a parent. If they bring germs in they'll transfer them around the house	I wanted to insist that the children wash their hands and changed their clothes as soon as they came in	This is a just a thought that they are contaminated and they'll get ill. Letting the children expose themselves to a few germs isn't irresponsible – it's normal! If they do get ill there's every chance they would get better again. Do the exposure by getting them contaminated

Loop Tapes

One option for intrusive thoughts that are significantly anxiety-provoking is to do exposure with a cassette loop tape (of the kind normally used in old telephone answering machines.) You would first record on the loop tape the content of the intrusive thought (e.g. Judith recorded her intrusive thoughts about her grandchildren dying: 'Rosa and Dheeresh have gone under a bus'). It is very important that you record only the thoughts that are anxiety-provoking and *not* your response, that is, any mental rituals or neutralizing (in this example Judith would normally say to herself: 'It's me going under the bus' to 'save' her grandchildren by neutralizing the thought which she had to resist). You would then listen with a pair of headphones to the recorded thoughts repeatedly on the loop tape without responding (e.g. with mental rituals or neutralizing) until the anxiety has subsided. You would monitor the effect of the exposure over time and then, if the anxiety is decreasing, repeat it at least daily until you're no longer anxious about the intrusive thoughts.

If, however, your intrusive thoughts and ideas:

- do not generate a high level of anxiety, or
- are not apparently linked to any mental rituals or neutralizing, or
- if they are associated with another emotion such as feeling depressed, ashamed, angry or guilty, then professional advice is required as exposure may not be helpful (and could even be counterproductive).

Here it may be more helpful not to respond to the intrusive thoughts in any manner; just to acknowledge the thoughts, to stop comparing or rating yourself, and to refocus your attention externally on the environment and other practical tasks (such as really listening to someone and talking to them).

It is usually helpful to make intrusive thoughts and images as concrete as possible. Examples include trying to draw or paint an intrusive image that is disturbing you (e.g. someone with an intrusive image of crucifying his children set about making a large crucifix in the garden with his children as part of the Easter celebrations). Intrusive thoughts and fears about being homosexual might require you to go and have a drink in a gay bar, or buy homosexual porn; if you have thoughts about the devil you might use a ouija board, watch the *The Exorcist*, and plaster the number 666 over your walls. Of course, we don't want to offend anyone's cultural beliefs; but sometimes when you're fighting OCD, you have to bring in the big guns.

Some Objections and Pitfalls

Treatment First, 'Normal' Later

You might be concerned at some of the suggestions we are making for exposure; but remember, they are a means to an end. As soon as your anxiety is reduced and you have overcome your OCD, you can bin them. Sometimes people complain that what they're being encouraged to do during exposure is 'abnormal' and therefore unreasonable. For example, someone who is asked to touch the sole of their shoe without washing their hands afterwards might say something like, 'Even someone without OCD wouldn't do that!' as if the therapist were being entirely unreasonable. (We are not saying therapists are never unreasonable: it's just that this is more likely to be a problem of misunderstanding!) We've also encountered family members, partners, friends, or even fellow professionals who have been more than happy to 'back up' the person with OCD in this respect, saying things like, 'Well, I certainly wouldn't do it!' (in which case they probably shouldn't be helping a person with OCD).

But if you think about it, many treatments for human ailments involve doing the unusual. How 'normal' is swallowing toxic chemicals every day? Chemotherapy for cancer involves just that. How 'normal' is it to wrap a leg in a cast? Yet if it's broken, this is very helpful. We accept these 'abnormal' activities as part of 'normal' treatment for physical problems. Part of the problem when tackling a psychological disorder such as OCD is that, because of the stigma and shame surrounding psychological and emotional difficulties, the normal processes of overcoming fears are not so readily discussed and understood.

So remember, if you're reading this book as part of your plan to overcome OCD, your exposure needs to be frequent enough, long enough, and 'potent' enough, and carried out without any safety behaviors, if it is to reduce your anxiety and discomfort significantly. Would you expect a medication to be effective if you took less than the recommended dose and less often than prescribed?

We realize that facing your fears is much easier said than done, but if you don't carry out potent enough exposures sufficiently frequently you'll drag out the recovery process, which can sap your motivation. In the worst-case scenario, experienced by many people with OCD who have made unsuccessful attempts to overcome it in the past, your exposure and response prevention program is insufficiently 'strong' or thorough to have a good and lasting effect on your OCD, and you end up feeling no better.

Why Stopping Rituals Often Isn't Enough

Because rituals are frequently the most obvious manifestation of OCD, it's an understandable error to concentrate on stopping rituals, without carrying out enough exposure. Although there is little doubt that stopping rituals is an important initial stage of overcoming OCD, it often is not enough to reduce a person's fear. Going that bit further, and deliberately seeking to activate your intrusive thought, image, doubt, or urge, and *stick with it until the anxiety reduces*, is essential if you're to overcome OCD fully.

Why is this? The problem is that while you may do well overall in reducing or stopping rituals in your day-to-day life, the time may well come when you encounter a trigger that you have not prepared for. Furthermore, people who concentrate on ritual prevention tend not to get long enough exposures to habituate fully to their obsession and alter their beliefs about the intrusive thought or urge.

Think of doing repeated and deliberate exposure as a way of providing yourself with enough opportunities to practice allowing intrusive thoughts to come and go without using rituals. If you want to get to the point where you can respond 'automatically' to your intrusive thoughts without anxiety or rituals, you will obviously need deliberate practice first.

Why Making Exposure Easier Doesn't Work

One of the main mistakes that people make when trying to overcome OCD is to make their exposure sessions easier on themselves by doing them with a certain degree of ritual, or transfer of responsibility, or reassurance. Ultimately, this has the effect of diluting the exposure and reducing (or stopping) its therapeutic effect. Here are some common pitfalls – all safety-seeking behaviors – to look out for:

- Only carrying out an exposure exercise after discussing its potential for harm with someone else.
- Only carrying out an exposure exercise after carefully calculating the risks involved.
- Running over the exposure session in your mind to check for any possible ways in which you may have caused harm.
- Always talking over the exposure task with someone after you've done it.
- Doing a ritual after exposure. (Remember always to transfer 'contamination' to your body or possessions to make this more difficult.)
- Carrying out neutralizing or a 'covert' (in your head) ritual in place of an 'overt' (behavioral) ritual during or after the exposure.
- Doing exposure, then using avoidance to try to 'contain' the exposure (e.g. touching the floor but then avoiding touching other surfaces).

Some Other Techniques, and Their Disadvantages

Response Reduction

Response reduction is a variation of response prevention that involves gradually reducing the frequency of the rituals. For example, Natalie was encouraged by her previous therapist to reduce her checking of the water taps, locks, gas taps, and electrical appliances, which took 1 hour 45 minutes, so that, initially, it took only 1 hour 30 minutes. In principle, this seems a good idea; but the method is inelegant and the individual often gets stuck and ends up still doing some rituals. Gradually reducing rituals can often become not a way to get to the ultimate goal, but rather a means of avoiding exposure and testing out one's fears. Another problem is that many individuals can speed up their rituals so they still feel 'comfortable' or 'just right' at the end of the procedure, while no change has really occurred.

We are not saying this approach should never be used, just that it should be used with caution. The approach seems attractive but it does not put enough emphasis on exposure or a behavioral experiment. You need instead to alter your criteria: instead of finishing when you feel 'comfortable' or 'just right', use a different yardstick – such as 'I will not check after I can *see* the appliance is turned off (even though I still feel uncomfortable and 'not right')'. In Natalie's case, she was taught to resist the urges to check altogether: if she was unable to resist the check, then she was asked to turn the tap on and leave the room. This was part of an experiment to test her belief that if she left the water tap on there would be a flood. In other words, the emphasis in change should be on exposure and behavioral experiments to test out your theories rather than just reducing the frequency of your rituals.

Rubber Bands and 'STOP!'

Some people have been taught to shout 'Stop!' at their intrusive thoughts or have a rubber band around their wrist and snap it when the thoughts arise. Fortunately, this method seems to be dying out, as it can make things worse. We saw in Chapter 2 that if you try to stop or suppress intrusive thoughts and urges, then their frequency increases (the 'white bear' phenomenon). It is important to identify clearly the obsession which you find anxiety-provoking and the way in which you respond to it (the compulsions and neutralizing which reduce your anxiety). Trying to stop an intrusive thought or obsession will just make it worse. Resisting a compulsion is of course helpful, but you do not need to snap rubber bands or shout to do this. If resisting a compulsion is a problem and you can't stop yourself, then ensure that you 'undo' the compulsion by following it with exposure. For example, if you do a mental compulsion that involves swapping an upsetting image of loved ones being killed in a car accident with a neutral image of the car driving along the road, follow it with exposure to the original thought and this time imagine the carnage on the road being much worse and your loved one dying in agony.

Building Alternative Explanations: Theory A versus Theory B

So far, we've discussed the principals of exposure and response prevention, which have made up the major part of behavior therapy since the early 1970s and for which we have to thank researchers such as Professors Isaac Marks and Edna Foa. One of the problems of using exposure and response prevention is that about 25 per cent of patients may refuse to do it, or drop out of treatment early. Cognitive therapy has therefore tried to refine and develop the principles, and this has given rise to the approach which we now call *cognitive behavior therapy*. The hope is that the 'cognitive' part of the therapy will reach the parts that 'behavior' therapy on its own has failed to reach, although this has not yet been proved in a research trial of people with OCD who have failed pure exposure and response prevention.

A critical contribution from cognitive therapy, which we

have to thank researchers such as Professor Paul Salkovskis for, is the process of building an alternative explanation of a person's intrusive thoughts, images, doubts, and impulses. This latter concept will help you to integrate the behavioral and cognitive approaches to overcoming OCD.

The essence of overcoming OCD by using the various techniques outlined throughout this book is to gather evidence to see 'which theory fits the facts'. As you learn more about the way your OCD works, by doing experiments and changing various aspects of the problem, you should become clearer as to which theory best explains what's going on. For example, Theory A might be that you really are a nasty pedophile and if you stop trying so hard to prevent yourself from abusing children then you will act upon your urges and abuse children. Theory B is that you are someone who cares a great deal about children; your problem is that worrying about being a pedophile, and trying too hard to prevent yourself being a pedophile, increase both your obsession and your distress.

Behavioral Experiments

A 'behavioral experiment' is a development of exposure and a way of putting a theory to the test in reality. Just as a scientist would carry out an experiment to test a theory, people can use experiments to learn more about the personal theories they have about their OCD. (Suitable forms to write down your theories and behavioral experiments are given in Appendix 5.) Progress will depend upon your acting for a limited time as if Theory B were true, and conducting behavioral experiments to test whether the evidence best fits Theory A or Theory B.

For example, the experiment might involve being alone with a child, and although thinking about abusing the child, not responding to such thoughts with any mental rituals or neutralizing. If Theory A is correct, then you would act upon your urges and be a pedophile. If Theory B is correct, then the worries about being pedophile will slowly fade.

Other types of behavioral experiment are designed to

improve your understanding of the nature of the problem (e.g. to see whether checking increases rather than decreases doubt), and to help you gather more information about specific obsessions (e.g. whether thinking about something bad happening increases the chance of it happening).

In some cases, behavioral experiments will mean you can conclusively test out a thought (e.g. 'If I don't get some form of reassurance I'll become more and more anxious and lose control'). In others, they can help you to gather evidence to discover which theory is in all probability most accurate.

Sometimes the therapist will volunteer to do an experiment to help you test out a theory. In the example above, one theory was that at least one person with OCD might have acted on their intrusive thoughts about abusing children or committing a murder. One of us once searched the database for the special hospitals – institutions that provide custody and treatment for those with mental illness who have committed crimes that make them a danger to others. Many hundreds of people have been admitted to these special hospitals over the past twenty years and yet, despite the many acts of murder, violence, and pedophilia they have committed, not one of these patients has ever been diagnosed with OCD. We could therefore safely reject any theory that an OCD sufferer is a pedophile or a murderer, and communicate to our patient and all health professionals that individuals with OCD are the safest group in the world. We can say they are *less* likely to act upon their intrusive thoughts and ideas than people without OCD. Someone who needs a babysitter or nanny to look after their children could do a lot worse than hire someone with OCD and intrusive thoughts about harming children!

Cognitive Therapy: Thinking about Thoughts

Cognitive therapy also focuses on the meaning we attach to events, thoughts, and images. The more negative the meaning we give something, the more negative the emotion we feel. Human beings easily misinterpret things, giving them a more negative meaning than they deserve. In the case of OCD, the heart of the problem is the way normal intrusive thoughts, images, doubts, and urges are misinterpreted as abnormal, unacceptable, or dangerous. Cognitive therapy helps people develop a more realistic and helpful way of understanding the mental events they worry so much about and to develop behavioral experiments to test out their theories. However, try to gain a better understanding of your own problem *before* you feel panicky and are having intrusive thoughts or urges. Be cautious about these techniques when you are highly anxious, as we don't want to teach you how to improve reassurance and mental rituals rather than eliminate them! We will return to this possibility below in the section entitled 'Be Careful CBT Does Not Become a Ritual'.

Cognitive therapy can also help you to reduce the chances of your OCD returning, by helping you to understand some of the thinking styles and philosophies that make you vulnerable to the problem. It can then give you tools to help reduce the chance of these problems recurring. We go into these, too, in more detail later in this chapter.

A third way in which cognitive therapy can be especially helpful is in reducing the obstacles to change, such as shame and depression, that many individuals with OCD encounter when as they strive towards overcoming it. This area is developed further in Chapter 5.

Thinking Errors

Understanding your 'thinking errors' (sometimes called 'cognitive distortions') is a key aspect of cognitive therapy. These inaccurate or unhelpful ways of thinking are by no means unique to OCD sufferers – on the contrary, nearly everyone tends to fall into them from time to time. Unfortunately, emotions such as anxiety, depression, guilt, and shame tend to increase the extent to which we tend to think in a distorted way, and these distorted thoughts can, in turn, lead to more emotions.

Magical Thinking

Magical thinking is the belief that one has the power to influence good or bad events, and leads on to superstitious behaviors. Magical thinking is common in OCD. The goal here is to accept intrusive thoughts, images, and urges without engaging in any mental activity or behavior that makes us think we can magically prevent them from occurring. 'Acceptance' means treating the thought as *just a thought* – for example, if you believe that you're contaminated and that you will lose control and go crazy, you are *having a thought* that you are contaminated and will lose control and go crazy. It's purely a mental event.

To strip intrusive thoughts and images of their assumed 'power', we recommend a positive pursuit of anti-superstition, to the point of *trying* to make bad things happen in our head and in writing to show that it can't be done. Bad things do occasionally happen to all of us, but by chance, not because we have willed it or 'tempted fate'. We have demonstrated this approach for you by trying deliberately to make bad events happen to our loved ones (see Box 3.1). The acting of writing and printing these statements in a book means that we have thought about them and we have not neutralized them or said a prayer to undo them. Over the past fifteen years we have shown our patients and trainees the attempt to kill off our respective loved ones in our heads many thousands of times, but it's never worked yet! If something does happen, then our consciences will be completely clear. Bad events like car crashes do occur, for reasons such as mechanical failure or bad weather, or simply being in the wrong place at the wrong time – for example, in the way of a drunk driver over whose behavior we have no influence. There are no known mechanisms for us to induce a bad event by thinking or writing something bad and not following it up with a ritual or prayer to 'undo' it; and if a bad event does happen, there are no thought police to investigate us.

So stand up and fight against OCD and superstitious claptrap! For example, if you're worried about unlucky numbers, make a goal of asking for 13 in various transactions and have pictures of 666 in your bedroom. They're just numbers!

> *I wish that my wife, Elizabeth, and my two daughters Camilla and Rebecca would die in a horrific car crash.*
>
> 1/1/2005   David Veale
>
> *I wish that my partner, Jessica, and my daughters Emma and Lucy will catch a fatal illness.*
>
> 1/1/2005   Rob Willson

Catastrophizing

As we've seen earlier, individuals with OCD have very often made a 'catastrophic misinterpretation' of an intrusive thought, intrusive image, a doubt, or an urge to act in an unacceptable or unusual way. One way of tackling this is first to identify your catastrophic misinterpretation, and think of some alternative ways of interpreting it. An example of a form to help you to do this before you get panicky was given in Table 3.2. However, be careful that using the record does not become a ritual and a way of reassuring yourself when you're anxious.

'Black-and-white' thinking

This refers to thinking in opposite extremes, or in an 'either/or' way. The problem is that when we think in extremes we tend also to feel and act in more unhelpful and extreme ways. Examples of black-and-white thinking in OCD are:

'Either I'm sure that my intrusive thought is safe, or it's dangerous'
'Either I'm responsible for causing harm or I'm not'
'Either I'm clean or I'm dirty'

The solution to black-and-white thinking is to think in degrees, like a thermometer. This is what we call the 'continuum method for tackling black-and-white thinking' (Figure 3.3).

The aim in using the continuum technique is to set the two ends of the 'either/or' continuum using the concept you have

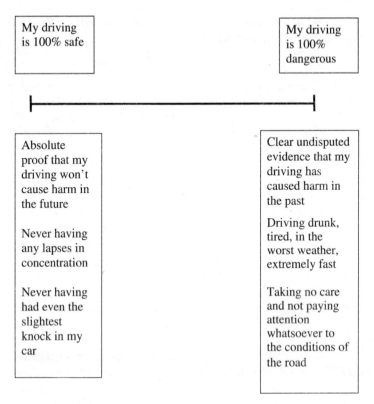

Figure 3.3   The continuum method for tackling black-and-white thinking

become caught up in, such as '100 per cent good person' and '100 per cent bad person' if you believe something like 'either I'm good in all I think or do or I'm a bad person'. Then define the qualities of each extreme and draw a line between the two, as in the figure. Now that you have the two ends of the continuum defined, you can step back and mark on the continuum where you truly fall. You can use this technique to be more realistic and less black and white about yourself on a number of scales, relating for example to your behavior, your thoughts, and your feelings.

Demands

'Must', 'should', 'have to', and 'ought' are all words that mean you are making demands of yourself or others. Examples of demands are:

- I should be in control of the thoughts and images that cross my mind.
- I must be certain that my actions or lack of action do not result in harm to myself or others.
- I've got to take every care not to pass on contamination.
- Because I'm a basically sensible person I ought to be able to get rid of my OCD without needing help or advice.
- Because my family know I become upset if they come into the house without washing their hands they absolutely should do so, whether or not they think it's reasonable.
- People ought to be more careful not to cause harm accidentally.

There are various problems with the demands we place on ourselves, other people, and the world around us:

- They're unhelpful, leading to painful, disturbed emotions (e.g. anxiety, guilt, shame) and counterproductive behaviors (e.g. rituals and avoidance) when they're not met. Even when we do meet them we quickly tend to become anxious about whether we'll be able to continue to meet them.
- They're inflexible, which makes them poorly suited to dealing with real people and the real world, which do not conform absolutely to rigid rules.
- They're illogical, in the sense that they do not logically follow from our wishes and preferences. For example, it's natural to want not to have images of the people we love being killed, but it does not make sense to say that because I do not like it (a preference), I must not have it (a demand).

The Problem of Trying Too Hard to Be Certain

As we have already seen, many individuals with OCD are driven by their need to banish uncertainty: undesired outcomes must not be allowed to happen. Our world is inherently uncertain, though, and no matter how hard you try to eliminate doubt, there is always going to be an element of it. Still, some people complain that to tolerate doubt is somehow sloppy and irresponsible, so they continue to try to make themselves believe that removal of doubt is possible, and probably essential.

At the heart of many emotional problems is the human tendency to take what is 'desirable' and elevate it in our minds to 'essential'. The 'need' for certainty is a good example of this. Here the idea that it would be nice to be certain (e.g. that we or our loved ones won't come to any harm) has been elevated into a need. The more you are able to practice the idea that *certainty about anything (yes, anything!) may be desirable, but is not essential*, the better you'll be able to tolerate the uncertainties and doubts that are a natural and unavoidable part of the world we live in without wasting needless time and energy on checks, rituals, and reassurance.

The Problem of Trying Too Hard to Control Your Thoughts

Learning to accept your thoughts

The idea that one should control one's thoughts is another common belief among individuals with OCD. The problem is that, as we have already seen, absolute control of one's thoughts is impossible and counterproductive, and results in more of the thoughts you were trying to get rid of, or their seeming to be even more out of control. Also, being able to choose the thoughts that enter your mind would almost entirely put a stop to any originality and creative problem-solving. It is so much easier and healthier to stop trying to control thoughts and feelings.

Imagine you are a bus driver and you are selective about who you want to get on and off your bus. The passengers are your thoughts, feelings, memories, and bodily experiences. Some of them look a bit scary in the way they are dressed, some are armed with knives, others smell a bit, and so on. Now, imagine trying to get some of these passengers off the bus or stop some of them getting on. It would be quite a struggle, and you would be unlikely to be able to drive very far while you are monitoring all your passengers and everyone who wants to get on! But this is precisely what you may be doing with your intrusive thoughts, images, urges, and feelings of anxiety. Being able to drive the bus and make progress means truly accepting and tolerating *all* your passengers and accepting them, even if they are a bit scary or smelly.

'Let them be' – detached observation and mindfulness

There is a trend in CBT towards the application of 'mindfulness' meditation in working towards an acceptance of emotion and suffering rather than trying to control such feelings. In many respects this approach fits neatly with contemporary psychological theory on how to manage intrusive thoughts, images, doubts, and urges. Mindfulness was originally (and still is) part of Zen Buddhist practice. However, researchers and clinicians have applied mindfulness without any of its religious connotations to helping people with mental distress. Mindfulness practice involves learning to be fully present in the current moment, but without passing judgment on that which you are experiencing. The application of this approach to overcoming OCD is obvious, since at the heart of the problem lie the making of extreme judgments about intrusive thoughts, images, doubts, and urges; these are the meanings and misinterpretations that give rise to obsessions.

Some people feel uncomfortable or confused about the spiritual connotations of mindfulness, whereas others find it helpful to think of it as an 'un-psychiatric' treatment. As yet no scientific studies have been done on formal mindfulness training in OCD, but theoretically it fits. Our experience is that it can be a useful *component* of treatment for some people with

OCD, especially when intrusive thoughts and urges are prominent. Mindfulness means acknowledging the intrusive thoughts and urges but not engaging with them, and instead refocusing your attention.

A useful analogy is to imagine the intrusive ideas as cars on a road. When you have OCD, you focus on particular cars and respond by trying to stop them or push them to one side (if you're not run over, that is). Alternatively, you may try to flag the car down, get into the driving seat and park it (that is, analyzing the idea and sorting it out until you feel 'right'). Of course, often there is no place to park; and then, as soon as you have parked one car, another one comes along.

Being 'mindful' means being on the footpath, acknowledging the cars that come past but just then walking along the footpath (that is, doing something else) and refocusing your attention on other parts of the environment (such as talking to the person beside you and noticing other people passing you and the sights and smells of the flowers on the verge). In other words, intrusive ideas have no other meaning than passing traffic – they're 'just' thoughts and images and part of the rich tapestry of human existence. OCD is a problem of misinterpreting normal thoughts and ideas and believing that you're able to prevent harm from occurring.

Questioning Thoughts and Reviewing the Evidence

A standard technique used in cognitive therapy is to question the content of a thought and to look at the evidence for and against it. For example, if you believe that a friend ignored you in the street, you might make yourself more depressed because you interpreted his actions as meaning that you're worthless and you will be alone all your life. Cognitive therapy would ask you to question the evidence for this interpretation and the logic that you have used to come to this conclusion. You might review your friend's behavior towards you in the past and come to an alternative explanation – for example, he may have been lost in his own thoughts and not deliberately ignoring you. You might then test this alternative theory by phoning him to see what had actually happened.

Be Careful CBT Does Not Become a Ritual

This is very important. The technique of questioning the *content* of an obsession is usually counterproductive in OCD. You may be making progress and resisting your compulsions and doing exposure, but still be troubled by obsessions. For example, Vic had fears of contamination. As soon he came near a 'contaminant' he would immediately experience urges to wash or think 'Get rid of it' or 'Don't let it touch anything else'. These urges are part of the original obsession. They're automatic and involuntary and are not something you can stop. However, he would respond by thinking, 'What would a rational person do?' or 'What would my friend say?' Alternatively, he would try to convince himself that it was not really contaminated and he had been told it was safe.

Now, this approach seems very sensible and some therapists and books may even teach you to do this. Such an approach sometimes 'works', and indeed Vic could get on with his life. However, it would often take Vic several hours to be sure in his mind that he felt comfortable and was certain that it was OK not to touch something without excessive washing. Questioning his intrusive thought had become a mental ritual, with the function of avoiding anxiety and uncertainty.

A similar problem occurs when you reassure yourself with the phrase 'It's just an OCD thought'. Here there are two problems. The first is that, as we saw in Chapter 2 (in the section 'The Overimportance of Thoughts'), the content of the thoughts in OCD is no different from that of the thoughts that occur in someone without OCD. Second, it is unhelpful to respond to such a thought: relabeling and reclassifying it as an 'OCD thought' has the function of reducing anxiety and uncertainty. We are not saying that relabeling thoughts is always unhelpful, but the timing is important. If you relabel thoughts when you're reviewing your OCD and what keeps it going, and deciding on how to tackle it, that's fine. *But* do not relabel thoughts at the time *when you are feeling anxious and want to reduce uncertainty*. This can become a mental ritual. It is more helpful to develop principles of acceptance and not engage with such thoughts and urges.

Marc, for example, had an intrusive thought about whether he had hit a baby in a passing baby carriage. He had been taught by an inexperienced therapist to question the evidence for and against this thought *when it occurred*. The trouble with this was that it taught Marc new mental rituals and encouraged him to reassure himself.

The problem is not the intrusive thoughts or urges (which are entirely normal) but the '*thoughts about the thoughts*' and the way you respond to them. Hence our detailed discussion on the meaning that you attach to intrusive thoughts in ways such as 'thought action fusion' (see page 96) and 'magical thinking'. OCD is a problem of misinterpreting normal thoughts and ideas as evidence that you are, for example, dangerous or bad, and believing that you're able to prevent harm from occurring. Beware, therefore, therapists who encourage you to challenge the *content* of intrusive thoughts and urges in OCD; what we're focusing on is the *process* – the *meaning* you attach to the thought and the way you *respond* to it. The content of the intrusive thoughts and images is perfectly normal. Questioning the content is probably something you already do but it increases your doubts and worries. Your goal in overcoming OCD is to not respond to your intrusive thoughts and urges. Acknowledge and note their passing nature, but do not engage with them.

Another problem with responding to a thought with a phrase that is reassuring is that it distracts you from following through with exposure and testing the beliefs in a behavioral experiment. The most powerful way of changing beliefs is to test them. An example is Naomi, who had intrusive thoughts about being in a parallel world and fears that her family and friends around her were 'false'. She found it difficult to articulate the 'awfulness' of being in a parallel world and, intellectually, she found the idea of being in a parallel world absurd. However, the idea made her extremely anxious and she was extremely handicapped, as she had developed a number of elaborate and complex behavioral rituals to avoid being in a parallel world. She had been taught to 'relabel' the idea of being in parallel world as 'just an OCD thought'. The problem was that she did this repeatedly when she experienced the intrusive thought so that the 'relabeling' became a safety behavior and somewhat reassured her. *Note again that 'relabeling' in the moment is a mental activity that involves engaging with the thought.* She remained very handicapped as she had difficulty in resisting any of her rituals.

It is also worth saying that cognitive therapy rarely ever involves just talking; it means following up mental activity with physical action to test your prediction. Naomi now needs to do exposure or a behavioral experiment to challenge the *idea* of whether she was in a parallel world. Naomi has two competing theories to test. Theory A is that she had a problem of being in a parallel world. Logically, she had to do everything she could to get herself back to the real world before any harm occurred. Theory B was that she worried excessively about being in a parallel world and being out of control, and that by trying too hard to control her thoughts she was increasing her worries. A behavioral experiment involved testing which theory best explained the phenomenon. For Naomi, this involved trying deliberately to jump into a parallel world and to stay there without any safety behaviors or rituals. (Who knows, it might even be better than this world!) She eventually agreed to try this and realized that her experience best fitted with Theory B, as her worries decreased when she stopped trying to escape from the *idea* of being in a parallel world. Doing this experiment was more effective than *intellectually* trying to relabel the thought and to convince herself that 'it was just an OCD thought'. You could teach a parrot to say 'It's just an OCD thought,' but it doesn't mean anything to the parrot, and in OCD making such a statement can become a ritual. It will not mean anything to you unless you follow it through with action and do the exposure to prove to yourself that it is *just* an interesting idea.

In summary, it is important to *acknowledge* an intrusive thought *when* it occurs. Don't attempt to suppress it or respond to it – for example, reassuring yourself that it is 'just an OCD thought' or 'just an obsession'. There is a danger that relabeling can become a ritual. Always try to act against the content of the thoughts by exposure and a behavioral experiment to test whether the data best fits Theory A or Theory B. If you're not sure whether you are responding, ask yourself what is the function of what you are doing. If you're trying to reduce anxiety or harm or avoid exposure, then you're responding to the thought.

Obsessions with a Sexual Content

A common intrusive thought is a doubt whether you're homosexual. It is of course perfectly normal to have such doubts, but again the thought needs to be seen in the context of your OCD. You may be horrified of being gay, so that the reason you have such worries or doubts is because you *fear* being gay and believe it would be devastating for you. You may then try too hard to banish such thoughts or ideas, or try to prove to yourself that you are *not* gay – for example, by visiting a prostitute or seeing if you can still get aroused with the opposite sex. Sometimes this backfires, because anxiety can interfere with normal sexual functioning, and this is likely to reinforce your fears that you may be gay.

It is very normal to have intrusive thoughts and worries about being homosexual, especially as an adolescent when you're beginning to develop your sexual identity and feelings. However, someone *without* OCD will treat such thoughts as just an idea, they might experiment, or they might accept that sexuality is not black and white. Just like any other intrusive thought, accept the thought and don't respond to it. Prove to yourself that it's just a thought by going to gay bars and being in the company of gay friends, and don't try to prove that you're heterosexual.

A similar situation occurs when someone with OCD becomes highly anxious about abusing a child. They may focus attention on their genitals to 'assess' their response to children or intrusive thoughts. They may notice sensations that are normally there and misinterpret them as signs of sexual arousal; they may notice arousal responses that are a consequence of anxiety, and misinterpret these as a sign of desire. Again, the more you gain confidence in these explanations of what is happening, by trying them out in reality, the sooner your obsession will subside. We should emphasize over and over again that having intrusive sexual thoughts towards children is perfectly normal. They pass through the minds of many people without OCD but no one pays much attention to them: they are irrelevant, just thoughts. Someone with OCD, by contrast, treats such thoughts as dangerous and starts to notice reflex sensations in their genitals as a sign they are aroused, and so the vicious circle of avoidance and mental rituals begins.

The Problem of Trying Too Hard to Control One's Behavior

A common obsessional response to intrusive thoughts, images, and urges, where there is a fear of acting in dangerous or socially unacceptable ways, is to try too hard to control your behavior. For example, if you're a person who fears blurting out obscenities in church, you might try to keep tight control of your mouth and vocal cords. The unfortunate thing about this, apart from being a total waste of time and energy, is that it focuses your attention on your body and leads you to be acutely aware of physical sensations that you otherwise would not notice. This then triggers more misinterpretations of these sensations, which appears to be evidence that you're really on the verge of losing control.

One of the worst costs of keeping tight control of behavior is that it can lead the individual with OCD to conclude things like: 'I narrowly escaped doing something terrible; luckily I just managed to stay in control . . . this time. I'd better be extra careful next time.'

There is a famous illustration of this in the 'keeping the tigers from the train' story:

> *A man was travelling on a train. The train guard walked past and noticed that the man was throwing crumbs of bread out of the window. The guard stopped and asked: 'Excuse me sir, can I ask why you are throwing crumbs of bread out of the window?' The man, continuing his unusual ritual, turned to look at the guard and said: 'To keep the tigers away from the train.' The guard, still more puzzled, responded: 'But there are no tigers here, sir'. The man replied: 'That's right; you see, it works!'*

The trick, as with so much in overcoming OCD, is to carry out a test and see for yourself that if you allow the urges to occur, without trying to suppress them, (a) your anxiety will pass much more quickly, and (b) nothing terrible will happen – there is no need to try so hard. It is your 'solutions' that are the problem.

Key learning point

Anxiety can frequently lead people to *feeling* out of control and trying harder to keep control of thoughts and behaviors. This focuses their attention on their anxiety. It can also:

- lead to the false conclusion that it was the act of keeping in control that prevented the feared catastrophe from happening;
- prevent the person from discovering that their fear won't come true or that it is not as awful as they anticipated.

The 'As if' Principle

If at this point you can accept an alternative explanation for you OCD 'intellectually' but do not 'feel' it in your gut, don't worry – that is a perfectly normal part of change. The most effective way to move from superficial intellectual insight to deeper conviction and belief is to act 'as if' you already 'felt' the new idea. One of the easiest ways of thinking about how to overcome OCD is to strive towards thinking and acting 'as if' you did not have OCD. The 'as if' principle can be used at either a general or a very specific level. Some people who have had OCD for many years complain that they cannot remember how they would have behaved before their behavior was dictated by OCD. Unsurprisingly, this is a particular problem for people who demand certainty that their actions are responsible and risk-free. The truth is that most individuals with OCD can make pretty good judgments about 'reasonable' behavior but, as we've already discussed, tend to be underconfident about their judgment. We shall discuss some specific guidelines for dealing with this and other obstacles when we turn to how you decide on your goals in Chapter 5.

The 'OCD-Free Twin' Technique

This is a useful technique to use when you're trying to decide upon an alternative behavior. Imagine a person who is the same as you in every respect, but does not have OCD. Then imagine what your OCD-free twin would do, and act 'as if' you were your OCD-free twin.

Friends, family members, and caregivers can also use this principle if they are unsure how to interact with you. They can also imagine your OCD-free twin, and strive towards treating you in the way they would your OCD-free twin. We give more detailed advice for family and friends later in the book (see Chapter 9).

The Survey Method

If you really cannot decide (or cannot agree!) on an alternative behavior, try the survey method, and quiz family and friends about what they'd do in a specific situation. However, be careful that this does not become a ritual for seeking reassurance or a means of justifying a ritual.

The survey method can also be a useful way of gathering information about kinds of intrusive thoughts, images, and impulses. Take a poll of your relatives' and friends' strangest, most upsetting, or even funniest intrusive thoughts, images, or impulses. You may need to give them a few examples to get them started, but you'll probably be pretty surprised at what does go through the average person's mind! However, because it means nothing to them, they may not notice them very easily and forget about them easily, so beware of thinking that they don't have such thoughts if they say they can't call any to mind when you ask them.

Realistic Responsibility: The Responsibility Pie-Chart

You can use a visual method to see more clearly your personal responsibility for something. Here's a technique that might bring memories of being taught percentages and fractions at school. We'll show you how it works in principle here, and give you some more examples of how it can be used in Chapter 4.

First, think of an event you are afraid of being responsible for. Then think how responsible, on a 0–100 per cent scale, you would consider yourself if this actually happened. Chances are you will have given yourself a pretty high percentage (if not 100 per cent).

Now list all the other possible contributing factors to this feared event occurring, placing your role at the bottom of the list.

Now draw a circle (your 'pie') and begin to divide up the pie up among the various contributing factors (Figure 3.4), giving each a rough percentage and leaving yourself until the very end. Now step back and consider the new percentage of responsibility you will have given yourself. We hope you experience a degree of relief now that you realize you do not carry sole responsibility.

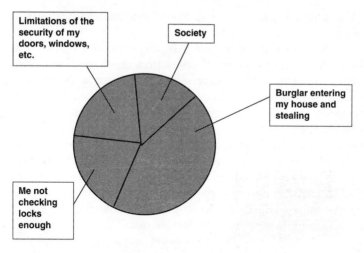

Figure 3.4   An example of a pie chart of being burgled

Correcting for Bias in Attention

If you have been pregnant, or have wanted to become pregnant, you may have noticed that suddenly the world seemed to be flooded with pregnant women and babies. How about if you have just bought a new car? Have you found that you kept noticing the same make on the road? It's not that there are more babies being born or more cars of the same model being bought; it's just that our attention is seeking out the subjects that interest us. It is common for people to have biases in attention because what is on our minds will influence what we notice; it's just part of how the human brain works.

How about someone who is anxious about spiders or insects? Have you ever observed that they see them where and when you hadn't noticed anything? When people are anxious about something they tend to be more *vigilant* for examples of it. This is of course one of the helpful aspects of anxiety should we be in a genuinely threatening situation; for example, it's helpful to be watchful if we are at risk from being attacked by a wild animal.

In OCD, this *attention bias* is an often-overlooked factor that keeps the condition going. People with fears of contamination, for example, will frequently tend to monitor what they or others have touched. People with fears of causing harm will tend to notice sharp objects and chemicals. Their attention will also be focused internally on how they 'feel'. Because they feel anxious, this will tend to be magnified and used as evidence that there is a danger from which they need to escape. Other people will be focused on their intrusive thoughts and ideas, and in just the same way these will tend to be magnified and appear more frequently. Overcoming OCD will mean taking *everything* in, not just focusing on what you fear or your obsession, and refocusing your attention away from your inner world.

What Do You Think You Tend to 'Over-Notice?'

Take a moment to consider the past day or past week, and try to identify what you tend to notice more of than the average person in the street.

I'm over-aware of _____

Tackling this part of OCD has two important components.

The first is recognizing that biased perception will very likely lead to biased conclusions. For example, monitoring the transfer of contaminant by hands will increase a person's sense of how contaminated and dangerous the world is. Thus you can helpfully correct for this bias in your mind. Imagine riding a bicycle that tends to veer to the right when you point the handlebars straight ahead. What would you do to make the bicycle go straight (before you had a chance to fix it)? In all probability you would correct for the bias towards the right by steering slightly towards the left. You can do exactly the same in your mind: so, if you know that you tend to overassume danger, you can correct your thinking by deliberately assuming you or those you care for are safe.

The second is recognizing that trying *not* to notice something, as an attempt to correct this bias, is doomed to failure in the same way that it is impossible to not think of something. However, you can improve the extent to which you focus on other things. So practice being absorbed in a particular task (like having a conversation), or the sights, tastes, smells, sounds, and physical sensations of the world around you. When you notice your attention is drawn excessively towards something you are overmonitoring in an attempt to reduce risk, refocus your attention away from it on to something else around you. Similarly, if you're excessively focused on how you feel or you're thinking about harm, refocus attention externally on the task in hand or the environment.

We appreciate that this is a difficult skill to acquire and requires frequent practice. In the future, we anticipate that therapists will develop new ways of helping you to practice refocusing or retraining your attention.

Taking Physical Exercise

There is good evidence for the benefit of physical exercise in overcoming mild depression. We do not know of any published research on exercise in OCD, but some of our patients with more severe OCD have found it helpful in giving relief in the short term.

> *Audra told us that the only time she escaped from her extensive mental compulsions was when she exercised at high intensity. Step aerobics was her personal preference because she was engaged in doing a choreographed routine that constantly changes, on a step, with an instructor leading a group, and music playing loudly. If she did a mental ritual, she would either mess up the routine and stand out or fall off her step (note that at this moment, Audra was focused on the cost of ritualizing). Having realized this, she joined a week-long trekking expedition to climb*

Mount Kilimanjaro. Kilimanjaro is the highest mountain in Africa and cannot be attempted by anyone without a reasonable level of fitness. The environment itself led to a sense of inner calm as there are only the sounds of Africa, such as squealing monkeys. In simple terms, daily survival instincts took over and there was no room for her OCD. Walking for an average of eight hours a day, at altitude, through all types of climactic regions is exhausting. While walking, her thoughts and actions revolved around putting one foot in front of the other, putting extra layers on, taking layers off, drinking plenty of water, and eating snacks (again, notice that Audra was in a state of focusing externally and concentrating on living, not psychological perfection). While walking she was with a group of people whom she enjoyed talking to. By the end of the day, when she desperately wanted to do a mental review in her head, her body was so physically exhausted that it made her sleep.

We are not suggesting exercise is a 'cure' for OCD, but it may help to break a vicious circle when rituals are so automatic. Even if you do not use exercise as an aspect of tackling your OCD, it will almost certainly help you reduce some of the stress of tackling such a thorny problem and improve your mood.

In general, sustained activity like brisk walking, jogging, or swimming has been shown to have the best psychological effects for depression. However, any form of exercise you can add to your weekly routine will be helpful.

4

Overcoming Obsessive Compulsive Disorder: How It Actually Works

To help bring to life the process of overcoming OCD, we are going to show you in this chapter some examples of people with OCD and describe some of the things they did to overcome it. It is inevitable that you will have symptoms that are somewhat different from any of theirs, even if you have the same 'type' of OCD. Beware of concluding that because there are differences, the principles don't apply or will not work for you; instead, use the examples creatively to draw up the *general principles* you can use to tackle your own OCD.

Edna's Fears of Contamination

This example focuses on overcoming fears of contamination, one of the most common forms of OCD. Although dirt, germs, bodily waste, environmental contaminants (e.g. asbestos, radiation), toxic substances (e.g. bleach, solvents), animals or insects, and sticky substances tend to be the most common feared types of 'contaminant', there is a wide range of possible contaminants that can be a source of worry. Not all are physical objects or substances; others include traumatic memories, feelings, or the personalities of other people or places that can 'stick to' or 'contaminate' objects by association. Some individuals believe that certain parts of their body, such as their hands, feet, or hair, may become contaminated because they regularly come into contact with the world. Fears of contamination may be driven by a fear of illness; a sense of dirtiness, mental pollution, or mental uncleanliness; and occasionally religious obsessions or perfectionism. They are associated with compulsive hand-washing, showering, bathing, tooth-brushing, grooming or bathroom routine, and excessive cleaning of household items. There is nearly always avoidance of certain areas or objects that are regarded as too contaminated. Fears of contamination are generally more common in women than in men.

Edna was very anxious about contamination from human or animal excrement and, to a lesser extent, nasal catarrh, urine, and sticky substances. She was also worried about contamination from cleaning products like bleach and other chemicals. Her main compulsion was washing her hands, which she did about fifty times a day in a meticulous order with antibacterial soap; she frequently used disinfectant wipes as well. She also insisted that her husband and children stick to a strict hygiene routine and discouraged them from going into the garden.

Edna would avoid shaking hands and using public toilets unless she absolutely had to. Whenever she had to use anything she thought was contaminated, she employed a range of safety behaviors. For example, when she used a toilet she would hover over the seat rather than sit on it. At home, she would pull down her sleeve to open the door or pull a toilet handle. After using the toilet she wiped herself very thoroughly, getting through more than a roll of toilet paper a day. She would use much more paper when she opened her bowel, so, in order to minimize the extent to which she had to use the toilet she followed a strict diet with reduced roughage, so that she only opened her bowels about once a week. She avoided touching certain clothes and shoes which she felt might be contaminated, and cordoned them off in their own cupboard. She threw away several items of clothing which she thought had been contaminated when she had been away from home. She used gloves to put waste in the waste bin outside. She avoided leaving her hair down and had two or three showers a day.

Edna's main fear was that she might contract a lethal illness and leave her children motherless. When she was very anxious, she had an intrusive image of her children in distress at her funeral. Edna interpreted this image as an indication that if she did not 'act responsibly' and try to prevent it, then the disaster would occur.

Because of her excessive hand-washing, Edna's hands were sore and cracked. She interpreted this as a reason to try even harder to avoid contaminants and wash her hands thoroughly, because germs could more easily get into cracks in her hands. She would also rinse the taps with water. She would monitor closely what she and other people touched, what was touched next, who touched that, what they then touched. These areas in turn would become contaminated. When her family doctor challenged her about her excessive hand-washing, suggesting that she might have OCD, she became angry and defensive. For a while she complained that because people really could become ill from germs it was reasonable to take precautions.

Her tendency to monitor the 'transfer' of contamination made her OCD much worse because it fueled her preoccupation, keeping her excessively aware of every possible chance of contamination. Her tendency to wash to decontaminate, and insist that her family followed suit, prevented her from becoming used to living with a realistic tolerance of possible dirt and germs.

Edna's Alternative Explanation

The first step was for Edna to seek a good psychological understanding of what her problem was and what was maintaining it. There are two competing theories for an explanation of Edna's problems:

- Theory A: she had a problem of being contaminated by germs and having to prevent serious harm to herself. Her solution was therefore to avoid contaminants and wash herself excessively. It seemed to work because, at least in the early days, it reduced her distress, and she had not so far died.

- Theory B: her problem was one of worrying about contamination, and her solutions, in trying to prevent harm, made her worries worse and kept her problem going.

An example of how Theory B is manifested appears in Figure 4.1. We call this kind of diagram, which you will see repeated for each case we describe in this chapter, a 'vicious flower' diagram, because the circling thoughts and responses that keep the obsession going look like petals on a flower. It describes a typical situation in which Edna received change from a shopkeeper. This activated a doubt that the change could be contaminated. This, in turn, triggered the image of her children being distressed at her funeral. It is not surprising that she felt anxious because the image felt very real and for her was like a portent for the future. However, when she felt anxious, Edna interpreted this as evidence that harm would occur. Feeling the sweat on her palms also made her feel contaminated. She then tried harder to get rid of the contamination by washing; however, the more she washed, the stronger became her fears and her conviction that harm would occur. Avoiding touching anything she thought might contaminate made her more vigilant and increased both the frequency of her worries and the level of her distress. Thus her problems were being maintained by the meaning that she attached to the image of her children being distressed and by the way she was responding to this image.

Edna began to realize the enormous cost of her solutions, and in particular the psychological damage they were causing to herself and her family. She finally agreed to test whether Theory B best fitted her experience. The prediction from Theory B was that if she treated her problem as just thoughts and dropped her avoidance and safety behaviors, then her worries would fade away. She would then feel less contaminated and be able to function normally.

Figure 4.1   Edna's 'vicious flower' diagram

Edna's Awareness of 'Magical Thinking'

First, Edna learned that images such as her children being distressed at her funeral are extremely normal for someone who cared a great deal about her children, as she did, and worried about how they would cope if she were to die. Had she not cared so much, she would never have been haunted by these images or worried about her children becoming motherless. She learned that the images were no more than pictures in the mind, and by themselves had no power – in imagining otherwise, she had been falling into the error of magical thinking. Dwelling on negative events such as her funeral and her children's distress cannot make these things happen (**see p. 54**). Furthermore, she had limited influence over when she would actually die. Trying too hard to prevent her untimely death with her extensive avoidance and safety behaviors was maintaining her worries and would ultimately destroy her ability to care for her children.

Edna needed to accept that the image of her children at her funeral was just a 'picture in her mind' and had no other meaning. She also needed to:

- drop all her avoidance and safety behaviors in a graduated manner;
- shower once a day for five minutes without any rituals;
- wash in a non-ritualistic manner and only before or after agreed activities;
- make practical arrangements for her death, including making her will and appointing a guardian for her children.

Edna's Plan of Action

Table 4.1 shows Edna's hierarchy of triggers, which she used as the basis of her exposure and response program. For each of her rituals, she worked out an alternative response that allowed her to make progress, steadily working through the list to overcome her fears.

It was important for Edna to tackle her compulsive washing *first*; if she persisted with this, she would merely undo the good work she was about to embark on with the exposure. In general, as we noted in Chapter 3, there is little or no benefit in doing exposure if it is followed by a compulsion. Edna therefore monitored how often she was doing compulsions on a daily frequency chart. There were three different activities to monitor on a daily basis:

- when she had an urge to do a compulsion (e.g. washing) that she resisted;

Table 4.1 **Edna's hierarchy of triggers and program of exposure**

Exposure and response prevention goals (object, word, place, person, situation, substance)	Estimated anxiety or discomfort (0–100)	Actual anxiety at end (0–100)
Touching a public toilet seat without washing my hands, and then touching my face and body	100	
Touching the toilet seat at home without washing my hands, and then touching my clothes, purse, and keys	95	
Touching the waste bin outside with my bare hands, without washing	95	
Wearing contaminated shoes from the garage without being careful where I walk around the house	95	
Wearing contaminated clothes from the garage and mixing them with other clothes, and sitting down around the house	90	
Wearing contaminated clothes from the wardrobe and not being careful where I sit around the house	80	
Going to the toilet (number two) and washing my hands only with water	80	
Going to the toilet (number two) and washing my hands briefly only with ordinary soap and water	70	
Eating a normal size meal with vegetables and fruit every day	40	
Shaking hands with my husband without washing or avoiding afterwards	40	
Eating an apple	30	

- when she did a compulsion that she did not resist but followed it by exposure (e.g. touching the floor);
- when she did a compulsion that she did not resist and did not follow by exposure.

Her goals were to follow the guidelines on washing (see p. 167) before or after any activities such as defecating and to do so in a non-ritualistic manner. The most important aspect of washing 'normally', without which it would be impossible for Edna to make progress, was to stop using an internal state of feeling comfortable as the measure of completion. Edna needed to finish washing while she still felt 'uncomfortable'. In this way, she gradually cut back on her ritualistic washing, starting off with the easiest rituals and then moving on to the more difficult ones. She started by restricting herself to one shower a day in the morning, unless she was going out to a social event in the evening. She then tackled washing her hands in no particular order and without rinsing the taps with water. She later used ordinary soap and gave up the antibacterial soap and disinfectant wipes. If she did wash ritualistically when she thought she was contaminated she recontaminated herself (e.g. by touching a toilet seat). Washing in a non-ritualistic manner did mean that she felt anxious and she experienced the image of her funeral. At first it was difficult, but she tried to accept the image as just a picture in her mind and not to modify it.

Once she had learned to wash in a non-ritualistic manner, Edna could then embark on her program of exposure. By the end of the exposure program she was able to redo some of the tasks such as touching the toilet seat whilst deliberately creating an image in her mind of her funeral with the children distressed.

As is the case for many people, Edna's OCD was not prepared to go down without a fight. She decided to work through her doubts and reservations about giving up her rituals with the aim of becoming less obsessional about dirt and germs, using the format shown in Table 4.2. Edna made sure she did this task when she was not panicking about contamination.

How Edna Maintained Her Recovery

As Edna began to overcome her fear of contamination, she became more aware that she had a tendency to keep things excessively ordered and symmetrical in her home. She resolved to do daily exposure and response prevention to tackle this and was very pleased at how quickly she was able to make progress.

Table 4.2 **Working through doubts or reservations**

Doubt or reservation	Response
Where dirt and germs are concerned the risk is real – it's not like other types of OCD	It's true that germs may offer a slight risk of illness in some people, but you need to offset that small risk against the substantial cost of OCD and the relative ease of treating an infection
But living with that risk is different for me – I've got OCD and I'll feel anxious	I'm no different from anyone else in terms of the level of risk I'm taking, and my anxiety *will* reduce when I *stop* carrying out rituals and avoiding
You say I shouldn't use antibacterial soap, but normal people use it so why shouldn't I? They wouldn't make these antibacterial and cleaning products if they weren't a good idea, would they?	It's true that other people use these products. However, manufacturers have created a market by generating fear and then providing a 'solution'. Antibacterial soaps are only required for certain medical conditions or by surgeons

Edna resolved to fill the gap in her life left behind by OCD with hobbies and interests. She rediscovered her love of going out with her friends, and began to do so much more often. Initially, her husband found this change a bit difficult to adjust to, joking that at least he saw her when she had OCD. However, he soon began to appreciate how much easier life was without Edna's obsessions, and in fact began to enjoy going out with Edna more often himself. To help keep her fears of contamination at bay, Edna also found it helpful to carry out occasional exposure sessions, which she thought of as 'booster shots', like a vaccination.

Jack's Fear of Killing a Cyclist

Intrusive thoughts, images, or impulses about being aggressive and harming either yourself or a vulnerable person are a common obsession. Examples of such obsessions include thinking of, or having the impulse to, poison, kick, or hit a child; push someone in front of a train; blurt out or write obscenities or insults; steal something; stab someone; cause a car crash; do something embarrassing; stab yourself with a dirty needle, or cut yourself with a broken glass or a razor. The fear may either be that you will act in such a way in the future (which leads to marked avoidance, safety behaviors, and self-monitoring) or that you might already have acted in such a way (which leads to marked checking behavior and mental reviews of your actions). Mothers with newborn babies very commonly experience aggressive obsessions.

Jack had become consumed with a fear that he might run over a cyclist in his car without realizing it. More and more often he would experience intrusive doubts that he might already have accidentally hit someone with his car while driving. He would experience an image of a body lying in the street covered in blood. He became extremely alarmed when sometimes he would have the thought 'Kill. Go on Jack, do it,' as if he could deliberately mow down a cyclist. He found these thoughts especially repulsive and thought there must be some evil part of him that would act upon the urge, and that he should be able to just get rid of the thoughts he did not want. He reasoned that if he had these thoughts, surely he might kill someone even though he didn't want to?

He had been taught incorrectly by a therapist to say 'Stop!' and to transform the thought into 'Kill your speed', which had not helped him. He had begun to believe that the only way he could allow himself to relax about his driving was to become absolutely certain that he had not hurt anyone. When driving he would pay extra attention to anyone near the side of the road, and try to give them a wide berth if he could. This once nearly led him to drive into another car coming in the opposite direction. To try to put his mind at rest he would often retrace his journey, looking for signs of an accident. As he got out of his car he would check it for any evidence that he might have hit someone, and seek reassurance from his parents. On one occasion he had given in to the urge to call the police to check that no accidents had been reported. On another occasion he had tried to obtain closed-circuit TV footage of part of his journey. Frequently, to try to reassure himself further when he arrived at his destination, he would replay the journey in his mind to check for any memory of a collision, such as a bump, shout, or evidence of other drivers looking at him in an alarmed manner.

Jack's Goals

Jack made his goals to:

- accept intrusive thoughts and images of killing a cyclist as a normal human experience without responding to them in any way;
- drive the way he used to drive before he had OCD, without excessive safety behaviors;
- stop retracing his journey, phoning the police, conducting mental reviews, and seeking reassurance at the end of his journey.

How Jack Developed an Alternative Meaning for Intrusive Thoughts

Like so many other people who have OCD, at the heart of Jack's obsessions was the meaning he attached to his intrusive thoughts.

Before treatment, Jack was basing his interpretation on the assumption that he was a careless and bad driver, and so had to try very hard to prevent harm occurring to vulnerable cyclists. We label this as Theory A. The solution to Theory A seemed to work, because so far as he knew he had not harmed any cyclists. Theory B provided an alternative explanation: namely, that Jack's problem was worrying excessively about harming a cyclist, and that by trying too hard to solve it as a careless driver problem he was making his worries worse. His problems were, therefore, being maintained by the meaning that he attached to the *thought* of a cyclist being run over and the way he had responded to this image in his avoidance and safety behaviors. He believed that the *thought* of killing a cyclist *must* have some relevance, otherwise it would not pop into his head, and that it was a warning to him to be more careful. He found the intrusive thought 'Kill. Go on Jack, do it' even more upsetting, interpreting it as a sign that he was a 'dangerous murderer' and that he must control his behavior.

With encouragement, Jack began to entertain the alternative explanation that he was in fact a very responsible person who had become excessively worried about causing harm to a vulnerable cyclist. Jack collected evidence supporting this theory by looking at a specific episode in which he felt his car bump (see Figure 4.2). As we can see from the 'vicious flower' diagram (Figure 4.2), his problem was driven by the way he interpreted his intrusive thoughts. He misunderstood these thoughts to mean that he was a dangerous and bad person; his solution was to be overcautious and to seek reassurance, which only served to feed his beliefs about being bad so that they became self-perpetuating.

Jack's Behavioral Experiment on Reassurance

It was important for Jack, as for most people with OCD, to start by tackling his compulsions, before he embarked on a program of exposure.

When Jack first read the advice not to seek reassurance he found it hard to understand that 'quickly asking to put his mind at rest' was causing him trouble. After experimenting with asking for *more* reassurance for two days, and comparing the effect to that of his usual level of reassurance-seeking, he discovered that his obsessions increased rather than reduced.

Imaginal Exposure

Jack was quite right to be unsure of the advice of the therapist who had taught him to say 'Stop!' and to transform his thought

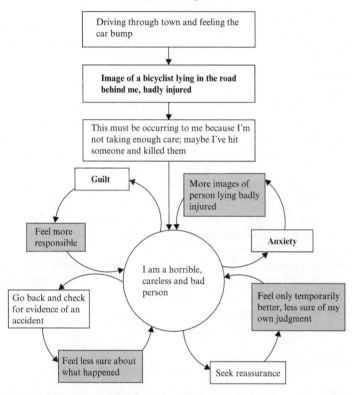

Figure 4.2 Jack's 'vicious flower' diagram

into 'Kill your speed'. In Chapter 2 we showed how trying to suppress or neutralize intrusive thoughts will only increase their frequency. It is important to stop mental rituals; but the inexperienced therapist had just taught Jack to suppress the thought and to adopt a type of neutralizing by trying to transform it. It would have been more helpful to do the opposite of what the therapist had advocated, and to ask Jack to imagine a scenario in which he deliberately ran over a cyclist. Initially, Jack was very unsure about deliberately imagining hurting someone, because he thought it was a callous and uncaring thing to do. However, he later decided that it was a reasonable way to test out Theory B. Because he was not actually hurting anyone, and he was so concerned about the effect his OCD was having on him, he felt it was worth doing something 'abnormal' to tackle the problem.

So, for around forty-five minutes a day for two weeks, Jack deliberately imagined himself hitting a cyclist in his car. He conjured up a picture of the body lying on the road covered in blood, and followed that by a scene in which the police arrived to arrest him. At first Jack wrote the scenario out in detail in order to help himself focus on it. During the exposure he tried to keep the imagery as vivid as he could; he also tried to draw the scene. He found it helpful to think of this as 'taking the horror out' of the mental picture, not belittling the event should it ever happen.

As he persevered, Jack found that his distress reduced when he practiced holding the image in his mind and not responding to it. If he did experience any spontaneous intrusive images he found that his discomfort began to reduce as he increasingly practiced keeping the image in his mind.

'Real-Life' Exposure and Response Prevention

Jack's experience of doing real-life exposure is a good example of '*It's not what you do, it's the way that you do it*'. You see, several of the safety behaviors he used while driving were quite subtle – undetectable to anyone observing him unless they knew what to look for. At first, Jack became quite frustrated when he learned that he would have to practice a different way of driving in order to overcome the obsessions related to it. He thought, 'I've done lots of driving and all that's happened is that my obsessions have got worse. I just can't see how driving more will help.' After thinking more carefully, he realized it wasn't just *more* driving he needed to do to overcome his OCD; he had to drive *differently*. He practiced driving '*as if*' he were his twin brother who did not worry excessively about harming a cyclist. This meant resisting the urge to give cyclists an unnecessarily wide berth, resisting checking in his rear-view mirror after passing a cyclist, and resisting the temptation to retrace his car journey if he did experience anxiety about hitting someone. He also became aware that he was listening carefully as he drove for anything that might sound like a collision, and that he was scanning the road ahead for cyclists. All these are 'safety-seeking behaviors' and are counterproductive, because at times they can be dangerous (like giving an extra-wide berth to a cyclist and nearly colliding with oncoming traffic, or not focusing enough on the road ahead). Safety-seeking behaviors also prevented Jack from testing out his Theory B, as each time he carried out a safety-seeking behavior he believed that he had had a close shave and might have killed a cyclist had he not taken evasive action.

Frequency Recording

Jack found it helpful to keep records of the frequency of his rituals, and he used a mechanical tally counter for this. He paid particular attention to the extent to which he was seeking reassurance and rerunning car journeys in his mind, because he found that these were the rituals he would most easily slip into.

Jack's Responsibility Pie Chart

Before starting to overcome his OCD, Jack believed that if he did accidentally kill a cyclist it would be entirely his fault: that is, he thought he would be 100 per cent responsible. As part of developing a more helpful way of thinking about accidentally knocking down a cyclist in the road, Jack developed a responsibility pie chart (Figure 4.3). He listed all the factors that might contribute to such an accident, and placed himself last on the list. He then divided a circle into segments that roughly represented the level of responsibility for each contributing factor.

The list of possible contributing factors he developed included:

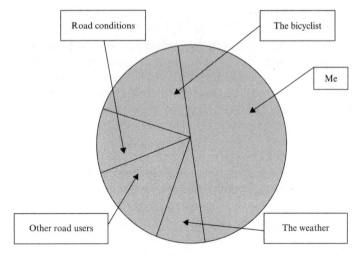

Figure 4.3   Jack's 'responsibility pie chart'

- the road being poorly lit if it was dark;
- the cyclist not using lights or bright clothing, making it difficult to see him;
- the road being bumpy or uneven, causing the cyclist to swerve unpredictably;
- other road users parking badly or driving badly, causing Jack or the cyclist to swerve, or leading Jack to be distracted;
- the cyclist not taking proper care or not paying attention;
- bad weather, leading to skidding or poor visibility;
- Jack not driving with proper care or attention

Jack found that working through the responsibility pie chart helped him to 'really' see that it was very unlikely that accidentally killing a pedestrian would be his fault entirely. He concluded that, although it made sense to take some safety measures such as having his car maintained, being aware of other road users, and not driving excessively fast, he had really been overdoing his 'precautions'.

Developing an Appropriate Sense of Responsibility

As we have seen already, a central theme in many people's OCD is a fear of being responsible for harm coming to either themselves or others (indeed, the two can overlap). Here we focus on the fear of causing harm to someone else, commonly someone that we perceive as being vulnerable. Two key demands that people with this kind of OCD tend to make are 'I must be sure that I don't to something that will cause harm' (such as accidentally knocking someone down a flight of stairs) and 'I must be sure that I don't fail to do something that might protect someone from harm'. Whereas most people will try to live somewhere within the spirit of these ideals, individuals with OCD will tend to try to follow them to the letter as prescriptions – at least in a specific aspect of the world about which they have had an intrusive thought.

The attitude to adopt in order to overcome this form of OCD is to assume an appropriate, flexible, and non-extreme level of social responsibility. The balance to strike is attending to the protection of others on the one hand, while on the other allowing yourself the usual rights to a life that is not plagued by anxiety and guilt.

Jack ultimately concluded that he could allow himself to be free of his excessive concern about hitting a cyclist with his car when he considered the following practical points:

- The precautions he was taking would reduce the chance of his having an accident by only a tiny amount.
- OCD was not the most effective way of living according to his wishes to be a 'decent' person, and was in fact preventing him from making the best contributions to society of which he was capable.
- His OCD was itself causing harm to both himself and his family (distress, worry).
- Giving up obsessional excessive concern was not proof of lack of caring, just proof of the need to tolerate a small

degree of risk in order to function in the real world – just like everyone else!

Mark's Fear of a Burglary

Checking is one of the most common compulsions and is associated with an obsessional fear that one will cause harm (e.g. burglary, fire, flood). Important elements here are the catastrophic interpretation of the *thought* of a bad event, the exaggerated sense of power to prevent harm, and feelings of lack of confidence and uncertainty. However, repeated checking tends to *decrease* confidence in the accuracy of your relevant memory and *increase* your sense of uncertainty: so the more you check the less sure you are in your memory that you have checked! This is another example of trying too hard with the aim of increasing certainty, while in fact it actually increases your doubts. After checkers complete a check for safety they feel even more responsible and also that the likelihood of harm occurring is greater. In short, checking sets off a vicious circle in which the more you check the more responsible you feel, the more you feel the likelihood of danger, and the worse your memory gets. Hence it recurs.

Checking can also be carried out by proxy and by transferring responsibility to others through repeated requests for reassurance (e.g. 'Is it safe?' 'Is the door locked?')

Mark first became anxious about checking his front door when he moved into a new neighbourhood and was told a crime wave had recently occurred. He realized that his house might be burgled. He thought that if this happened and he was responsible, he would lose his wife and children, because his wife would be so angry with him. He decided that he must make certain that his house was secure, especially if he was responsible for locking up. He would then repeatedly check doors and windows when going to bed or leaving the house.

Mark noticed that over time he needed to check more and more. He began to wonder if his memory was poor, because he knew other people would leave their homes without checking and suffer less anxiety than he did. He resolved then to tackle his 'memory problem' by trying harder to remember that he'd locked the doors and windows. He would stare at his front door; turn the lock on and off four or five times, and try to force his mind to 'take in' the image of the key turning in the lock. Later, he added saying the word 'locked' in his mind to try to make it more memorable. He would later review his actions in his mind as an aid to remembering the exact sequence of events. However, this often made him more confused, and he would return to check the door again. He would often shake the door back and forth until he felt 'comfortable' and was absolutely convinced that it was locked. Mark continued to feel anxious and worried even when he left the door locked. When his OCD was at its worst, he would normally take about 90 minutes to leave home or to go to bed.

Sadly, none of these 'solutions' helped; in fact, Mark's OCD got progressively worse, and he would spend many hours checking the locks and looking out of the window for an intruder. He would ensure that his curtains were closed, the gas taps and oven turned off, and the water taps fully tightened, which had led to their breaking on a few occasions. He repeatedly checked that light switches and electrical appliances were all turned off and his cigarette was fully stubbed out. He repeatedly checked that his credit card was still in his wallet, his keys were in his pocket, and his cell phone and keys laid out in exactly the same position on the table. When he left his car anywhere, he would check that all the doors were locked, that the windows were fully shut, that the handbrake was left on, and all the lights fully turned off.

He found it very difficult to get to sleep at night, as he never felt comfortable. This led to much discord in his family and eventually other members took over responsibility for many of the tasks of locking up and leaving the home last. However, this then led to further family arguments, as Mark wanted to check with them that they really had locked the doors and turned off the taps satisfactorily.

Mark's Alternative Explanation

One of the important things researchers have discovered about people with OCD is that they do not have poor memories, but rather lack confidence in their memory. Mark's demands on his memory, like 'I have to be certain that I've locked the door', would also make him more likely to worry about whether the doors were locked. Mark had made an enormous investment in ensuring that nothing bad happened, as the 'bottom line' of what he was worried about was losing his wife and children. The reality was that they were more annoyed with his OCD than anxious about the possibility of being burgled.

Mark developed two possible theories about his difficulties with locking the house and his fear of burglary:

- Theory A: I have a poor memory which means my judgment about whether I have locked the doors or windows cannot be trusted and I must try harder to check whether I have locked up.
- Theory B: I'm a person who is very worried that we will be burgled and I lack confidence in my memory. However, trying too hard to make sure I have locked the doors and windows increases my worries.

An example of Theory B in action in a specific episode is shown in Figure 4.4. Mark had a catastrophic thought about the consequences of the house being burgled. He was trying too hard in a number of respects to make himself sure, and used emotional criteria for stopping checking, like feeling 'just right' or 'comfortable'.

Mark's Behavioral Experiments

Frequency recording

Initially, to learn more about the possibility that this was a problem of excessive worrying about causing harm, Mark recorded the frequency of his checking, both in his mind and

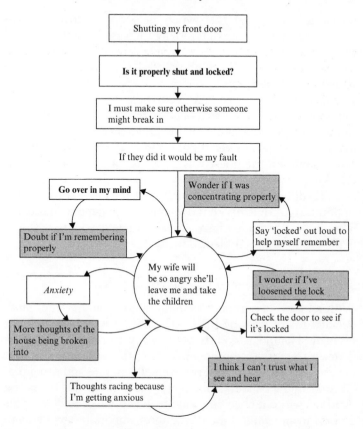

Figure 4.4   Mark's 'vicious flower' diagram

in his behavior (using the 'Frequency Record' chart in Appendix 5). At first, he was quite alarmed that he was checking so much. His initial response was to 'check better', which basically meant concentrating harder and doing his checking rituals for longer. Unsurprisingly, this did not help. Luckily, his wife picked him up on this and he then decided to see what would happen if he reduced his checking on one day and compared it with a day when he maintained his previous level of checking. He found that when he stopped checking, his worries and level of anxiety briefly increased but that overall his urges decreased.

Responsibility holiday

It helped that Mark's wife wanted to help him recover from the very start. They discussed using a temporary 'responsibility holiday' to demonstrate that his problem was influenced by anxiety. Thus they agreed that for a week she would assume full responsibility if the house was burgled as a result of Mark not checking excessively.

Mark discovered that his urge to check lessened, and – importantly – that his confidence in his judgment improved. This helped Mark to have more confidence in the 'worry' explanation of his problem, Theory B.

Exposure and Response Prevention

With a lot of support and encouragement from his wife, Mark decided to try treating his OCD 'as if' it were a confidence problem. He understood that the best way of improving confidence is to do the exposure unconfidently and uncomfortably. He drew up with his wife a program of exposure and ritual prevention, and set about deliberately practising closing doors and windows without checking what he had done or reviewing his actions in his mind. One of the most important steps was to alter the criterion he used to finish a check from an internal state of feeling 'comfortable' or 'absolutely certain' to a more objective state of having seen that the door was locked and tried to reopen it once. A second step was to turn as many of the checks as possible into exposure tasks – for example, rather than checking that his taps were fully tightened, he did an experiment over several days to see what would happen if he left them dripping. He increased his exposure by making sure he was the last to go to bed, or the last to leave the house.

Mark devised some specific goals he wanted to achieve in his exposure:

- to check his front door only once after he had locked it;
- to leave his curtains open;
- to leave gas taps and oven turned off without checking;
- to be able to leave his water taps slightly dripping;
- to be able to leave light switches and electrical appliances turned on;
- to resist the urge to check his cigarettes;
- to resist the urge to check his wallet, keys, and credit cards, and accept that they might not be in his wallet;
- to check his car door only once after locking it;
- to check once that car windows and handbrake were secure and lights off by a quick glance.

Mark recognized that this meant he would need to practise 'staying with' doubts and intrusive thoughts if they occurred during the day without trying to reassure himself. He enjoyed a big sense of achievement when eventually he and his family went away for the weekend and he was the one who locked the house, with barely any checking.

Establishing Criteria for When and When Not To Check

Mark began to realize that, even with really important actions and decisions, using certainty as the benchmark did not make sense – there is always room for doubt. Mark decided to try to think in terms of chance and probability rather than certainty, and to use the fact that he was 'fairly sure' that he'd locked the doors and windows as 'good enough' rather than checking to feel 100 per cent confident and comfortable. He also set himself the rule of thumb 'If you're doubting, it's OCD' to help keep himself some distance from his doubts. Eventually, Mark concluded that it was virtually never essential to check, having discovered that allowing himself 'just one check' would very often lead to more.

Isaac's Obsession with Order and Symmetry

Some people with OCD feel a need for order, symmetry, or exactness that takes the form of having to have objects arranged in a certain order or position. Alternatively, you may have to perform actions is a precise fashion: for example, to walk through a door in exactly the middle and always to sit at 90° to others. Another example might be a compulsion to 'even up' all your actions so that they are equal on both sides.

Sometimes an obsession with order or exactness is associated with magical thinking: that is, if an object is not in the correct position then a bad event will occur. Sometimes a person cannot articulate any meaning behind his action, and regards his compulsion as a habit or as a kind of perfectionism. The desire for order and exactness is often associated with tics, and there is some evidence that this may have some implications if you want to try medication (see Appendix 1). When a desire for order, precision, and exactness is very severe and rituals are performed very slowly, then the condition may be termed obsessional slowness (we discussed this briefly in Chapter 1).

Isaac's OCD was characterized by compulsions to keep his possessions in order – tidy and symmetrical. His desk at work and study at home were particular sources of concern for him, because these were 'his territory'. He would spend many hours a day readjusting items such as his pens, papers, books, and computer disks, or putting them in their correct place – for example, his watch had to be placed precisely in its box. At home he would compulsively order his shopping before items were put away in kitchen cupboards and his clothes before they went into the wardrobe (e.g. his shirts had to face the same way, be matched for colour, and checked so that there were no creases.) His possessions had to be placed 'just so' until it felt 'right'. In addition, when he took his shoes off, he had to make sure that he took the left off first and ensure that they did not touch one another. The laces then had to be folded neatly. He had to read the messages on his cell phone three times and write them on line number 3. He had to switch off the TV remote control on Channel 3 and place it to the right of the set. He had to ensure that his shower bottles did not touch one another and were neatly lined up.

Isaac also had to remember exactly where items had been placed and spent hours mentally reviewing his actions. He had become significantly handicapped as his isolation increased and he ceased being able to have any social life or fun. His employer had expressed concern about his performance at work. His symptoms tended to be worse when he was under more general stress, but nothing else in particular made his OCD worse. Because he never resisted any of his rituals he was unable to identify any feared consequences of not doing a ritual or what motivated him to act in the way he did. Isaac, like many people with OCD, had become so good at carrying out his rituals (at substantial personal cost) that he had largely managed to avoid experiencing any anxiety. His OCD had just become a way of life for him.

Breaking Down Isaac's OCD

The first step for Isaac was to find out what it was he was afraid of. He made a determined effort to resist one of his ordering rituals on his desk, and observed what went through his mind as he became more anxious (see Figure 4.5). He discovered that he was afraid that he would be paralyzed with fear, lose control, and become totally unable to function. In fact, as long as Isaac did not use a different ritual or safety behavior, his anxiety would reduce over time, rather than escalate out of control.

It was only when Isaac began to experience some anxiety that his behavior started to make any sense. Because he feared losing control so much, his solution was to try harder to prevent disorder and untidiness; but the harder he tried, the more he noticed imperfection and disorder, and the less able he became to tolerate things not being in order.

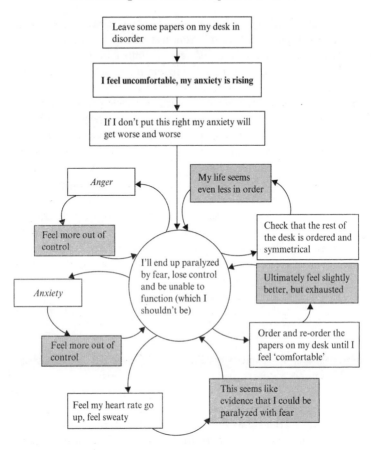

Figure 4.5   Isaac's 'vicious flower' diagram

Isaac's Alternative Explanations

Isaac developed two alternative explanations for the thoughts and behaviors that made up his OCD:

- Theory A: there is a problem with chaos and disorder that I have to prevent and if I don't I won't be able to cope with life.

- Theory B: I have a problem with being *afraid* of chaos and disorder and being unable to cope with life.

Isaac's Behavioral Experiments

Having acknowledged the possibility that his 'need' for order and symmetry was in fact based on a catastrophic prediction that he would be unable to cope with disorder (a thought causing his fear) rather than on the need to keep a real catastrophe away (a real threat causing his fear), Isaac decided to design an exposure and response prevention program to see which theory was true.

His exposure program involved gradually increasing the degree of disorder and asymmetry in his personal possessions over about six weeks. Isaac made sure that he would be aware of the disorder, letting it affect visible areas such as his desk, but refrained from tidying and ordering again.

Cost–Benefit Analysis and Reframing OCD

Because Isaac found the discomfort of his self-directed exposure and response prevention program so difficult, and easily slipped into ordering his possessions, he decided to set out the pros and cons – the 'costs' and 'benefits' – of carrying on as he was and of changing. He filled in two cost–benefit analysis forms (see Appendix 5). On the first he set out the costs and benefits of carrying on with his order and symmetry rituals and related avoidance, and on the second, the costs and benefits of learning to tolerate disorder and asymmetry. Isaac found he needed to make a clear distinction between the short-term relief from discomfort that his avoidance and rituals brought him, and the extra strain and hassle they brought him in the long term.

The cost–benefit analysis helped Isaac reframe his OCD. That is, he moved from considering it to be something that reflected his individuality and self-discipline to a sort of restricting, nerdish entity. By giving it a persona, Isaac found it easier to think of overcoming his OCD not as giving up his order and symmetry, but as standing up to OCD and regaining control over his life.

Isaac wrote out the disadvantages of carrying on doing what the OCD wanted him to do, and the advantages of being more flexible, on a sheet of paper that he referred to when his motivation was flagging.

Isobel's Fear of AIDS

Isobel's obsession was that she might have HIV and develop AIDS. Her fears are an example of 'health anxiety' or 'hypochondriasis', one of the family of obsessive compulsive disorders that has been identified as a separate condition, as we noted in Chapter 1. In other people with health anxiety, the fears and doubts about an infectious illness might focus on hepatitis, or a sexually transmitted disease.

> *Isobel had had a small tattoo drawn on her body. This was against her better judgment, as she was normally quite cautious, but she had let a girlfriend persuade her into it. It was done at a reputable clinic and they used new, sterilized needles. However, after the tattoo had been drawn Isobel began to experience doubts about whether she might have caught HIV. She had expressed some of her fears to the artist and he had joked, 'Well, you're not dead yet!' She replayed in her mind exactly what everyone in the clinic had said or did, and how they might have infected her. Although she was able to function, the doubt was at the back of her mind most of the time. She had seen her doctor after three months and the doctor had arranged an HIV test which was negative. This briefly reassured her, but after a few days her doubts returned. What if the doctors was wrong and HIV could only be detected after another few months? She replayed in her mind how she might have been infected, and all the possible reasons why the clinic might perhaps deliberately have infected her.*
>
> *She had another HIV test after a further two months, which was also negative. However, this led to further doubts – what if her blood sample had been mistakenly switched with that of*

another patient? Could there be a new strain of HIV that did not show up in the text? She was beginning not to cope in her job and was becoming more withdrawn. She started to take more precautions. She avoided meeting anyone whom she thought might be gay or could be infected with HIV. She tried to get her boyfriend to have an HIV test because of her fear that she might have got him infected, but he refused.

For a while Isobel spent a few hours every day researching AIDS and how HIV could be caught, in magazines and newspaper articles and on the internet. She would check her body repeatedly for signs of weight loss or lumps, and her skin for rashes. She thought she found something once under her arms and this made her panic. She would repeatedly seek reassurance from her friends and family, who became increasingly frustrated at her incessant questioning. She therefore sought help on an AIDS helpline, ringing up every day at least once. She also had a number of superstitious rituals – for example, when someone said, 'You are so lucky', then she had to neutralize it by touching wood or saying to herself, 'Don't say that', in case something bad happened to her.

She became increasingly worried that even if she did have HIV it would not be detected as her doctor would think she was 'crying wolf' and not take her seriously. She also worried that she did in fact have HIV, but her family was managing a conspiracy to make sure that she was not told because, she feared, they thought she would not be able to cope if she knew. She was getting increasingly desperate and low in her mood.

Breaking Down Isobel's OCD

As is the case for so many people with OCD, Isobel's problem had begun with a doubt that became a demand for certainty. She was insisting on having a total guarantee that she could not have HIV. This is of course impossible. There are no guarantees in life, apart from death and taxes – and the guarantee that, while she continued to demand certainty, the OCD would persist and even perhaps worsen, and her fear of HIV would persist.

Having a concern or doubt about getting HIV from having a tattoo is normal. The difference in OCD is that the sufferer overestimates the likelihood of getting HIV, and treats the doubt as if it were a fact. All this was happening in the context of a happy and successful life in other respects; the idea of getting HIV was a catastrophe to Isobel. She was worried that she would lose everything that was good about her life, as she associated AIDS with ending up dying alone and being very distressed. Furthermore, she believed that she had power to prevent HIV from occurring. Hence Isobel's solutions involved trying to find out for certain whether she had HIV, with extensive checking, reassurance-seeking, and replaying her memory of the trigger event in her mind, along with magical thinking and superstitious rituals to 'fend it off'. Realizing that her desperation was increasing and that she was simply not coping, Isobel embarked upon a program of self-help.

Isobel's Alternative Theory

The first step for Isobel was to achieve a good psychological understanding of what her problem was and what was maintaining it.

There were two competing theories to be tested:

- Theory A (which Isobel had been following): I might have HIV, for which I will need to get diagnosed and treated as quickly as possible.
- Theory B: I have an excessive worry about having undiagnosed HIV.

Theory B is summarized in Figure 4.6, which describes what happened when Isobel noticed a rash. At the centre of the vicious flower is the belief that is activated whenever she is anxious.

How It Actually Works

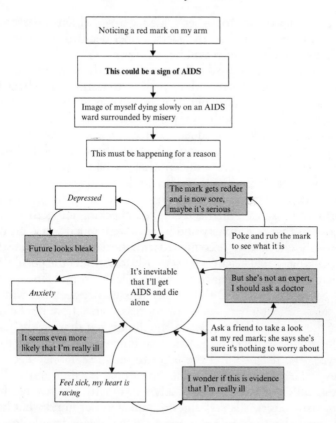

Figure 4.6   Isobel's 'vicious flower' diagram

Isobel's Behavioral Experiments

Isobel had spent several months pursuing Theory A and trying to prove that she had HIV. So far, this had not worked, as she was no nearer a conclusion. In fact, the opposite was the case, since she was more confused and distressed now than when the problem had started. She therefore agreed to test out Theory B, that she had a problem caused by worrying about *HIV* and that by trying too hard to treat it as an *HIV* problem she was making her worries worse. To gather evidence to see which of these two theories best matched the facts, Isobel decided to see if her checking had any effect on her worries.

First, she was advised to keep a chart of the frequency of her checking. From this record she realized that she would check by looking at or touching her body more than thirty times on an 'average' day, more if she was particularly worried. This inspired Isobel to work hard to reduce the frequency and duration of her checking. Noticing the frequency of her checking helped Isobel to feel a little bit more confident that she had a problem of worrying about HIV rather than HIV itself. She then experimented with comparing days in which she increased her checking against those in which she stopped checking altogether. She noticed that her anxiety and worries were much worse on the days she checked more compared with the days when she resisted checking. Isobel began more seriously to consider the possibility that her checking behavior played a role in her problem.

She now extended this to her reassurance-seeking, with a goal of resisting her urge to ask for reassurance from her family or the AIDS helpline. Again she discovered that on the days she stopped checking her anxiety briefly increased, but that over time it faded and the urges to seek reassurance became less. She promised herself that she would have no more HIV tests unless it was medically advised. Finally, she resisted her superstitious rituals and urges to replay in her mind what had happened in the clinic as she realized that she had made herself more confused and that, whenever she performed these rituals or mental reviews, her doubts and worries had increased. Now, whenever she had such an urge, she made a point of refocusing her attention away from memories on to the 'here and now', for example, what she saw, what she heard, or what she smelt. In this way she learned to retrain her attention to focus externally.

Exposure

To put her two theories to a real test, Isobel decided to see what happened if she treated her fear of HIV 'as if' it were a problem with worrying about HIV. It was predicted that if the problem were related to an obsessional worry then exposure would decrease her fears. If, however, she really did have an HIV problem, then exposure would make little difference to her behavior. She embarked upon a hierarchy of exposure to triggers for her fear of HIV without any checking or seeking for reassurance.

This included sitting on the train near people she thought might have AIDS or HIV; visiting a less-reputable tattoo parlor to look at tattoo styles; looking at magazine articles on blood-borne illnesses; going to a gay bar; meeting people with AIDS as a volunteer at a hospice – all without then checking or looking for reassurance. As she repeatedly confronted her fears, without checking, rituals, and reassurance-seeking, Isobel's fear steadily reduced.

Paul's Religious and Sexual Thoughts

Before we describe Paul, we should warn you that you might find his story more upsetting than the others in this chapter, because his obsessions are of a sexual and religious nature. We do not apologize for including Paul's story, because such symptoms are typical of OCD so we cannot avoid dealing with such problems.

Paul had been brought up in the Roman Catholic church. He did not have a particularly strong personal faith, but he had respect for his priest and religion. He became increasingly troubled by the idea that he would blurt out obscenities against Christ or God. When sitting in church listening to a sermon he would experience sacrilegious thoughts and an urge to stand up and shout an obscenity. He tried very hard to push the urge away each time it arose and to think of something 'nice'. He would say 'Sorry God', and try to neutralize the thought by undoing it with a prayer that he repeated twelve times. He found that he could not concentrate on the sermon properly. He became increasingly concerned that he would be sent to hell for eternity as a sinner and that his family would be destroyed by the devil's disciples. Each Sunday before he arrived at church he would decide that this time he would make sure he kept his mind clear of any blasphemous thoughts. However, he continued to experience the urge, and began to dread going to church. He began to avoid reading the Bible or having any contact with his priest. Paul prayed every night until he felt comfortable, and tried to apologize to God and seek forgiveness. He now began to think of a revolting penance to punish himself, by asking himself what was the worst thing he could think of? However, this developed into a whole new intrusive thought.

When there were stories in the media about a famous pop star being accused of pedophile activity, Paul started to experience an intrusive image of having oral sex with one or both of his daughters. These images were often triggered by seeing his children or by looking at certain pictures. He was very frightened because he thought on some occasions he had a tingling sensation in his penis. He tried to challenge the thoughts logically and reassure himself. Alternatively, he tried to think of something else or distract himself by going for a run. He believed that morally he should not have such thoughts. He ruminated on why he had them and why they didn't just stop. He generally believed he would not act upon the thoughts, but when they were strong he avoided being near his daughters. He would check to see if he was still attracted to his wife or other women, but because he was feeling down and his libido was reduced, this strengthened his doubts that he was attracted only to his daughters. He now had little doubt in his head that he liked what he saw in the image. Finally he thought he could no longer go to church because of the fear of having the intrusive thoughts of his daughters in church.

Paul's Alternative Theory

There are two competing theories for Paul's problems:

- Theory A: Paul was sick and evil, a pedophile and blasphemer. The implications of this theory (which Paul had been

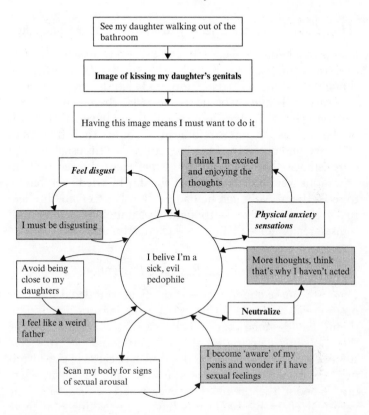

Figure 4.7   Paul's 'vicious flower' diagram

following for some time) were that he had to try very hard to control his impulses.

- Theory B: Paul was a person who cared a great deal for his church and his daughters, but was very worried about harming his daughters. Trying too hard to control his intrusive thoughts maintained them (Figure 4.7).

How Paul Tested the Effect of Resisting Intrusive Thoughts

Paul used a behavioral experiment to see for himself the effect of resisting his intrusive thoughts. He spent a day resisting his thoughts of abusing his daughters, and recorded the frequency, intensity, and duration of the thoughts. He then spent a second day trying harder, as hard as he could, not to have any thoughts of abusing his daughters and again recorded their frequency, intensity, and duration. Then he returned to his usual amount of resistance. The results of the experiment showed that his obsessions were indeed worse on the day he tried even harder to resist them. Although he had previously accepted 'intellectually' that his resistance thoughts was unhelpful, seeing it for himself really helped Paul to reduce his rituals.

Exposure and Response Prevention

One of the more important questions Paul considered about his obsessions was 'How did he explain having not acted upon them?' Paul realized that he believed that it was his resisting the thoughts, carrying out rituals, and avoidance that had stopped him from abusing his daughters. Because of the 'awfulness' of actually carrying out this act, Paul was at first very unsure about 'risk-taking'. However, when he focused on the very real effect his OCD was having in making him more distant from his daughters, and contemplated the long-term impact this could have, he felt more able to try facing his fears.

Paul developed the exposure and response prevention hierarchy shown in Table 4.3 for his fear of thoughts about abusing his daughters.

Once Paul gained confidence that he could safely allow his intrusive thoughts about abusing his daughters to come and go, he felt much more confident about his blasphemous thoughts and impulses. He did deliberate exposure and response prevention in church and while reading the Bible, 'allowing' the impulse to blurt out blasphemous obscenities to happen, without apologizing to God or repeatedly praying.

Table 4.3 **Paul's hierarchy of triggers and program of exposure**

Exposure and response prevention goals (object, word, place, person, situation, substance)	Estimated anxiety or discomfort (0–100)	Actual anxiety at end (0–100)
Letting the girls get into bed with me in the morning	95	
Giving the girls a bath without neutralizing my thoughts	95	
Sitting on the girls' bed to read them a bedtime story	80	
Helping the girls to get dressed	75	
Letting the girls sit on my lap in front of the TV	70	
Giving the girls a hug	65	

Re-Evaluating Faulty Beliefs

At the heart of Paul's OCD was the extent to which he regarded his thoughts and images as being important. As he became more successful in overcoming his OCD, Paul began to see that intention and action were much more important than the thoughts and images that might cross his mind. He concluded that although he certainly would *prefer* not to have blasphemous or inappropriate sexual thoughts cross his mind, there was no reason why he *must* not have them, since he was only human. Anyway, trying to resist such thoughts had clearly led him to have more of them, and the fact that he had tried so hard to resist them in the past was proof of what a gentle and caring person he was.

Gail's Hoarding

Obsessional hoarding is less common as a primary form of OCD than some of the other types discussed in this chapter. However, hoarding occurs in a milder form in up to a quarter of people with other types of OCD. Hoarding is best understood as a tendency to keep, collect, or avoid throwing away items that for the most part have no real benefit to the individual. Hoarding almost always results in chaotic clutter, which steadily takes over the person's home. One of the important differences between obsessional hoarding and the kind of 'collection' that someone might build as a hobby is that where hobby-type collections tend to give the person pleasure, obsessional hoarding is a source of anxiety and distress. Hobbies usually enhance a person's life; obsessional hoarding often overtakes and significantly impairs the person's life.

It is generally agreed that hoarding is a difficult form of OCD to overcome (although clear goals for change and motivation make a huge difference), so patience and persistence are the watchwords here.

Gail's avoided throwing any paper items or bags away. She lived in dread of accidentally throwing something away that she might need. Her house was full of piles of paper, letters, newspapers, and plastic bags containing plastic bags. Her fear of losing possessions had begun after she had had difficulties with her insurance company following a car accident. She had to correspond with her insurers regularly and became increasingly anxious about losing any of the correspondence. Even though the insurance matter was resolved, whenever Gail attempted to throw something away she checked carefully to ensure that nothing of importance had become attached to or mixed up with it. When it came to newspapers she tended to believe that, because she could not be 100 per cent certain that there was nothing important in between the pages, she must err on the side of caution and keep the newspaper 'just in case'. She had been married but her husband became unable to tolerate her behavior. He pleaded with her to seek help and overcome her fears, but in the end he decided they had to separate. Her home became a fire hazard and it was extremely difficult to negotiate a passage through it. She had lost many of her friends and was too embarrassed to invite anyone to her house.

A couple of years earlier, Gail had had her house cleared following the intervention of some family friends. Gail was par-

tially grateful to these friends but was also very angry and resentful because she had been unable to find some letters that were important to her, and was convinced that they had been thrown away in the clearout. Regrettably, this had meant that Gail had resolved to be even more careful in the future about what she threw away. The friends who had initially tried to help ultimately broke off contact with Gail when they became unable to tolerate her persistent calls and visits for reassurance about what they had discarded. Gail's profound sense of isolation ultimately led to her to prize her possessions even more greatly, saying that she would rather burn with her possessions than lose them in a house fire.

Breaking Down Gail's OCD

Gail's OCD was characterized by a demand that she must be absolutely certain not to accidentally throw away a personally meaningful item or important document. Unfortunately, because her extreme belief left no room for doubt, it led to very extreme and excessive precautions. Her isolation was an important maintaining factor, since it meant that she tried even harder not to lose her possessions.

Her original belief or 'Theory A' was 'Because I have doubts and anxiety about losing something important, this means I could easily lose something and must take great care to ensure I do not do so'. Her alternative explanation for her doubts, or 'Theory B' was 'I get so much doubt and anxiety about losing things because I'm so afraid of it, and I need to gradually stop trying so hard not to lose things in order to reduce my fear'.

How Gail Overcame Her Obsessional Hoarding

Initially, Gail found the idea of change very daunting, because she had begun to lose touch with other aspects of her self and the world around her, and was afraid that she might 'lose everything' and become paralyzed with fear.

Gail's Cost–Benefit Analysis

To help build up a sense that trying to change was worth the effort, Gail prepared two cost–benefit sheets or 'pros and cons' sheets. One focused on 'carrying on as I am' and the other on 'throwing away things I don't need and keeping my home free from waste'. She found it very helpful to focus on the probable practical benefits of change, rather than possible losses, and transferred these benefits to pieces of card that she stuck up around her home.

Exposure

It became clear to Gail that her previous attempts at getting rid of her hoarded waste had been too 'all or nothing'. She thought of the process of clearing out as like crash dieting, which she had always thought was silly since the weight loss was inevitably not sustainable and people who did it always gained weight again. She decided instead that she would start a routine of throwing things out that she thought she could sustain. Gail systematically went through her possessions, considering: Is this useful (now, not some time in the future!)? Is this beautiful? Is this valuable? Do I have space for it? As she sorted through her clutter she divided her possessions into three sets of boxes:

1 throw away;
2 give to charity;
3 keep and store.

Gail decided that the way she stored possessions was important, and 'banned' herself from stacking things up on her floor, bed, and furniture. 'If I run out of storage space it's time for another clearout!' she told herself.

Initially, she threw away a sack of waste every day; in the long run she would probably only need to do this every two or three days.

However, it was the *way* Gail threw things away that was her most important change. Instead of checking everything before she threw it away, Gail resolved to resist this compulsion and throw things away without checking.

Gail developed a hierarchy that involved different areas of her home and different kinds of items. She also put inviting people into her home on her hierarchy and planned to resist the temptation to seek reassurance from her visitors or check them as they left.

Changing Attitude

Gail found it especially helpful to build up her 'frustration tolerance'. She practiced the idea that losing something important would 'be difficult, but not the end of the world, and *I could stand it!*' Gail worked hard to restore a sense of identity that was separate from her possessions, and deliberately made herself treat possessions 'as if' 'they're important, but there's much more to me than my junk'. She kept a note of all of the evidence that showed she had things going for her.

Gail eventually reduced her hoarding of unwanted possessions substantially, and she learned to keep an eye out for warning signs of clutter building up. She made throwing things away part of her daily life, which helped it seem much more normal and less frightening. From talking to others, she learned that doubts about losing things were quite common, and that her own doubts didn't mean that she was somehow more careless. Undoubtedly, the greatest result for Gail was to be able to start a part-time job, and to build some new friendships.

5

Getting Ready to Change

Defining the Problem and Setting the Goal

To start preparing to change, you will need to set about finding the answers to several important questions about your OCD:

- What has made you vulnerable to OCD?
- Are there any triggers or life events that might have activated or worsened your OCD?
- What is now maintaining your OCD?
- How bad is your OCD now?
- In what ways would you like to feel and behave differently?

By the time you have worked through this chapter as we suggest, you will have

- defined your problem;
- set your goals;
- gained some useful information and learned some practical techniques on how to deal with obstacles you may come up against.

Any attempt to solve a problem is only ever as good as your definition of the problem. This is especially important in overcoming OCD, because having a more accurate understanding of what the problem *is* forms a large part of recovery. For example, a faulty definition of the problem (e.g. 'Having intrusive thoughts about punching a baby means I'm dangerous') leads to solutions that become the problem (e.g. 'I must try hard not to have intrusive thoughts about punching babies and must stay away from them'). An accurate definition of the problem (e.g. 'I worry too much about my intrusive thoughts of punching a baby because it means I could act upon my urges'), leads to an appropriate solution (e.g. 'accepting my intrusive thought of punching babies as normal, and being close to babies while having the thought about punching them to prove that the thoughts have no power').

Thus overcoming OCD begins with two distinct steps:

1   A definition of the problem, which includes: (a) a description of your intrusive thoughts, images, doubts, or urges; (b) the *meaning* you attach to these experiences; and (c) the way you *respond* to these experiences, for example, the rituals, avoidance, and safety behaviors you use. When you change, these responses will need to be 'unlearned' and alternatives tested out to gather supporting evidence for your new meaning.

2   A description of your goal, which includes: (a) accepting the intrusive thought, image, doubt, or urge but with a realistic, non-catastrophic meaning; and (b) changing the way you respond to these experiences so that your behavior ceases to handicap and distress you.

Moving towards the realistic, non-catastrophic, compassionate understanding that intrusive thoughts, images, doubts, or impulses are normal is a critical step in overcoming OCD. It will help to begin to reduce both your feelings of anxiety, guilt, or discomfort and the frequency of the intrusive thoughts. So a clear definition of the problems points the way to helpful solutions.

Defining Your Problem

Rating the Severity of Your OCD

How bad is your OCD right now? Rating the severity of your OCD now and later will help you to monitor your progress and assess whether what you're doing is effective or not. You will need to repeat the rating exercise at regular intervals, for example, every four weeks. We have reproduced in Appendix 4 several rating scales that measure OCD symptoms: using these will both help you to identify different aspects of your OCD, and give you a score that you can use as a basis for comparison later. You can use these even if you decide not to use any self-help and are prescribed medication instead, or if you decide to have an alternative therapy.

Try to organize your problems using the following system:

1 What is the main intrusive thought, image, doubt, or urge you experience? Use a separate sheet for each group of problems. (If you need help, use the Yale–Brown Obsessive Compulsive Symptom Checklist on page 302 (Appendix 4).)

2 What do you think the main intrusive thought, image, doubt, or urge means about you, or what do you think will happen if you accept the thought?

3 What do you tend to avoid because of your intrusive thought, doubt, or urge? Don't forget to include what you avoid *thinking about*.

4 How do you respond to your intrusive thought, image, doubt, or urge (e.g. your main rituals and neutralizing strategies)? Again, don't forget to include things you do in your head as well as ways you behave.

You can then summarize and rate your problems using the forms in Appendix 4. Make a separate problem statement for each of your obsessions. Frank, for example, defined his problem thus: 'Recurrent intrusive *thoughts* of blasphemy and sacrilegious images about Jesus Christ which means I will burn in hell with the devil's disciples. This leads me to avoid churches, priests, and the Bible, and to attempt to suppress my blasphemous thoughts and repeat frequent prayers for forgiveness.' Before he started his self-help program, he rated his obsession and compulsion as being 8 out of 8 on a scale of distress.

Where Might Your OCD Have Come From?

In Chapter 2 we discussed some of the factors that might make someone vulnerable to OCD, such as a genetic vulnerability, and also possible triggers, such as various life experiences. Frank's vulnerability factors included a possible genetic predisposition – there was a family history of alcoholism, most recently in his uncle – and a strict Catholic upbringing by his parents. (We are not saying that the Catholicism *caused* Frank's OCD, but it may have influenced the form it took. If Frank had been brought up in a non-religious family, he would probably have developed a different sort of OCD.) The trigger for Frank's OCD was thought to be his father's death, as before then the problem had been mild and had not significantly interfered with his life.

Start to build a compassionate perspective on the development of your OCD by writing down your own ideas of how it has come about – the 'history' of your OCD, if you like – using the 'formulation' sheet in Appendix 5. This will help you to be less critical of yourself for having OCD, and also give you some ideas of the beliefs you will need to be aware of and to modify in order to help with relapse prevention.

What makes you vulnerable to developing OCD?

For example, do you have any family history of OCD or another mental disorder that might make you vulnerable? Have you always had an anxious temperament? Can you identify any bad experiences, like bullying or neglect, that might have made you vulnerable to developing OCD?

Can you identify the attitudes or rules that make you vulnerable to OCD?

Examples might be: 'Thinking a bad thought is as bad as doing it,' or 'It's irresponsible to ignore thoughts of harm coming to myself or other people.' You might find the Responsibility Interpretations Scale (RIS) and the Responsibility Attitudes Scale (RAS) in Appendix 4 helpful in identifying beliefs and rules that drive your OCD. Do any of the kinds of thoughts and beliefs outlined in Chapter 2 give you clues as to the kinds of beliefs you hold?

Can you identify any triggers that set off or aggravate your OCD?

Events that can act as triggers include an infection, a death, pregnancy, or a change in your role in life.

'I can't identify any factors that caused my OCD'

Don't worry if you can't identify specific factors that have made you vulnerable to developing OCD. It is often impossible to be certain why it happened, especially if OCD developed in childhood; we have to accept that, as yet, we don't fully understand all the causes of OCD. Uncertainty and constant questioning ('Why me?') can themselves become an obsessional rumination leading to a compulsive seeking of reassurance about the cause of OCD. Inevitably, you may read or be told different things by different therapists or doctors. However, the more opinions you seek, and the more books or websites you read, the more your doubts will increase. We explained in Chapter 2 that some experts may emphasize the role of brain pathways and serotonin, whereas others may lay stress on your childhood experiences. The tasks here are to tolerate uncertainty: to accept that you will never know the 'exact' combination of factors that contributed to your present position, and that most of the 'causes' are probably in the unknown category.

A word of caution about seeking causes

Some psychotherapies endlessly encourage you to look for a cause rather than a solution, but this rarely has any benefit in OCD. If you are down a hole, you don't need to know the route you took to fall into it – you want to be able to get out of the hole. Just say *no* to any therapy that offers to find the route you took into the hole. Insist on a proven psychological treatment for OCD that helps you get out of your hole!

Sometimes memories about the onset of OCD can be identified *during* therapy, when you're confronting objects or activities that you've been strenuously avoiding. For example, when one of us was helping a woman to confront a fear of contamination or dirt and avoidance of a wide range of situations, she began to experience images and memories of a sexual trauma when she was much younger which was clearly relevant to the development of her OCD. Ever since then she had felt 'dirty' and humiliated, but these feelings had become generalized so that she avoided virtually everything that she regarded as dirty. This masked the original trigger. However, the relevance of the original trigger was identified only because of the focus on solutions to overcoming her fear and avoidance. She then needed therapy similar to that used for post-traumatic stress disorder – for example, talking about the trauma in detail, giving up her self-blame, and developing a compassionate attitude towards herself – as well as the standard approach used for overcoming fears of contamination.

Maintaining Factors: What Keeps OCD Going

In Chapter 2 we emphasized the importance of identifying the factors that *maintain* the problem and keep it going in a series of vicious circles. In this chapter we have used Frank's case as an example to show a typical trigger, the meaning he attaches to the obsession and his response. These are set out diagrammatically in Figure 5.1, using the 'vicious flower' model we introduced in Chapter 4.

You can do this for your own problems using the 'vicious

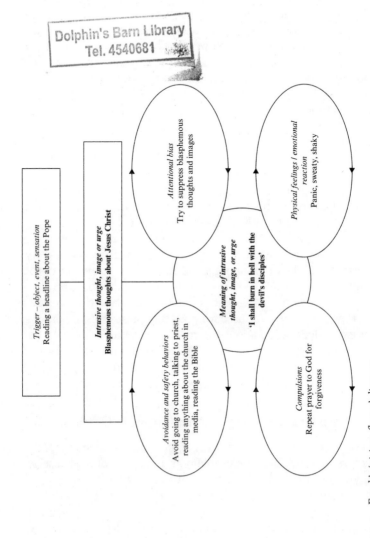

Figure 5.1 Frank's 'vicious flower' diagram

Trigger – object, event, sensation
Reading a headline about the Pope

Intrusive thought, image or urge
Blasphemous thoughts about Jesus Christ

Attentional bias
Try to suppress blasphemous thoughts and images

Physical feelings / emotional reaction
Panic, sweaty, shaky

Meaning of intrusive thought, image, or urge
'I shall burn in hell with the devil's disciples'

Avoidance and safety behaviors
Avoid going to church, talking to priest, reading anything about the church in media, reading the Bible

Compulsions
Repeat prayer to God for forgiveness

flower' diagram in Appendix 4. First write down a typical trigger (a), and the intrusive thought, image or urge in (b). Next identify the catastrophic meaning of your intrusive thoughts, images, or urges in circle (c). Next complete the features of attentional bias (d), mood (e), compulsions (f), and other avoidance and safety behaviors (g), which reinforce the obsessions and the catastrophic meaning they have for you. Once you've identified the maintaining factors in the vicious circles, you'll be able to define your goals and apply the strategies described in Chapter 6.

Setting Your Goals

Goals are fundamental to overcoming OCD by self-help with CBT. You need to know what you're aiming for and to measure your progress towards these goals at regular intervals. Frank had two main goals:

1 To accept blasphemous thoughts and images as a normal human experience and a sign that I care a great deal about my God.
2 To read the Bible, go to church, and speak to the priest while experiencing the thoughts.

He rated his progress towards these goals as '0' at the beginning of his program on a scale of '0–10', where '10' represented complete achievement of his goal. You can rate your own progress towards your goals at regular intervals on the 'Problem and Goal Sheet' in Appendix 4.

Don't start your program until you have written down and rated your problems and goals, so you know what you're trying to achieve and can assess at regular intervals how far you've come. Setting goals can be tricky, especially for those individuals with OCD who have lost sight of what is normal or have forgotten how they used to behave. So in this part of this chapter we will cover goals in detail, taking some of the main themes of OCD in turn. First, though, some general points need to be made that apply to all your goals, whatever form your OCD takes.

Make Your Goals Specific

The first rule is to make your goals as specific and objective as possible, so that your progress towards them can easily be monitored. An example of a goal for someone who had a problem with excessive showering might be 'To shower once a day and to finish within 5 minutes even if I feel uncomfortable'. This is better than making a non-specific goal like 'To shower normally'. That could be interpreted in many different ways; so, for example, it might leave room for you merely to speed up your showering rituals.

Develop a Group of Goals

When you have more than one type of obsession and compulsion, try to group goals which are related – for example, one person grouped goals related to (a) fears of contamination and compulsive washing, (b) thoughts about causing harm to children and compulsive checking of his actions, and (c) hoarding of objects. *In general*, start on a group of goals that is easier to tackle, and set yourself a realistic timetable with a target date by which you intend to move on to the next set of goals.

Within each goal devise a series of tasks, which are the means towards that goal. This may include specific acts of exposure, or testing specific theories by behavioral experiments. Set out the tasks within goals in a hierarchy, too, so that you begin with easier tasks and work your way up to more challenging ones.

Make Your Goals Realistic

Many individuals with OCD have forgotten what is normal and may set themselves goals that are unrealistic. They may not be sure how long it takes to wash their hands 'normally', or how often most people check their front door when they leave their house, and so on. A rule of thumb is to try to revert to how you used to behave before you developed OCD. Some people may like to ask around among their friends to find out what is 'normal'.

In case you're reluctant to ask questions that you feel might embarrass you or others, we now go on to discuss suitable goals for the most common compulsive behaviors, including hand-washing, toilet routines, checking, and keeping order.

Goals for Contamination Fears

Goals for Washing Your Hands

Only 150 years ago, filth and contamination were everywhere in most people's lives. Horse manure filled the roads, and human excrement was heaped on the streets or thrown into rivers. Foodstuffs were frequently riddled with bacteria or dirt. As a consequence, there were epidemics of infectious diseases like cholera, typhus, and typhoid. Increasing knowledge of how such infections are spread led to many cultural changes that put increasing emphasis on cleanliness, to the point where some people equated cleanliness with godliness. The pendulum has now swung so far that today our society is cleaner than ever, but we have become fearful of dirt and disease. Even some individuals without OCD become very concerned about dirt, believing it might harm them or their children, which is highly unlikely.

There are some interesting cultural differences. For example, the Japanese have a particular concern with germs on bedlinen, children's toys, or stationery, which have to be sterile. They use a lot of antibacterial products, but there are not fewer infectious diseases in Japan than in other developed countries.

Our society has in many ways become 'too clean' and this may have led to a rise in autoimmune diseases such as eczema or asthma. The theory is that in the absence of real germs, we react to substances such as dust mites and pollen that are usually harmless. Children with pets or several older siblings are less likely to have asthma or allergies. The body seems to need some of the bacteria and microbes in the 'dirt' to develop a healthy immune system. Without a healthy immune system, you may be vulnerable to developing an autoimmune disease.

We comfortably live with many bacteria all the time. About fifteen minutes after washing your hands, 'germs' such as *Staphylococcus* are back on the surface of your skin, as they live deep in our pores, so you can't wash them off. They just reappear! Moreover, these bacteria live with us to fight other potentially harmful bacteria. Our skin also excretes natural oils and fatty acids that will kill many harmful bacteria. *Excessive hand-washing in hot water removes these essential oils so that your skin becomes dry and chapped or cut and therefore more vulnerable to infection and contamination.* This is another example of how trying too hard to prevent the event that you fear actually makes it worse. If your hands are excessively dry and damaged, please make sure you use a moisturizer that contains urea (e.g. 'Eucerin').

Many people with OCD and fears of contamination have forgotten how to wash to 'normal' hygienic standards; so we have set out in Tables 5.1 and 5.2 some guidelines for setting your goals on when and how you wash your hands. Keep in mind though, that '*normal*' is different from '*treatment*': so, in order to get sufficient exposure to overcome your fear of contamination thoroughly, you will probably need to have some sessions that leave you less clean than your OCD-free friends would be.

It is not usually *necessary* to wash your hands after urinating (although it may be customary, and it's not a problem as long as it's not done compulsively), as urine is sterile. Nor is it necessary to hover over public toilet seats or to cover them with toilet paper unless you can *see* dirt or excrement on the seat. In such situations, make decisions on the basis not of how you feel but of what you can see. It is worth remembering that workers who clean toilets all day clearing up other people's messes have no increased risk of contracting disease and don't wash excessively.

Table 5.1   **Suggested goals for when you wash your hands**

To wash my hands
  before I handle uncooked food
  before I treat a cut or wound
  before I tend to someone who has an infectious disease
  before I put in my contact lenses
  after I have defecated
  after I have handled raw meat or fish
  after I have handled or petted a wild animal or one in a zoo
  after I have cleared up animal excrement
  after I have changed my baby's diaper
  after I have treated a cut or a wound
  after I can *see* that my hands are dirty (e.g. after gardening)

Table 5.2   **Suggested goals for how you wash your hands**

Aim to wash your hands within 30–40 seconds with the following procedure:
  wet your hands thoroughly with *warm* (not hot) water
  apply liquid or bar soap and lather well
  do not use soap if your hands are dry or chapped but use a hydrating cleanser, which contains urea, is free of fragrance and is non-irritating
  rub your hands together and scrub the surfaces for between 1 and 15 seconds
  only scrub under your nails if you have been doing a messy job and can see (not feel) dirt under your nails
  rinse well under running water for about 10 seconds and dry your hands: pat gently with a soft towel if your hands are dry and chapped

Similarly, bank cashiers or butchers or all those other people who work in occupations constantly touching things that you might think of as 'contaminated' are no more likely to have an infectious disease than the rest of the population.

When you wash, don't hold your arms up like a surgeon – unless, of course, you are doing surgery! Don't wash with excessively hot water, bleach, antiseptic or antibacterial spray, or antibacterial soaps. Antibacterial soaps are 'overkill', as is using disposable wet-wipes or towels on your possessions. These added safeguards are necessary only in certain situations, for example, for a surgeon before conducting an operation, or in an intensive care ward.

While you are washing your hands, don't count up to a particular number or wash in a specific order, as these are all rituals.

If you are unable to resist washing ritualistically, ensure that you re-expose yourself to something you find contaminating afterwards, like touching the floor or the toilet seat, and then touch your face, body, and possessions.

Don't dry your hands excessively and make them further chapped – if this is a problem, make a goal of completing the drying process within thirty seconds and finishing while you feel uncomfortable.

Avoidance in Contamination Fears

Some people with OCD get so fed up with all their washing and cleaning that they develop elaborate avoidance behaviors to prevent cleaning rituals. Examples include using rubber or disposable gloves, pulling your sleeve down to use a toilet handle, kicking a door open, or keeping separate clothes within the house and other 'contaminated' clothes to use outside the house. In Chapter 1, we described how Howard Hughes gave up using clothes altogether and had most of his possessions covered in paper tissues. Needless to say, you need to remove all the safety-seeking behaviors like using gloves and tissues, and all your clothes need to be mixed up: your goal here might be 'To use my clothes flexibly and for 'contaminated' clothes to be used within my home and not kept in a special contaminated box'.

Work out goals to cover all your avoidance behaviors related to contamination. For example, another goal might be 'To sit daily on public toilets with the seat against my skin and to use the toilet handle to flush the toilet without covering my hand'. One of the goals for another person who had an obsession about catching HIV from a gay person was to 'To visit a crowded gay bar and try to brush against strangers'.

Goals for Showering or Bathing

You may bathe or shower once or twice a day, but aim to finish within five minutes (or ten minutes if you are also washing your hair). As with washing your hands, don't count up to a particular number or wash in a specific order: just allow yourself to be on automatic pilot. If you need help in determining when five minutes is up, then set an alarm clock or timer and when it goes off, have a final rinse from soap and immediately get out of the shower. More important than leaving after a specified time is to leave your shower or bath even if you feel uncomfortable. If you complete a ritual until you feel 'comfortable' or 'just right', you will need to make yourself feel uncomfortable or not right again by recontaminating yourself – for example, by touching the floor or a toilet seat and then touching yourself all over your face and body.

Another way of monitoring your progress is to count up the number of bars or bottles of soap that you use, as this is often a good indicator of the severity of excessive washing. You could set a goal of reducing the amount you use by a specific proportion.

Goals for Toilet Routines

Excessive toilet routines are problematic for many people with fears of contamination. It may be necessary to set a limit on the amount of toilet paper you use, or the time and frequency of going to the toilet, depending on the nature of the problem. An example of a goal for defecating might be to wipe your bottom twice with up to four pieces of toilet paper folded over.

Some women with fears of contamination wipe themselves excessively hard on their genitalia after urinating, leading to a skin irritation. A goal after urinating would be to use two or three sheets of soft paper, which are patted gently over your genital area.

If using an excessive amount of toilet paper is a problem, then you may need to count up the number of rolls of paper that you use in a week, or the number of times the toilet gets blocked, and set a realistic goal to reduce these numbers.

Some individuals with OCD change their diet or use drugs to constipate themselves so that they will not have to use the toilet so much. Needless to say, all such safety behaviors will need to be added to the tasks you set yourself to work through your hierarchy for exposure, so that you allow your body to function normally and don't abuse it.

Goals for Grooming or Shaving

Rituals to do with grooming one's hair or shaving may be especially relevant if you have problems to do with obsessional slowness or symmetry, or a form of body dysmorphic disorder. People with these obsessions perform grooming or shaving too meticulously and in a specific order, or to achieve a symmetrical appearance, or to avoid the risk of getting a cut, which becomes very time-consuming. Here the goal would be to groom or shave in a specific time (e.g. five minutes) and to finish when you feel 'not right' or 'asymmetrical' or fear that you are doing it in the 'wrong' order.

Goals for Cleaning Around the House

The same remarks about washing your body or grooming can also be made about cleaning surfaces or objects around the house. Some people with OCD are preoccupied with keeping surfaces sterile and use bottles of antibacterial spray or bleach. Again this is overkill; there is no need for sterile surfaces, antibacterial sprays, or disposable wipes in a normal home unless, for example, a pet has accidentally defecated on a surface. In normal circumstances, use a cloth with soapy water and decide to finish cleaning on the basis of what you can see and not how you 'feel'. You need to aim for a 'clean enough' home, not sterile perfection.

Experiments have been done whereby subjects were asked to touch 'contaminants' such as money or toilet door handles with one hand while keeping the other hand 'clean'. Fingerprints from both hands were then imprinted on blood agar plates, which are normally used by microbiology laboratories to grow bacteria. When the cultures developed, normal bacterial flora was found from both hands. No dangerous bacteria were found.

Try to clean only when you can *see* that your home is dirty, rather than when you 'feel' that it is dirty. In the kitchen, wipe surfaces when food and spills are apparent using a detergent and cloth. Vacuuming or washing floors is very unlikely to need to be done daily; once or twice a week is usually enough. When you do clean your floors or surfaces, keep each wipe or 'sweep' to a minimum. A suitable goal may be to limit the frequency of cleaning (e.g. to twice a week) and the time spent cleaning each room (e.g. 10 minutes). We're not saying that you won't feel anxious because of your fears, but you won't come to any harm from contaminants.

Goals for Checking

People without OCD don't demand complete certainty, and as a consequence feel more confident that they probably did the action in the first place. There is very rarely any need to carry out 'just one check', or 'another quick check'. Fast OCD is still OCD. Do you really think you would do the check if you did not have OCD? If you're not sure, go against the OCD – it's no friend of yours. Checking 'just to be on the safe side' is one of the most seductive and hazardous routes to keeping your OCD going.

Checking Gas Taps

It may surprise you, but the majority of people without OCD don't bother to check their gas taps before they leave the house. If you don't believe us, do your own survey. This is because you can smell a gas leak, which would be apparent within the house. Again, the rule is: don't go by how you feel, and resist checking even when you feel uncomfortable.

Checking Water Taps

Most people don't bother to check water taps when they leave their home either. Make a goal of resisting checking even if you feel uncomfortable. Turning off taps can be done within five seconds, and you shouldn't normally need to overtighten the tap. Go by what you see or hear, not how you feel. If there is a risk of flooding, then you will see the water gushing. As a means towards this goal, it's often helpful to leave the taps running to prove to yourself that there is no significant risk.

Checking Lights or Electrical Appliances

Again, most people don't check all their lights or electrical appliances and plugs, so there is no reason for you to do so. Even checking once is an exercise in OCD. Only use objective information – for example, you can see if a light is on, so leave even though you feel uncomfortable. Don't then turn it on and off until you feel comfortable. Some people might prefer to check certain appliances like an iron: here a quick glance at the switch is sufficient, and placing your hand near the iron will also provide sufficient objective information to determine that it is turned off.

Checking Doors are Locked

It is within the boundaries of normality to check a door lock or window once before you leave your home, but most people without OCD will be able to trust their memories at least most of the time, and will not, for example, check a door or window they have not opened that day. You can use objective information – for example, try to open the door *once* after you have locked it and then leave, even if you feel 'uncomfortable' or it does not feel 'right'. Don't, for example, shake the door until it feels 'right'. A normal check after locking will take less than five seconds.

Checking That You Did Not Make a Mistake

This covers a multitude of sins, from nurses who want to check that they have dispensed the right dose of medication to an accountant who has to check his figures or reread information. It's amazing how many people protest that in *their* profession they really must not make mistakes. Do you really act the way your OCD-free colleagues do? If not, use them as role models. Again, a key criterion in the goals is finishing the check while feeling uncomfortable or 'not right'.

Goals for Repeating Actions

This covers routine activities such as crossing thresholds, getting up and down from a chair, dressing and undressing, or climbing stairs. The goal may be to complete each activity once without repeating it and to finish when feeling 'not right'. This may be part of a behavioral experiment to complete the activity while deliberately thinking of the feared catastrophe to determine if it is just a thought.

Goals for Hoarding

A critical goal for hoarding items such as newspapers or useless objects is to reduce clutter and make your living space more practical, safe, and pleasant to live in. This may involve several smaller goals: (a) throwing away or 'moving on' waste and unnecessary possessions; (b) having healthy criteria for acquiring objects in the future; (c) storing and organizing your possessions according to categories (and not so you can see them all the time).

To assist with throwing away or recycling, consider: Do I like it or is it beautiful? Is it valuable or a family heirloom? Do I have a use for it (*now*, not 'possibly' in the future!)? If you decide that the answer is no (and 'If in doubt, throw!'), then resist the temptation to check the item. Even if you decide not to throw a hoarded item away, would you really keep it if you did not hoard? Could you find it a better home? Consider passing it on to a charity shop, for example, if it has some monetary value. When you buy new items, try to use the criterion that it will be useful to you, rather than an emotional 'fix'. Devise a system for storing your possessions that does not involve piles of things on the floor or on your furniture. If you run out of storage space, this may well be a clue that it's time for another clearout!

Goals for Intrusive Thoughts and Superstitious Behaviors

These goals are relevant for a range of intrusive thoughts about causing harm to others (e.g. stabbing a baby, pushing someone into the path of an oncoming train, having sex with your mother, blasphemous thoughts) and various superstitious and neutralizing behaviors that you perform in order to prevent the bad event from occurring.

It is true that there is a range of superstitious behaviors in our culture, many of which are practiced by people who don't have OCD, but this does not mean you have to follow such superstitions. In general, the goals should be to accept intrusive thoughts, images, and urges without engaging in any mental activity or behavior to prevent the catastrophe from occurring or appearing immoral. Make your own goals from your intrusive thoughts. For example, if you worry about stabbing your baby, then your goal might be 'To deliberately experience thoughts and images about stabbing my baby without neutralizing them and while being alone with my baby with a kitchen knife in my pocket'. If you have intrusive images about having oral sex with your son, your goal might be 'To allow my intrusive images about having oral sex to pass through my mind without trying to alter the image and while being physically close and alone with him'. If you are heterosexual and have intrusive thoughts about being homosexual, then a goal might be 'To allow my intrusive images about being homosexual to pass through my mind without trying to engage in the thoughts and while being in the company of a gay person'. Paradoxically, these approaches will reduce the frequency and distress of the images.

Goals for Order and Symmetry

A demand for order and symmetry in one's possessions can be turned into goals of achieving disorder and asymmetry. Interestingly, this does not usually need to be chaos: the slightest deviation from the previous position is usually sufficient to create a feeling of being 'not right'. Most other people wouldn't actually be able to notice the difference, but as long you feel 'not right' or 'uncomfortable', then the disorder is sufficient.

Now that you've defined your problems and set your goals, your next step is to get yourself ready to commit to overcoming OCD. You can help yourself to do this by focusing on the benefits of freeing yourself from OCD, and tackling any of the psychological obstacles to overcoming it.

Managing Obstacles to Overcoming Your OCD

One of the main difficulties in helping people overcome OCD is not that the principles we've outlined don't work, but inspiring people to try them out. One thing we do know from using CBT to overcome OCD is that starting to change early on gives you a better chance of success. Long deliberation about engaging with the principles of overcoming OCD is often an exercise in OCD in its own right, and can lead you to feel demoralized. So clearly it's important to tackle any obstacles to getting started as soon as you can, so that you can get on with the business of freeing yourself from OCD.

Some of the more common obstacles are:

- shame;
- pride;
- depression and a sense of hopelessness;
- pessimism about your chances of recovery;

- 'losing touch' or overvaluing ideas;
- an exaggerated sense of responsibility;
- wanting guarantees that no harm will occur;
- anger;
- guilt;
- a sense of being a 'martyr';
- perfectionism;
- 'I've tried it before . . .'
- 'My OCD is different' ideas (almost everyone believes this!): e.g. 'My thoughts/doubts/urges/images are so bad/odd/unacceptable they really do mean I'm bad/dangerous/weird, etc.'

Shame and OCD

Shame is defined as 'an intense negative emotion when you believe you fall short of your ideal, such as a 'flaw' or 'weakness' being revealed to others'. Shame can have a number of consequences: making you less inclined to seek help or to disclose important obsessions, increasing your isolation, increasing your attempts to suppress obsessions, making it difficult for you to accept responsibility for overcoming your OCD, or giving you a tendency to blame others for your OCD.

On average, a person with OCD puts up with the condition for ten years before seeking help. For many people this is because they feel ashamed of their thoughts or behaviors. This can also mean that they don't discuss their problems with friends, family members, or partners. There are several consequences of this. First, not discussing your symptoms means not getting feedback that intrusive thoughts, doubts, and urges are normal. Second, it can increase a sense of isolation, which can contribute to a low mood. Third, it can deprive you of the support that can be so helpful when combating OCD.

Here are some of the things people with OCD report feeling ashamed about:

- intrusive thoughts and images;
- rituals;

- avoidance behaviors;
- not carrying out a ritual;
- having a 'mental' problem;
- impact on their close family;
- disclosing their condition to others.

Hiding your intrusive thoughts

It's not unusual for people with 'unacceptable' intrusive thoughts to find it difficult to share them with other people, even trained health-care professionals. They fear that anyone they tell will share their own extreme misinterpretation that having such thoughts means they are bad, crazy, or dangerous, that they will be misunderstood, or that talking about the thoughts might have dire consequences. You might think that if people found out the things you think, they'd be bound to think less of you (reject me/take my children away/lock me up), so you can't possibly disclose them. These are examples of shame. Try to treat these beliefs as a theory to be tested out with a few individuals and see what happens.

How shame affects thinking

At the heart of shame is the meaning you attach to an event – for example, what you believe about having OCD. If you feel ashamed about something you may then tend to think about that thing in exaggerated or distorted ways, for example:

- overestimating how abnormal, weird, or 'weak' you are as a person;
- overestimating the degree to which you think others will disapprove/ridicule/be horrified if you reveal what you're ashamed of and how long they will think about/remember it.

How shame affects behavior

If you feel ashamed, you may find that it affects the way you feel inclined to behave. For example, you might:

- Withdraw from others, so that they won't realize you've got a problem. This tends to feed depression and ruminating.
- Avoid eye contact and find it hard to look other people in the eye. This leads to people believing you're not interested in them and want them to give you a wide berth.
- Criticize others to save face. This can be a major problem when people around you want to help you and mention your OCD. If you feel ashamed you might then be overly critical of others in order to 'save face' and draw attention to other people's weaknesses. The problem is that you're only doing this because you feel bad about your own problem, and it does nothing to improve the situation.
- Use a ritual to get rid of 'shameful' thoughts and images.
- Conceal the problem from others. As we've seen, shame can lead many people with OCD to keep their thoughts and rituals secret, meaning they suffer alone.
- Minimize personal responsibility. This is another self-defeating 'face-saving' exercise, in which the person feeling ashamed believes they would be revealed as weak and inadequate if they took a good measure of responsibility for overcoming their problem. The reverse, of course, is true: it takes strength and determination to tackle a problem like OCD. Sometimes, too, people overlook self-help because they confuse it with being to blame for the problem.

Overcoming shame: self-acceptance
Self-acceptance is based on the principle that condemning the whole of yourself as 'weak', 'inadequate', or 'inferior' is an error of overgeneralization. You are, in reality, a complex, unique, ever-changing, fallible, human being. As we have seen, rigid demands for physical, mental, or behavioral perfection are unrealistic and will lead to distress and frustration. Flexible thinking and unconditional self-acceptance are much more constructive and better for your psychological, emotional, and physical health. Treat yourself as you would treat a friend with the same problem. For more detailed advice on self-acceptance,

we'd recommend consulting Windy Dryden's book *How to Accept Yourself* (Sheldon Press) and Melanie Fennell's book *Overcoming Low Self-Esteem* (in this series). You can also do the 'Big I, Little I' exercise in the last section of this chapter.

The steps to take in overcoming shame

1 Accept that you have an emotional problem and face up to its consequences. Give up rating *yourself* as weak, inferior, 'inadequate'; stop comparing yourself with others and accept *yourself* as a complex, unique, ever-changing, fallible, human being of whom OCD is just one aspect. The most important aspect of shame is accepting yourself, so that even if there are isolated individuals who will condemn you or rate you negatively, you can recognize that this is their problem, not yours.

2 Take a compassionate and understanding view of your OCD and assume a good degree of responsibility for the fact that it has persisted.

3 Understand that there is no reason why you *must not* have any kind of intrusive thought, image, urge, or doubt: all these are normal. Accept yourself as a normal human being, including this experience.

4 Think realistically about the extent to which others will condemn you for your thoughts or actions and how long any disapproval will last. You might like to review the evidence of people's reactions so far. If you did get a poor response, is there an explanation for this that lies in a misunderstanding (e.g. because of lack of knowledge)? If others know that you have intrusive thoughts that you think will be unacceptable (e.g. about being a pedophile), accept that you can't know or control exactly what others will think about you. If you ruminate over this or to try to 'solve' it, you will disturb yourself for many years to come.

5 Talk openly about your OCD when appropriate, for example, to your family and mental health professionals involved in your care or in an OCD support group.

6 Increase your social contact and openness (you may wish to do a cost–benefit analysis on this: see the last section of this chapter), and deal constructively with misunderstandings. Try a behavioral experiment to check out whether you get the kind of reaction you fear from other people, and see to what extent you can educate them about the nature of OCD.

A final word on shame about obsessions

Are high standards, strong morals, and a desire to prevent harm or disasters really something to be ashamed of? OCD is symptomatic of trying too hard to uphold values and moral ideals. It's very hard to imagine that anyone should feel ashamed of doing their utmost to succeed with these aims. The good news is that giving up OCD only involves giving up trying too hard, not the values themselves.

Pride

It's often said that 'pride comes before a fall'. It can also be an obstacle to overcoming OCD, and can lead people to resist approaching their OCD differently because they are afraid to lose face. Pride, in this sense, is usually linked to shame, and is usually a 'compensatory strategy' aimed at preventing you from the feelings of shame you might experience if you accepted that the way you have been trying to cope with your OCD has been less than ideal. Of course, there is absolutely no shame in this. Debate still rages among researchers as to the best way to help people overcome OCD, and even professionals get it wrong sometimes.

The following is a list of some of the attitudes that can lead you into the defensive trap of unhelpful pride, along with our answers.

- *If I give my rituals up, especially those I've insisted other people go along with, my friends and family will think I'm a fool.*
  Answer: They are more likely to think your behavior foolish if you don't attempt to give up your rituals.

- *I should resist attempts to change me, otherwise it feels like they've won.*
  Answer: If you don't change yourself, the OCD has won and is in control.
- *The principles of exposure and response prevention are simple and since I'm basically an intelligent person, I should be able to work out how to get rid of my OCD without any help or advice.*
  Answer: The principles of exposure may be simple, but the implementation is not.
- *It's ridiculous to suggest I can help myself – if I could do that I would have done so years ago!*
  Answer: It's rare for someone with OCD *simply* to stop their rituals. You need to understand how self-help works before you implement a program.

Depression and OCD

Because of the marked impact OCD has on people's lives, it's hardly surprising that many who have OCD also experience depression. However, feeling down and depressed can lead to hopelessness and pessimism about the prospect of recovery, and this in turn can affect an individual's ability to engage with the tasks required to overcome their OCD. This can then mean that OCD drags on for longer, and seemingly confirms the view that the problem will never go away, and so the vicious circle is complete.

Which came first: OCD or depression?

Did your depression come after the onset of the OCD? Alternatively, if the OCD was sorted out, would you then feel much better in your mood? The vast majority of people with OCD report that depression did indeed begin after the onset of OCD and find that, as their OCD starts to improve, their depression also begins to lift.

However, in a small minority of individuals, OCD appears to be secondary to depression. Here the depressed mood comes first and the OCD follows in the context of the depression or a history of bipolar disorder (manic depression). In this case, OCD might consist of troublesome ruminations and guilt about something the person has or has not done in the past.

Determining whether you are suffering from depression, and if it is secondary to your OCD, is best done by a psychiatrist or a psychologist experienced in OCD. You can, however, complete a screening test for depression to assess whether you are likely to be suffering from it. In Appendix 4 we reproduce such a test, the Hospital Anxiety and Depression Scale.

If you score 10 or more on the depression scale then you are probably suffering from depression, and should read the rest of this section. If you scored fifteen or more, you may find it difficult to follow a self-help book on OCD. Overcoming OCD is hard work, so you will need to be motivated to do your homework consistently and regularly. For this reason, if you are seriously depressed it would probably be advisable for you to seek professional help, to tackle your depression as well as your OCD.

Suicide
If you're feeling hopeless about the future, and have thoughts of killing yourself, please *see a doctor right away*. We are glad to report that suicide is relatively uncommon among OCD sufferers. It is worth emphasizing again: people who have OCD *can get better* – it is never hopeless.

Behavioral activation
One of the first steps of CBT for depression involves changing your behavior. This alone has been shown to be as effective as standard treatments such as antidepressant medication and cognitive therapy alone. The approach is called behavioral activation and we know from our own experience that it can help in the depression that occurs in OCD.

Behavioral activation is based on the observation that when you are depressed, everything becomes an effort and you tire easily. You avoid things that are uncomfortable. You might avoid making difficult decisions or conflicts. You do less, and become socially withdrawn and inactive. You might then blame yourself for doing less and probably tell yourself: 'You should be able to pick yourself up and get on with life.' You become more negative about yourself, ruminate, and believe you can't do anything; you become more depressed and a vicious circle is established. You may stay at home or in bed during the day, distract yourself watching a lot of television or playing computer games, and give up your normal activities. Your lifestyle changes so that you may eat little or eat only junk food, and you no longer exercise.

Avoiding activities may stop unpleasant feelings in the short term (hence it becomes reinforced and maintains the vicious circle). However, as with OCD the solution has become the problem, as not engaging with the world and being inactive means a less rewarding life without any positive experiences. Being inactive makes you more likely to ruminate on the various losses and things missing in your life, and again fuels the vicious circle, making you more depressed. You now have two problems. First, you have OCD and a life that's not going particularly well; and now you have retreated from the world, which is going to make you more depressed.

Reversing this process can significantly improve your mood and motivate you to tackle your OCD. The first step is to monitor your daily activity on a chart that breaks the days of the week into one-hour blocks (see Appendix 5). A cognitive behavior therapist using behavioral activation would conduct a detailed analysis of your behavior to find what you were avoiding and what therefore was maintaining your depressed state. Your therapist would then try to target specific changes in your behavior that would help improve your mood. They would do this by homing in on the inertia and the activities you are avoiding, aiming to break the link between doing less when you feel low. You would be encouraged to increase your activity levels and then timetable future activities.

When activating yourself, it is especially important to act according to a plan or goal, regardless of the way you feel. If you wait until you feel motivated or derive pleasure from an activity, then nothing will change. However, the more you act towards your goals, the more likely you are to come into contact with more pleasant activities, thereby deriving more pleasure from life experiences and improving your mood.

Christopher Martell was one of the clinicians who developed the program of behavioral activation and has published a self-help book, *Overcoming Depression One Step at a Time* (New Harbinger). He has a way to remember what to do: use the word ACTION!

A Assess to see if what I am doing is avoidance.
C Choose either to continue to avoid and be depressed or to do a different activity.
T Try the activity chosen.
I Integrate my new behaviors into a routine. One is not enough as old behaviors are well-established patterns.
O Observe the results.
N Never give up: keep trying this as an experiment.

Depressive ruminations

At some point, you may need to tackle depressive ruminations or excessive worry. This way of thinking is similar in some ways to OCD ruminations, as it involves dwelling on a problem over and over again without getting anywhere. To assess whether you do this, ask yourself:

- Do you spend a lot of time thinking about yourself and how you feel?
- Do you worry a lot about the future, or question yourself a lot about the past?
- Are you constantly judging or rating yourself?
- Do you rate and check on how badly you are doing against some ideal that you think you should follow?

Ruminations about the past tend to begin 'Why . . .?' (e.g. *Why is it me that has developed OCD? Why am I even bothering to try to overcome my OCD? I'm bound to be one of those people who don't recover so what's the point?*).

These 'Why?' questions generally can't be answered definitively.

A pattern of worry about the future usually takes the form of 'What if . . .?' (e.g. *What if my OCD gets worse? What if people I've told about my OCD don't like me? I'm sure other people can learn to accept their intrusive thoughts, but what if I can't accept them?*). Often worry questions have no answers or are nonexistent problems.

Key points in understanding worry and depressive ruminations are:

- they make you feel worse and more depressed, anxious, or tired;
- they rarely solve anything, and instead generate more questions ('But what if . . .?' or 'Why . . . ?') for you to ruminate over;
- they lead you to avoid making decisions, performing activities, or solving problems, and to procrastinate (and waste time that could usefully be used for exposure and behavioral experiments).

If you have a real problem or problem that can be solved, then overcoming ruminations will involve turning 'Why . . .?' type questions into 'How can I . . . ?' type questions.

An example might be if a car breaks down before you have to go to an important appointment. You could ruminate on thoughts like 'Why does it happen to me?' 'It will be a disaster,' 'I am so useless,' which will lead to procrastination, missing your appointment, and further depression. Or you could turn the question into 'How am I going to get to my appointment?' and then evaluate whether to call a taxicab or whatever. When you are feeling depressed about OCD, refocus your ruminations on to what you can do by your own actions, or who you can obtain help from in overcoming your OCD.

If you are planning to set about problem-solving, make sure that you are dealing with the right problem. For example, Ed worried about whether a woman he had told about his intrusive sexual thoughts about children would think he might actually be a pedophile and tell others and ruin his career (even though she had been very supportive). Ed tried to reassure himself that the risk of her thinking he was a pedophile and ruining his career was extremely low.) This is an example of a nonexistent problem, and if you try to solve nonexistent problems then all that happens is that you get more 'But what if . . .' questions and further uncertainties (e.g. 'What if Ed told someone who doesn't understand about OCD?'). Nor is it a problem that can be solved, as you can't control what people think.

The best way of dealing with: (a) problems that can't be solved, and (b) nonexistent problems, is not to engage with them, but instead to use the same strategy that is recommended for intrusive thoughts, doubts, or urges in OCD. Just accept them as merely thoughts and try not to engage in any mental activity with them to deal with them. *If* and when an actual problem arises, then you can your use problem-solving skills. If, however, it is a problem that can't be solved (e.g. 'What will happen when I die?') then don't even attempt to engage with the question or try to solve it. Only if there is a significant risk of a bad event happening are you allowed to prepare for it, and then only if it involves action. For example, it's sensible to prepare for your death by writing a will or appointing a guardian for your children. In Los Angeles the emergency services practise how they will cope in an earthquake. These are actions you can do – as opposed to ruminations that stop you getting on with life.

Cognitive therapy and depression
If behavioral activation and not responding to ruminations don't work, then cognitive therapy can also be used to overcome depression. This approach is based on the observation that depression is associated with negative thinking. We are not saying that depression is *caused* by negative thinking, but that there is a vicious circle involving thinking negatively and feeling depressed and becoming inactive. You may believe that you are worthless or a failure, that you are helpless to change

your situation, and that the future must be hopeless. Challenging the way you think and looking for alternatives can improve your mood. It is beyond the scope of this book to describe all the cognitive therapy techniques for depression. Look at *some* of the self-help books for depression (e.g. *Overcoming Depression* by Paul Gilbert, in this series) and *Feeling Good* by David Burns (Avon Books). Both books are based upon CBT and take you through a self-help program.

Another powerful way of overcoming pessimism is to treat your thoughts as a theory to be tested out. This means acting against the way you feel and doing so consistently and regularly. If you are having trouble with pessimism and hopelessness about recovery, hang on to the fact that *recovery is possible*. Try out the principles outlined in this book, and make a date with yourself in eight weeks to review if they are helping.

Low self-esteem

Another problem that can be difficult to overcome is chronic low self-esteem. Many people with OCD have had their lives affected by it from a young age and have missed out on normal activities or friendships while growing up. They have developed a sense of being alone in the world, and regard themselves as worthless or unlovable. They may not be suffering from clinical depression, but they have difficulties in social situations and are very sensitive to the slightest sense of criticism or rejection. They may overcompensate and demand impossibly high standards or be perfectionists. Such problems usually require long-term therapy, but a good start would be to read *Overcoming Low Self-Esteem* by Melanie Fennell (in this series) and *Reinventing Your Life* by Jeffrey Young (Penguin Putnam USA).

Antidepressant medication

Medications that are used for the treatment of OCD (see Appendix 1) can also be prescribed for moderate to severe depression. Drugs that act on serotonin receptors are also better at treating depression in OCD than other types of antidepressants. Improvements are usually seen within four to six weeks.

It is not a sign of weakness to take an antidepressant. It is a pragmatic approach, as you need to be in the best possible state of mind to tackle your OCD. If you prefer to take a natural substance, then there is some evidence for the benefit of St John's Wort for treating mild to moderate depression (and possibly OCD). Synthesized antidepressants have, however, been researched more and are 'purer' than St John's Wort. If you plan to take St John's Wort, it is important to tell your doctor if you are taking other prescription drugs. St John's Wort may not mix with some prescription drugs, including the contraceptive pill, which becomes less effective. Unfortunately, it is not known what the optimum dose of St John's Wort is for depression.

Lifestyle changes

We noted above some of the lifestyle changes that often come about with depression. Here is a summary list of lifestyle factors that may aggravate depression and therefore OCD:

- a restricted or chaotic diet;
- eating large amounts of junk food;
- staying up late at night and getting up at irregular hours;
- not exercising;
- increased alcohol or illegal drug use

You probably know that these are unhelpful and contribute to a depressed mood. It is important to regulate your appetite and sleep. The best approach is to plan eating and rest into your activity schedule so that you sleep regularly and eat normal amounts of food at regular times. Drinking excessively and using many recreational drugs (especially cocaine and amphetamines or 'speed', and possibly marijuana and ecstasy) make depression and OCD worse in the long term if you are vulnerable.

The Comfort Trap

The comfort trap can be a big obstacle in overcoming OCD. The most common problems arising from the comfort trap, which stems from a low frustration tolerance, are:

- Not tolerating anxiety long enough for it to subside. This means that new learning can't take place, so you can't finish your experiment and test out your predictions. Hence there is little progress in overcoming OCD.
- Procrastination – putting off the uncomfortable process of resisting rituals and facing fears. Unfortunately, this means being left in the uncomfortable position of living with OCD in the long term.

The goals are, therefore, to develop a high frustration tolerance and to act 'as if' your problem was one of *worrying* and thoughts about causing harm. If you have a worry problem, the solutions are quite different from the ones you are pursuing. The following list sets out some thoughts that often come to people caught in the comfort trap, and suggests answers that will take you out of it.

- *The anxiety and discomfort of doing exposure are just too hard to bear.*
  Answer: The anxiety and discomfort of doing exposure are hard, but not *too* hard, and if you do nothing about your OCD, they will probably just get harder.
- *I need to reduce my anxiety first, then I'll change my behavior.*
  Answer: This is putting the cart before the horse – act first, then your anxiety will reduce.
- *I need to build up my courage and confidence before I can confront my fears.*
  Answer: This is another example of putting the cart before the horse. Act uncourageously and unconfidently in order to get your courage and confidence.
- *CBT is all too much like hard work; I'll wait for my doctor to find the right medication.*
  Answer: If you have to try a series of different medications, then your chances of success with medication alone are diminishing. Furthermore, if you are on medication you will get the best result in the long term if you combine it with CBT.

- *When they tell me to stick with the anxiety and discomfort they can't possibly mean tolerating as much anxiety as I feel. I need to find an easier solution.*

  Answer: CBT is hard work, but not half as hard as living with OCD. There is no easier solution; if there was we'd have told you about it.

- *I can't possibly set aside enough time to work on my OCD; it'll interfere in my life too much.*

  Answer: If you don't set aside enough time to work on your OCD, your OCD will interfere in your life too much.

- *If change doesn't come naturally or easily then it's not genuine, and I'm just acting a part.*

  Answer: While you continue to uphold this attitude, we will guarantee that your OCD will persist. Change does not come naturally or easily. Acting against the way you feel is a temporary state while you overcome your OCD.

The 'If-Only' Trap

The 'if-only' trap can interfere with overcoming OCD by leading you to focus attention on largely insoluble problems or improbable solutions. This can result in wasting considerable energy, and can even be a contributing factor to depressive rumination (see above). Related to the comfort trap, it stems from the idea that certain conditions must exist before one can overcome OCD.

An example that often arises is when someone with OCD might remark to another person with OCD, 'If only I was worried about what you're worried about – I'd have no problem overcoming that.' This idea, of course, flies in the face of the fact that obsessions are a source of anxiety because of the unique personal meaning they have to the individual. So if you don't share the meaning, you couldn't have the obsession.

Losing Touch (Overvaluing Ideas)

Another possible obstacle for individuals overcoming OCD is that they can begin to lose sight of the fact that their avoidance and rituals are symptoms of OCD (and a factor that maintains the problem). They may feel that they are 'right' in their pursuit of cleanliness, hoarding, order, or whichever concern applies, and that it is others who are wrong. In this sense, cleanliness or hoarding becomes an *overvalued idea*, and not only a response to fear but also a goal in itself. In a sense, the individual seems to have lost touch with the real world and to have come to identify their whole self through their idealized value. The OCD is now in control and driving you around.

We discussed on **p. 100** the metaphor of being a bus driver and wanting to *control* the passengers (thoughts and feelings) that look scary, trying to throw them off the bus or to prevent them from getting on altogether; and we saw that this was an impossible and constant struggle. Eventually you might try to placate those passengers and do deals with them to keep them at the back of the bus where you can't see them. The deal you make with them is to do what they say so they won't come up and stand next to you and make you look at them. The problem with this deal is that you do what they want in exchange for getting them away from you.

Now the unwanted passengers have power over you. 'If you don't do what we say, we're coming up to you and making you look at us.' It's true they do look scary, and look as if they could do a lot more than threaten: they have tattoos, look very ugly, and smell. It looks as if you could be destroyed. The driver (you) is supposedly in control of the bus, but you have given up control in these deals with some of the passengers. In other words, by trying to get control over certain passengers, you have actually *given up* control. Soon they don't even have to tell you to 'turn left': you know as soon as you get near a left turn that the passengers are going to crawl all over you if you don't take it. Notice that the passengers threaten to do something horrible to you if you don't turn left, but it has never actually happened. In time you may almost pretend that they are not in the bus at all. You just tell yourself that left is the only direction that you want to turn.

The only way to overcome OCD is to admit that the passengers are controlling you, but to let them remain on the bus and to look at them in the eye. Test out your assumption that these passengers will destroy you. You are the driver and you can decide in which direction you want to turn. There is a route that you want to follow and these are your own goals and values – for example, you want a meaningful relationship with a partner and children, a job or career that is satisfying, and so on. Don't let the abnormal values of OCD drive you and then somehow convince yourself that this is what you want. Overcoming these idealized values is tough, and that's why it's so often a relative who desperately wants their family member with OCD to change rather than the person with OCD themselves taking the initiative to change. We discuss some of these issues in Chapter 9.

An important step in overcoming an abnormal or idealized value is to start to experience some anxiety and identify what it is that is driving you. It may then be helpful for you and a relative or friend to use cost–benefit analysis to assess: (a) the costs and benefits of carrying on and being driven by some of the passengers and the values of OCD; (b) the costs and benefits of ignoring the values of OCD, being in control of your own bus, and following your own values that you really believe in.

We describe how to do a cost–benefit analysis in the section at the end of this chapter on 'Techniques to Help You Overcome Obstacles'. Blank cost–benefit forms are given in Appendix 5.

The Responsibility Trap

Because of the powerful sense of excessive responsibility that underlies so many people's OCD, it's quite understandable that many try to solve the problem by shifting responsibility to others for the 'risks' you believe are being taken in overcoming OCD. The problem is that at best this is a 'sticking plaster' solution, and doesn't make you step back and reconsider the excessive sense of responsibility itself. At worst, shifting responsibility can neutralize any benefit from things like exposure exercises, and simply becomes an exercise in OCD itself.

This might seem to fly in the face of the notion that accompanied exposure can be helpful. But accompanied exposure is a bit like push-starting a car – fine to get things going if it's really needed, but not a good way to keep on the road.

Common examples of transferring responsibility are:

- asking another person if what you're about to do or have done is 'safe' or 'OK' (you may use a number of plausible arguments to persuade the other person to answer, e.g. 'I don't know how to do things properly because I have OCD,' 'I need you to answer otherwise I'll worry and have to carry out a ritual');
- 'discussing' a particular decision or action with someone without directly asking for reassurance – in the knowledge that if what you were talking about was truly dangerous that person would say something;
- only carrying out certain behaviors in the company of another person;
- entering into a lengthy discussion about the precise nature of an activity with someone, so that you can be 'certain' of what it is you are going to do, thereby shifting responsibility for that activity.

Reassurance-seeking and responsibility shifts are unhelpful *no matter who is involved*. In this sense, reassurance is no more helpful from a family doctor, psychiatrist, therapist, nurse, or volunteer than it would be from friend, family member, or someone on the street. What matters is the function of reassurance and the way it makes you feel more certain and comfortable about what you are worried about in the short term. However, the doubts then return – sometimes after only a few minutes, sometimes after a few hours. You can't be reassured out of OCD, no matter how hard you might try and irrespective of the efforts of those who care about you. Yet again, one of your solutions is now the problem, reinforcing your worries and making you more likely to want to seek reassurance or transfer responsibility again.

The Guarantee Trap

The guarantee trap stems from attitudes like:

- I have to be certain that no harm will result from my dropping rituals and carrying out exposure tasks.
- I need more guarantees from other people because I've got OCD and my judgment can't be trusted.

It drives the need for reassurance and endless checking. As we have said before, demanding guarantees as a way of overcoming OCD guarantees you just one thing – OCD. If your OCD were an insurance policy against that which you are afraid of happening, would you buy it? Is it worth the cost to you, your life, and the lives of the people close to you? The goal is to accept that there are no certainties or guarantees in life (except death and taxes) – and the fact that your OCD will continue to demand a guarantee that no harm will occur.

If you are struggling to come to grips with tolerating doubt, do a cost–benefit analysis (see the section at the end of this chapter, and Appendix 5) comparing the costs and benefits of (a) carrying on as you are with your demand for guarantees, and (b) facing your fears, resisting your checking and reassurance-seeking, and tolerating your doubt and uncertainty.

Anger

Anger at yourself or others is not unusual when you are suffering from OCD. People often become angry and frustrated with themselves for their thoughts and rituals. Individuals with OCD can also become angry with friends, family, or partners if they don't 'help' by giving reassurance or complying with requests to change their behavior to accommodate rituals or avoidance behaviors. An individual with OCD might think something like:

*Because I find things (e.g. dirt, disorder) so upsetting, other
people should make sure I don't have to confront them. If they
don't go out of their way to do so, it means they are uncaring and
don't understand.*

But why should other people fall in with the demands and com-
mands of your OCD? If they give way to your OCD it won't be
satisfied, it'll just want more.

The big problem with getting angry with other people for not
going along with your avoidance or rituals, apart from the harm
it does you and your relationships, is that it leads you to look
for change in entirely the wrong place.

Instead of being angry with yourself or with people who are
going about their business exercising their right not to be controlled by your OCD, focus on standing up to the bully that is
your OCD. See the anti-OCD bill of rights in the last section
of this chapter.

Guilt

People who develop OCD frequently have a very strong sense
of responsibility and morality, and high personal standards.
Although they can often seem selfishly preoccupied with their
rituals and obsessions, they are very often all too aware of the
impact their OCD is having on others and feel guilty about
this. Guilt can have some very important effects on OCD and
people's attempts to overcome it. It can often lower a person's
mood and contribute to symptoms of depression. Also, when
people feel unhealthily guilty they frequently expect to be pun-
ished, which can serve to fuel fears of harm coming to them or
those for whom they feel responsible.

Feeling guilty about resisting compulsions and taking risks
People with OCD frequently feel guilty when they try to reduce
their harm-prevention behaviors – despite the fact that they
and the people close to them stand to have a substantially
better quality of life as a result. For example, one man felt guilty

for not checking himself so carefully for toxic chemicals when leaving work, even though he was still at least as careful as any of his colleagues.

To help tackle guilty feelings and accept yourself, question the demand you place on yourself to put others' well-being so far ahead of your own. Consider whether you would choose such an extremely cautious belief system if you were starting from scratch; is it instead a symptom of your OCD which you would do well to ignore? Read the 'Anti-OCD Bill of Rights' at the end of this chapter to help you think about asserting your own rights against your OCD.

The 'Martyr' Trap

The martyr trap occurs when the person with OCD believes that it's better to sacrifice the quality of their own life than to expose a person (or persons) for whom they feel responsible for from a possible threat. For example, it's not unusual for people with fears of contamination to avoid hugging their children in order to 'protect' them from the harm of germs or some other contaminant.

Consider the long-term consequences of this on the children and on your relationship with them. Is the 'protection' you're offering worth it? Do the people who care about you and whom you trust agree this is a good idea? Does the person or people you're 'protecting' want you to carry on? Do you think they would if you asked them? Will they be grateful in years to come to learn that you have overprotected them?

The 'On-the-Safe-Side' Trap

Take a long look at what it is that's causing you the biggest problems in your life. Chances are your OCD is at the top of your list. However, one of the self-defeating attitudes that can keep your OCD alive is the idea that it's better to 'be on the safe side', or 'err on the side of caution'. This may be one of the styles of thinking that made you vulnerable to OCD in the first place, or it might be symptomatic of the condition. Either way, this style of thinking is doing you little good if you apply it to your exposure and response prevention plan, as it will probably guide you towards falling short of enough risk-taking and doubt tolerance to overcome the problem.

If you want to err on the side of caution, err *against* your OCD. Steer towards *more* tolerance of uncertainty and risk if you know you have a tendency to be overcautious.

Perfectionism

Waiting until you have completely assessed your own OCD, and have a perfect understanding of the treatment principles, can lead to long delays in getting started.

Perfectionism can also result in thoughts like this:

Since there's a chance that I might carry out the principles of overcoming OCD wrongly I must think about them and talk them over with someone qualified until I'm absolutely certain I won't make a mistake.

The problem is that attempting to overcome OCD perfectly is an exercise in OCD in its own right and is therefore doomed to failure. Instead, aim for a 'good enough' understanding and do what you think is *probably* the best thing. Act 'as if' perfectionism were not your most important value – aim for a high standard but be guided by flexibility and pragmatism.

'I've Tried it All Before'

Many individuals with OCD reading this book will have made a previous attempt to overcome their OCD without managing to overcome it fully. Roz Shafran, a noted researcher on OCD, once gave an excellent talk on this subject, entitled 'It ain't what you do; it's the way that you do it'. Her point was a crucial one: when CBT fails it's much more likely to be the way it was applied that was the problem, rather than the individual being 'untreatable'.

We frequently meet people who have tried exposure and response prevention before, and when we try to discover why they didn't make the progress they hoped for, discussion reveals that their exposure sessions were too short, or not frequent enough, or that they did not truly stop carrying out rituals, or that they changed over to mental rituals.

There is no good reason to assume that not because you haven't managed to overcome your OCD in the past you could not try again and succeed. Look at it another way: you now have useful experience to bring to the process, and in fact this may give you an advantage over someone who has never tried before – as long as you approach overcoming your OCD with an open mind and real commitment to tolerate your thoughts and feelings and not attempt to respond to them.

Techniques to Help You Overcome Obstacles

Cost–Benefit Analysis

Being free of OCD may change people's expectations that you get on with other aspects of your life. You may see this as a cost as it's a further pressure. Doing a cost–benefit analysis is also a way of deciding whether change is 'worth it', even taking into account the 'costs'. Deciding this in your mind will make it much easier to commit yourself fully to overcoming your OCD.

Doing a cost–benefit analysis means going over the pros and cons, the advantages and disadvantages, of two options. Apart from the most basic pair of options – staying with your OCD, or overcoming it – you could apply the technique to:

- trying out a particular technique like exposure and response prevention;
- deciding whether to continue a particular behavior, such as checking or reassurance-seeking;
- whether to confide in someone;

- considering two possible ways of looking at an intrusive thought.

Use two cost–benefit analysis sheets (see Appendix 5), one for each option, and list the costs and benefits, in the short term and the long term, for both yourself and other people. Once you have completed the cost–benefit analysis for both options, review them critically. Now check how realistic your perceived cost of change is, and whether the benefits of staying the same are genuine. Are you focusing on the long term or the short term? If you are deciding to change, write down the most important costs of staying the same and benefits of change, and put them somewhere you can refer to at moments when your motivation is flagging.

Remember, change is still only an experiment; you can always go back to your old way of thinking and acting if ultimately it's been proven to be more helpful than the new way.

Figure 5.2 shows an example of cost–benefit analysis using the responses of Vic.

The TIC–TOC Technique

The TIC–TOC technique is a useful tool to help tackle thought and attitude obstacles to overcoming OCD. The principle is simple; in the left-hand column write down the thoughts and attitudes that are getting in the way of you applying the self-help treatment principles in a consistent and systematic manner. These are your 'task interfering cognitions' (TICs). You can use the examples in the common 'traps' included above in the series of obstacles, but you may well also have thoughts that we have not listed. In the right-hand column respond to each of the 'TICs' with an alternative attitude that will help you tackle your OCD. These are your 'task orienting cognitions' (TOCs). You might want to conduct a behavioral experiment (see p. 202) to see whether your new attitude is more effective. An example of this technique is set out in Table 5.3.

Short-term cost	Short-term benefit
To myself	*To myself*
It can be very frustrating getting people to give a 'sure' answer Sometimes I feel more confused	I feel much better when someone gives me a clear and definite answer If I feel properly reassured I don't need to wash my hands
When I feel calmer I often feel embarrassed about asking so many questions	If I feel properly reassured I spend less time worrying
Reassurance only lasts a few minutes It reduces the effect of my exposures	I might be less likely to make myself or other people ill
To others	*To others*
I can tell people sometimes feel quite stressed by me asking so many questions	They know what it is that I'm worrying about
It's putting a strain on my relationships	They don't then get upset about me washing my hands because I don't need to wash if I've been fully reassured
Long-term cost	**Long-term benefit**
To myself	*To myself*
Despite all the reassurance I've had, my confidence in my own judgment has got steadily less over the past couple of years	I might reduce the chances making myself or other people ill, so I wouldn't feel guilty
I very rarely actually feel 'fully' reassured, and afterwards worry or wash anyway	
It feeds my OCD	
To others	*To others*
Getting slowly more fed up with me seeking reassurance	Other people might have a slightly reduced chance of me giving them a germ if I know what is or isn't safe

Figure 5.2(a)   Vic's cost-benefit analysis form for seeking reassurance about 'whether something I have touched is safe'

Short-term cost	Short-term benefit
To myself	*To myself*
It will be uncomfortable.	It's a step towards overcoming my OCD I'll feel less embarrassed about seeking so much reassurance It will help me to focus on other things
To others	*To others*
I might wash and my family will be upset	They don't have to put up with me seeking reassurance Will find their time with me less stressful Will be pleased to see me making steps in overcoming my OCD
Long-term cost	**Long-term benefit**
To myself	*To myself*
May have to take more responsibility as other people expect me to manage without reassurance	A move towards overcoming my OCD It will probably get easier to resist seeking reassurance the more I practice resisting it My relationships will improve
To others	
Tiny chance they'll be at greater risk of me passing on a germ	

Figure 5.2(b)   Vic's cost-benefit analysis form for 'resisting the urge to seek reassurance and tolerating the doubt'

'Big I, Little I': An illustration of the Complex Nature of Being Human

In the 'big I, little I' illustration in Figure 5.3, the 'big I' represents a whole person, and the many 'little i's' represent the huge number of facets that make up a human being. As a human being, you are extremely complex with many different aspects – for example, your personality, your likes and dislikes, your

Table 5.3   **An example of the TIC–TOC technique in action**

Task interfering cognitions (TICs)	Task orienting cognitions (TOCs)
If I don't resist my thoughts as is being suggested, then I'm taking a chance with my life, and that's irresponsible	For a start, being less responsible than I have been might feel irresponsible now, but that's just because my sense of responsibility has been so excessive
	Also, coming to accept my intrusive thoughts is part of dealing with my OCD – and that's about taking responsibility for my life!
If I let go control of my mind I might end up totally out of control and do something dangerous	This is what's called black-and-white thinking. It's not a case of either being in control of my mind or not, my brain isn't a speeding car. If I try out controlling my thoughts less I'll probably discover my brain can largely keep itself together – it's not as if I feel all that in control now!
I've made progress with my OCD before, and it's just come back, so what's the point in keeping trying?	It's true it's been disappointing that my OCD has come back before, but if I keep on trying I might learn more about staying better; and it's not as if I've got a lot to lose by trying.

values, your achievements, your aspirations, and everything that has happened to you since you were born.

The diagram is a simple illustration of the complexity of a person: use it to remind yourself that 'identifying' or 'condemning' the whole of yourself using words like 'stupid', 'worthless', 'bad', 'weak', 'useless', and 'inferior' is a gross (and very unhelpful) overgeneralization. Even if one aspect of you is negative (and let's not forget that the 'average' individual with OCD tends to have rather high standards), the whole person can't be considered to be negative. To rate yourself purely on the basis of one negative trait is rather like one saying one banana in a bowl of apples makes the fruit bowl full of bananas.

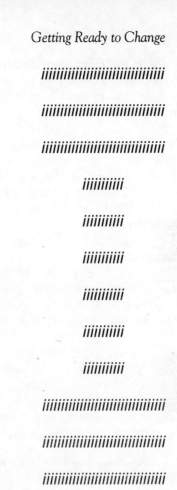

Figure 5.3 Big I, little i

At the most, OCD is only one little 'i' or one aspect of you, which, even if you rate it negatively, can't be the whole of you.

Standing Up to Your OCD: A Bill of Rights

Living with OCD can be like living with an oppressive dictator, whose sole interest is in keeping himself in power. Would you really choose the rules he/his state dictates you live by? Start your own revolution and claim your life back from OCD. The following are assertions of some human rights that your OCD may currently be violating:

1   I have the right to live my life free from rituals, avoidance, and unreasonable fear.
2   I have the right to place my happiness and fulfilment as a high priority in my life, without feeling guilty that I'm not doing as much as I could do, or used to do, to prevent harm from coming to others.
3   I have the right to enjoy physical contact with my loved ones without fear or guilt.
4   I have the right to walk down the street, in a park, or around the shops without worrying excessively about the harm I might do to myself or others.
5   I have the right to take everyday risks without undue anxiety.
6   I have the right to work, spend time with my family and friends, enjoy my hobbies, and take leisure time without OCD telling me what I can and can't do.
7   I have the right to allow intrusive thoughts, doubts, images, and urges to pass through my mind and assume they are safe without having to spend time and effort making sure.

Are there any other rights that your OCD isn't respecting, and you want to assert? Write out your own list if you wish, maybe including some of the above in a modified form.

6

Taking It Step by Step

You should by now have a more helpful interpretation of your intrusive thoughts, images, doubts, or urges, and a plan to try to 'test' how acting on that interpretation works out. For the most part, this will involve turning your OCD on its head: where you have been avoiding, you will be facing up to things; where you use rituals you will be resisting the urge to carry them out. This chapter is about working steadily to overcome your OCD and identifying and dealing with stuck points.

Putting It All Together – The Steps to Take to Overcome OCD

1 Define your problems and set your goals.
2 Understand what your obsession is about. For example, an intrusive thought of harming someone; an intrusive image of loved ones hurt; an impulse to stab someone; a doubt that doors are securely locked; an idea about catching an illness.
3 Understand the meanings and attitudes you've attached to these that are causing your distress and behavioral responses (Theory A). For example, 'If I think this, then it's likely to happen'; 'Having this image means I'm dangerous'; 'Taking any chances with illness is irresponsible'.

---

4 Identify the way you respond to avoid experiencing your intrusive thoughts or urges and feelings. For example, rituals, avoidance, neutralizing, reassurance-seeking.

5 Understand how these 'solutions' (i.e. attempts to avoid your intrusive thoughts and urges) are, to a large degree, the problem. For example, use a 'vicious flower' diagram to write this out; see how using more or fewer of these strategies affects the frequency, intensity, and duration of your obsessions.

6 Develop an alternative explanation (or meaning) for your obsessions (Theory B). For example, 'I have *thoughts* of being a pedophile'; 'Having so many intrusive images shows how much I don't want harm to come to my loved ones'; '100 per cent certainty is impossible – I'm trying too hard to be sure'; 'I can only expect myself to take a reasonable number of sensible precautions, and that's still being responsible'.

7 Act 'as if' you believe Theory B, to gather evidence on which explanation fits the facts best.

8 Keep 'turning your OCD on its head'. This means facing up to the things you've been avoiding, and resisting rituals, neutralizing, and reassurance-seeking (refer back to the principles of exposure and response prevention in Chapter 3 for guidance).

9 Deal with obstacles to progress (use Chapter 5 to help you here).

10 Develop a relapse prevention plan. We will deal with this in Chapter 7.

Things You Can Do to Help Yourself

Be Patient

For the majority of people overcoming OCD, recovery does not happen overnight, but requires patience and persistence.

Furthermore, recovery is never a smooth process – there are nearly always setbacks. You can learn from setbacks and use them to modify your approach so that it works better for you. What matters is the overall progress towards your goals in the long term. Be tolerant of the natural ups and downs of recovery: becoming anxious that you're not getting better quickly enough, or getting angry with yourself, will only fuel your OCD.

Keep Records of Your Progress

To help keep motivated it's really helpful to have a record of what you've done so far and how you are changing. When you get better from a cold you probably don't really notice how much better you feel, but rather take this for granted, and maybe focus on the fact that you still have a bit of a sniffle. It is a tendency of human nature to concentrate on what's not going well rather than what is; so get used to keeping records, using the forms we have referred to in the previous chapters and provided in Appendices 4 and 5. These will give you a helpful reminder of the work you have put in and the changes that have resulted. Repeating the measures of OCD, using the assessment forms, at regular intervals (we suggest between once every two weeks and once a month, depending on how quickly your OCD is responding) will help to give you a feel for how things are changing.

Reward Yourself

Overcoming OCD is like investing in a company that's very slow to return a profit. You have to take a substantial leap of faith that your investment (in this case, of time, energy, and tolerance of discomfort) will ultimately pay dividends. Luckily, overcoming OCD is a sound investment; but while you're waiting to see the results of your efforts it's important that you give yourself a reward for your hard work. This might be as simple as a hot bath with a good book, or agreeing with yourself that you can have a treat if you achieve a certain target. If you have been working through this book you'll probably be spending much of the time you are overcoming your OCD struggling alone. It will all be worth it in the end; but meanwhile it's really important you give yourself credit for your hard work.

Consider Finding an Ally in Overcoming Your OCD

Overcoming OCD can be a tough process, and support can be very helpful. In CBT such a supporter is often called a 'co-therapist'. This person might be a friend, partner, or relative. Such allies can be of enormous value and can help you in numerous ways, for example:

- Having regular meetings with you to review your progress. You might talk over how exposure and behavioral experiments are going, look at frequency records, and discuss ratings of progress.
- Sharing with you their own examples of intrusive thoughts, images, doubts, and impulses to help remind you how normal these are.
- Explaining appropriate behaviors (e.g. how they wash their hands or shut a door).
- Demonstrating exposure (e.g. touching a toilet seat without washing their hands, wishing something bad would happen to their own loved ones).
- Helping to come up with imaginative ideas for exposure and response prevention tasks.
- Helping to troubleshoot stuck points.
- Giving general support and encouragement – this is probably the most important part!

It makes sense for both the individual who's working to overcome their OCD and their ally to work through this book together, and review it together as things progress. Clearly, the person you choose will need to be prepared to act as your co-therapist – to read through this book, and to set aside sufficient time regularly to sit down with you (perhaps about half an hour a couple of times a week at the start). You should emphasize that they are there to act as a supporter in *your* plan to overcome *your* OCD. Hopefully, they will have creative suggestions and ideas; but it's critical that you negotiate a plan and both agree to it, before you begin to implement it. It is also worth deciding beforehand what you would prefer your ally to do or say should you become overanxious, stressed, or angry. Above all, you need to choose someone with whom you share mutual respect, someone whom you trust and who you feel understands, to some extent at least, your experience of OCD. What you don't want is someone who will provide endless reassurance and answers to your questions about whether something is safe or not; someone who gives in and takes responsibility for some of your rituals to 'keep the peace'; someone who will help you avoid objects or areas which you think are contaminated; or someone who is antagonistic to you and is aggressive, sarcastic, or critical of your OCD. We cover this idea of a helper or 'co-therapist' more in Chapter 9.

Stuck Points: Common Problems in Applying the Principles of Overcoming OCD

Obstacles to overcoming OCD can occur in three phases of treatment: getting started, keeping going, and staying well. Encountering obstacles to progress is entirely normal, and many of them can be overcome by returning to basic principles (see Chapter 3).

There are several 'internal' reasons for these obstacles, and we looked at some of these in detail in Chapter 5. They include depression, shame, demoralization, guilt, anger, discomfort intolerance, demands for certainty, looking for change in the wrong place, and insufficient application of treatment principles. There can also be a number of 'external' obstacles. These may include critical partners or family members, absence of appropriate support, or partners or family members unwittingly 'cooperating' with OCD.

One of the most common complaints from people attempting to overcome OCD is: 'My anxiety isn't coming down during my exposure and response prevention sessions.' The principles of exposure and response prevention can appear quite simple, and indeed they are – but *simple* does not necessarily mean *easy to follow*. In the remainder of this chapter we set out a few common problems that arise in overcoming OCD, with some suggestions of how to tackle them.

Little or No Exposure

Check that you've understood why exposure is important in overcoming your OCD, and that you've got a clear hierarchy to guide you. Are there any thoughts getting in the way (see the various 'traps' discussed in Chapter 5 for some suggestions)? Use the 'TIC–TOC' form introduced in Chapter 5 to list any thoughts that are getting in the way of your recovery, and put alongside them responses that will help you to move forward in your efforts to overcome your OCD. If you're finding the exposure you've set too difficult, consider tackling another task lower down your 'hierarchy of triggers'. Even if this seems too easy, it will help you to get into the 'mode' of facing your fears and discovering that your anxiety lessens of its own accord.

Boost your motivation by going over the costs of staying the same and the benefits of overcoming your OCD.

Exposure Too Short

Check that your exposure and response prevention sessions are long enough for your anxiety to reduce by at least half. Especially in the early sessions, this can take anything between 20 minutes and 3 hours.

Rituals Used Alongside Exposure

Reread the section on response prevention in Chapter 3 and check that you understand the rationale. Be firm with yourself and resist any subtle reassurance or rituals; review your list of rituals to remind yourself what to look out for. Use the symptoms checklist in Appendix 4 to help you determine the rituals you need to resist. Broadly speaking, anything you do in your behavior, think in your mind, or say to yourself for reassurance that results in you thinking that you have reduced the potential for harm and reduced your anxiety is likely to be a safety behavior or ritual. If you do accidentally slip into using a ritual when you've done some exposure, whenever possible re-expose yourself so that you undermine the value and effect of the ritual.

If you can't manage response prevention, then try delaying or reducing your rituals to build up to it; but take care not to stay with this as an easier option, as if you do it will take longer for you to recover.

Replacing Overt ('Behavioral') Rituals with Covert ('Mental') Rituals or a Safety-Seeking Behavior

This is a common obstacle to overcoming OCD. Many people believe they have found a creative solution to the need to carry out time-consuming and embarrassing behavioral rituals by carrying out a ritual in their head instead. For example, one man stopped checking his front door, but would mentally review the process of locking his door instead. Unfortunately, the result was that he needed to spend more and more time carrying out his 'covert' ritual, which is ultimately harder to stop than the behavioral version. Reread the section on **p. 100** that describes how responding to your intrusive thoughts with reassurance can turn into a mental ritual.

If you have found that a covert ritual has replaced an overt one, start doing response prevention for this, and make sure you re-expose yourself to the intrusive thought if you do ritualize.

7

Keeping Obsessive Compulsive Disorder at Bay

Once you've made good headway in overcoming your OCD, it becomes important to start thinking about how you're going to *stay better* now that you've got better. There are several things to consider about staying better from OCD:

- Have you made a written summary of how you've been overcoming your OCD and the gains you've made, in a way that's easy for you to remember? It is often best to do this as you go along; if you wait 'until it's done' you will forget. You may need to recall what you did in the future; also, as well as being extremely useful, this exercise can help you feel justifiably proud of the changes you have made.
- Have you removed all the rituals (behavioral and mental) and avoidance behaviors that were driven by your OCD? If not, what can you do to continue to reduce them (e.g. response prevention for rituals, exposure for avoidance)?
- Have you managed to reduce your fears of thoughts, doubts, images, and urges? If not, what can you do to reduce these further (e.g. strengthening alternative meanings, doing more exposure and response prevention)?
- Are there any 'lesser' obsessions or compulsions that are not causing you significant difficulty at the moment, but that might 'step forward' now that you've reduced other fears? If so, what can you do to reduce them (e.g. design an exposure

and response prevention plan, build helpful attitudes and beliefs)?

- Have you managed to accept that doubts, urges, intrusive thoughts, and intrusive images are an entirely normal part of being human? If not, what can you do to build the strength of your conviction of this fact (e.g. surveying others, doing behavioral experiments, allowing for some doubt while still being 'sure enough')?
- Have you 'filled the gap' left by your OCD with interesting, pleasurable, absorbing, or satisfying (or simply un-OCD) activities (e.g. new hobbies, work, building relationships)?

The rest of this chapter offers some ideas on how you can best be on your guard against OCD.

Key Questions to Help You Prevent a Relapse

One of the most helpful things to do to prevent yourself returning to your former level of OCD is to be clear about what has helped you to get better. These questions are designed to help you reflect on this:

- What have been the most useful things you've learned that have helped you overcome your OCD?
- What have been the most helpful techniques you've applied in overcoming your OCD?

Make a written summary that you can return to if and when your OCD returns, so that you can immediately nip it in the bud.

Keeping Psychologically Healthy

Try to think of keeping mentally healthy as similar to keeping physically healthy. Even if someone has given us some medication to help treat a physical problem, most of us still believe that we need to eat healthily, take appropriate amounts of exercise, and get enough rest to keep in good shape. Unfortunately, people all too often seem to think that psychological health is something that can simply be taken for granted and, as anyone who has read this book will know by now, this is not so. The following are some ideas for keeping you in good psychological health, and therefore reducing the chances of OCD returning.

Filling the Gap Left by OCD

OCD loves a vacuum. Any 'space' left in your life will tend to be filled by OCD if you are prone to it. Everyone needs some space in their lives, and many people find it very therapeutic to sit quietly and allow thoughts simply to pass through their minds without engaging with them. However, OCD can be a very time-consuming and energy-consuming problem, and research has shown that the extent to which people who are recovering from OCD absorb themselves in other activities can have a significant effect on their chances of relapsing. Putting it simply, keeping active and interested will reduce the chances of developing OCD again.

Many people who have had OCD notice that aspects of their lives were restricted or 'put on hold' because of their fears and rituals. Think of all the different things you can do now that you are no longer so handicapped and constrained by your OCD. What interest or pursuit have you wanted to take up, only to find that fears or lack of time have prevented you? Here is a small range of possibilities (in no particular order) to give you some ideas:

Chess	Tennis	Football	Dressmaking	Sailing
Walking	Quizzes	Baking	Flower arranging	Fishing
Swimming	Gardening	Decorating	Pottery	Painting
Jogging	Wine tasting	Cycling	Motorsport	Singing
Languages	Mechanics	Raquetball	Basketball	Pets
Enamelling	Antiques	Astronomy	Jewellery making	Cooking
Martial arts	Reading	Writing	Voluntary work	Drama

Work and Career

Do you think that your OCD has interfered with you seeking work or studying? If you're working, do you think it has interfered with you making progress in your career, or perhaps changing careers? This is a common experience for people who have OCD. As you get better, start to set goals for how you would like to see your working life develop, and build a realistic and practical action plan for how you will move towards these goals.

Relationships

As we have seen earlier in the book, OCD can have a very detrimental effect on personal relationships. We also know that a supportive relationship from a 'significant other' (e.g. partner, parent) can reduce the chances of OCD returning. Furthermore, there is good evidence that a network of social support, and a person in your life you can confide in, helps to reduce the chances of you suffering from emotional problems in general. Improving your relationships and spending more time with other people doing things you find enjoyable or worthwhile will also help fill the gap left by OCD as you overcome it. Put simply, your relationships with other people are vitally important in keeping OCD at bay.

Improving Your Relationships

Consider how you would like things to be different in your relationships with other people. Who would you like to make things different with? For example:

- partner or spouse;
- children;
- relatives;
- friends;
- colleagues;
- neighbours.

Good relationships are sustained by time, thought, and effort, and many changes in your relationships will happen naturally, as you become less preoccupied with your fears and more able to focus outside yourself on the world around you.

People recovering from OCD often find they have additional problems, however, such as their OCD having restricted the amount of time they have spent socializing, their drive for reassurance having shaped their conversations for years, or fear of being responsible for harm leading to avoidance of close physical contact. These behaviors tend to impede normal relationships. Establishing healthy relationships and rebuilding those that have suffered from your OCD will be a crucial part of your recovery.

Communicate Effectively

It is often said that the lifeblood of any relationship is communication. Keep in mind that we communicate not only by what we say, but also by the way we say things, when and where we say them, and by a variety of non-verbal methods (e.g. eye contact, body language, spending time with someone, a hug). Here are some tips to improve communication:

- If you've something important to discuss with someone, find a mutually good time with enough time set aside for both of you to talk and listen.
- Use 'I feel' statements: for example, 'I feel disappointed that we couldn't meet up last week,' rather than blaming: for example, 'You made me so angry . . .'
- If you want to give feedback to someone on their behavior, keep it clear, brief, and specific. Remember it's OK to give positive feedback: for example, 'I'd really like to thank you for . . .', as well as saying how you'd like things to be different: for example, 'I'd really appreciate it if you could . . .'
- If you have given someone some feedback, check how they feel and what they think of what you have said.

- Try to avoid getting stuck in the trap of thinking there is a right or 'true' way of doing something. Value the differences in others, and seek a compromise if appropriate.
- Deal with critical remarks by finding some part of the criticism to agree with, and invite the person to tell you more. This will enable you to evaluate the criticism effectively and respond in a non-defensive, self-accepting way. For example, 'You're right, my OCD has made life more difficult for you. I've often worried about the effect it has had on you. What particularly would you like to be different?'

Spirituality

As we have seen, some people with OCD can find their religion becoming entangled with their disorder, and establishing a healthy relationship with their religion can be an important part of their recovery. For others, spiritual matters can provide an important element in an OCD-free life: for example, becoming more involved in practicing your religion, meditating, praying, or going to a place of worship.

Relapse Prevention and Dealing with Setbacks

There is a helpful distinction to be made between a relapse and a setback. A relapse means a 'back to the beginning' slide into your OCD, whereas a setback is a slip backward on the road to recovery. The good news is that neither is a hopeless situation; but by dealing effectively with setbacks you can dramatically reduce the chances of a relapse. *Setbacks are a normal part of recovery.*

The 'two steps forward, one step back' experience is common in many earnest attempts to achieve, and overcoming OCD is no different. Don't panic if you slip back, but do try to see if you can learn anything about why it happened. Here are a few examples of possible triggers, and the lessons you can draw from them:

- Encountering a previously avoided trigger; now it can become part of your exposure hierarchy.
- Allowing yourself 'small amounts of ritual', such as a 'quick check', which then escalates: this can serve as a reminder of how firmly you need to resist rituals.
- Discovering that you've been relying on certain conditions to do exposure and response prevention (e.g. after discussing it with someone) and then finding it difficult to manage without these conditions. Redesign your exposures to be more independent.
- Having become complacent about exposure and response prevention without having done sufficient work to remove the fear, allowing your fear to grow. Return to the program and put extra effort into doing it thoroughly.

So, although setbacks are disappointing, you can make the most of them if you use them as an opportunity to learn about the strengths and weaknesses of your recovery, and then plan how you can pick up the momentum again in a way which builds on your strengths as well as minimizing your weaknesses.

Try to make a plan on how to deal with setbacks by considering the following questions.

What Events or Situations Might Trigger a Setback?

How could you plan to tackle these events or situations to minimize their impact? What could you do to practice coping with them?

Act Sooner Rather than Later

To reduce the chances of a setback becoming more serious it is helpful to take action to tackle it as early as you can. What might be early warning signs that your OCD is beginning to creep back in?

Take a Long-Term View

One of the biggest mistakes we see people make is the decision to settle for 'manageable OCD'. In our view this is a bit like trying to aim to stay 'a bit pregnant' – sooner or later things are going to develop further! Such a decision leaves you vulnerable to relapse. So, in the same way that someone who has a bad back needs to strengthen his back and tummy muscles, people who are recovering from OCD need to strengthen their psychological capabilities, such as doubt tolerance, realistic responsibility, decatastrophizing, risk-taking, and flexible thinking. They must remain aware of their vulnerability.

A few people may ultimately need to accept a reduced, 'manageable' level of OCD in the long term, but this will only happen if they continue to work at minimizing it and keeping psychologically healthy.

Keep asking yourself: in order for you to maintain your gains, what are the main things you need to work at?

Keep Weeding Out Your OCD

Think of your life as a garden. Obsessions, rituals, and avoidance behaviors are weeds that have taken root, and probably grown over time. Hopefully, you've succeeded in pulling up those weeds (possibly with the help of a little weedkiller in the form of medication), and planted some desirable plants in the form of new or increased activities and interests, and more helpful attitudes. Now you need to think about maintaining the garden, which of course means continuing to 'pull up' avoidance behaviors, rituals, and the catastrophic misinterpretations that cause obsessions should they arise.

One of the best ways of reducing the chances of weeds growing back is to make sure you pull them up and get the roots out rather than just nipping off the tops; otherwise part of the weed is left in the ground and can grow back again, especially when the conditions are right. The parts of OCD that are left in your life might be very subtle and something you feel you can live with (e.g. 'mini' rituals, slight avoidance, resisting certain thoughts). To reduce the chances of them growing into something bigger, especially under the 'right' conditions, such as at times of stress, keep working to get rid of them. Alongside this, you will need to take care of your new activities and attitudes to make sure they flourish. Good luck and happy gardening!

8

Children and Adolescents with Obsessive Compulsive Disorder

In many ways, OCD in children and adolescents is the same as in adults. OCD in young people is common (affecting about 1 in every 100), but it is often not diagnosed or treated. If untreated, it not only causes great distress, but may also disrupt schooling and normal social and emotional development. When OCD is more severe, a child's peers may tease and make fun of the symptoms or even bully. Eventually, the child becomes isolated and wants to avoid school.

The Importance of Early Recognition

Therefore, the earlier a young person starts therapy and/or self-help the better, as otherwise the rituals and avoidance behaviour will have time to strengthen and the OCD may spread to other areas. Statistically, half of adults with OCD also had it as children. However, some children have only minimal symptoms as an adult. OCD may, however, change over time – for example, children may have more unusual symptoms, such as 'evening-up' and making things 'just right', as well as the more familiar symptoms such as washing and checking. A child who was a washer may become a checker as an adult. For some, OCD follows an episodic course in which symptoms disappear and return at times of stress. For others, it follows a chronic and unremitting course. We don't know what determines why some individuals have just a single episode as a child and others develop a chronic condition. What we do know is that *early recognition and treatment can improve outcome*, so it is important that everyone is alert to OCD developing in a young person.

Making the diagnosis of OCD in children is the same as in adults, with the exception that they cannot always be expected to show the same insight into their condition. Unlike adults, children may not recognize that their obsessions and compulsions are unreasonable or the result of an illness (although even very young children can explain that their rituals are 'silly' or unnecessary). Because OCD in children under the age of about 12 differs somewhat from that in adolescents, we discuss younger children separately.

OCD in Young Children

Among children with OCD, boys outnumber girls by about two to one. Boys are also more likely than girls to have a family member with OCD or Tourette's syndrome, or to show tic-like symptoms. The youngest child reported with OCD was diagnosed at 18 months; his mother also had OCD. Here, the toddler spent most of the day anxiously ordering and reordering his toys. However, it is not possible to be certain about a diagnosis of OCD until a child is older, as there are other conditions, such as autism, to consider. Six is about the earliest age at which it is possible to make a firm diagnosis.

The most common compulsions in childhood OCD consist of ordering and counting rituals. Younger children are less likely to describe the consequences of not doing a ritual other than feeling 'not right' or 'uncomfortable'. At this stage in their development, children are less bothered by what other people think of their compulsions, are less inhibited and are less likely to hide OCD.

We discussed in Chapter 2 the many possible causes of OCD, and how different factors can apply in different combinations from one individual to another. In childhood OCD, a biological or genetic predisposition is likely to be a prominent contributory factor.

Research is under way on a small group of children whose OCD or tics appear to have been triggered by infection with the *Streptococcus* bacterium, a common cause of a sore throat. It is thought that some children may produce antibodies to fight the streptococcal infection that react with nerve cells in the brain, and that this reaction in the brain may be the cause of the emotional and behavioral changes. This disorder has been called PANDAS, an acronym for Paediatric Auto-immune Neuropsychiatric Disorder Associated with *Streptococcus*. This may explain why some children experience a sudden onset of OCD which develops after a throat infection and recurs with subsequent infections. Children with this type of OCD should still be treated in the same way as other children with OCD, namely with CBT and, if needed, medication as well. You may read about treatments using antibiotics or dialysis; these are carried out only as part of research studies and remain experimental.

OCD in Adolescence

OCD during adolescence affects equal numbers of girls and boys. As with adults, adolescents may take up to 10 years or even more to seek help, by which time, of course, they will be adults themselves.

If you were unaware that your adolescent had OCD, then you might notice them:

- avoiding touching certain objects, parts of the body, or hair, and spending an excessive amount of time in the bathroom;
- excessively checking locks and seeking reassurance;
- getting up very early, or being late for school without an adequate explanation;
- expressing superstitions about preventing bad events from happening;
- compulsively touching, counting, ordering, or arranging objects;

- excessively checking mistakes from schoolwork, leading to procrastination in starting schoolwork, avoiding it altogether, or staying up very late to finish it;
- excessively praying in a way that is different from that recommended by your religion.

OCD in young people is often linked with other problems – for example, it often occurs with anorexia nervosa, where it is likely to include a need for order or exactness and symmetry. OCD may also occur with Tourette's syndrome, where it is more likely to consist of touching, counting, and blinking compulsions.

If you see significant changes such as those mentioned above in your teenager, it is important to encourage them to seek help. Perhaps there is nothing much to worry about – it may just be ordinary adolescent grumpiness or rebellion. But adolescence is also the time when serious mental health problems such as depression or schizophrenia can begin, so it is always a good idea to be alert to changes in behavior.

Overcoming OCD in a Young Person

Overcoming OCD using self-help and CBT in a young person is much the same as overcoming OCD in adults. There are, nevertheless, specialist self-help books written for children with OCD; we would recommend *Up and Down the Worry Hill* by Aureen Pinto Wagner and the companion book for parents, *What To Do When Your Child Has Obsessive-Compulsive Disorder: Strategies and Solutions*, also by Aureen Pinto Wagner (both published by Lighthouse Press).

Where the child with CBT is younger than 12, one or both parents will usually need to be involved in the therapy. Many teenagers will like to have a parent as an ally or 'helper', as long as the role has been negotiated sensitively. However, the child is at the centre of the therapy, and must be able to express preferences and take part in making decisions. Like adults, children have to become their own therapists. For teenagers, the therapist will want to negotiate how much information can be shared with parents, and the therapist will want to know how involved the parents are in OCD rituals and avoidance behaviors. When OCD is severe and affecting schoolwork, it is often helpful to inform the child's teacher. Other children's teachers do not need to be told.

Issues related to living with OCD in the family are discussed in Chapter 9. If possible, many parents find it helpful to meet other parents coping with a child with OCD. In specialist centres, young people with OCD often gain great benefit from meeting others with the same problem. It helps them know they are not alone, not 'crazy', and young people are great at sharing tips for recovery.

Young people respond to medication in exactly the same way as adults, and we discuss this in Appendix 1. However, the initial treatment for a young person is usually CBT. There are, however, few cognitive behavior therapists specializing in child and adolescent OCD. Providing CBT to a young person with OCD requires not only training in CBT, but also an ability to modify the therapy according to the child's development. For example, in young children, the belief that 'having a thought' is the same as 'doing an action' is quite normal – for example, everyone encourages young children 'to make a wish', and they believe that wishing something can influence events. Thus highlighting the difference between normal intrusive thoughts about causing harm and the meaning attached to such thoughts in OCD can be trickier than in adults. Family therapy may be offered, but this needs to be as an adjunct to any CBT for the person with OCD – the family disturbances are a consequence of OCD, and if the OCD is addressed, then it's a lot easier for everyone to develop healthier roles.

How One Family Helped a Child Overcome OCD

David was nine years old, and had been suffering from OCD for two years. His main fears were about death and dying, and he worried that household cleaning products like dishwashing tablets, bleach, oil, and toilet cleaner would poison him. David would avoid going to the toilet if it had toilet cleaner in it, or if it had a 'cleaning' smell about it. On occasion, David had wet his pants because of being unable to use the bathroom despite having been fully toilet-trained at two years of age. He would refuse to go out shopping or to visit friends in case he needed to use the bathroom and could not because of bleach or other cleaning products. He also worried that he would die by choking. He was fearful of sleeping at night in case he choked on the cotton in the bed sheets, and he worried about eating things that had not been prepared by his mother. When preparing food, David's mother had to follow special rules. To prevent food being poisoned, David required her to wash her hands before and after touching food and to make sure the lid was properly on the pot during cooking. To prevent choking, David would eat only soft foods, and he would become angry and upset if foods that he could not eat, for example, meats or crunchy vegetables, were served to him.

In addition to his fears of death and dying, David felt compelled to order and arrange things until they were 'just right'. These rituals were most evident when doing his schoolwork, and David would spend up to two hours arranging his pencils and books on the table around him. Sometimes David would not get any homework done at all because all the time to be spent on homework was used up in the preparation. David would become very upset if anyone disturbed him while he was doing this, and he would then check that everything he had already arranged was still in place before continuing to order whatever items were remaining. When asked by his parents why he needed to do this, David could not explain it, except to say that he just had to and it just felt right.

David's OCD symptoms were having a significant impact upon the rest of his family. His parents were exasperated and exhausted by his continually seeking reassurance that he was safe, and that he would not choke or be poisoned. David could not go to sleep at night without having one of his parents sit with him and reassure him that he would not choke or die during his sleep. It would take him a long time to fall asleep, and he would frequently do so only after crying and begging his mother or father not to leave his bedside. In order to try to alleviate David's distress, his parents had stopped using many household cleaning products, and instead his mother was cleaning with warm water only.

David had fallen behind at school. As a result of his ordering and arranging, he would often not complete the required work within class, and he was required to make up incomplete class work at home. However, because David was often unable to complete his homework, he rarely got to finish any set work.

David had an elder brother, Rob (aged thirteen) who was also very frustrated with David's behavior. Rob felt that his parents were giving David special privileges and attention. Rob felt as though he had to do all the chores around the house because of David's concern about cleaning products, and he thought it was very unfair that David did not have to go to sleep before he did. When he became particularly frustrated or angry, Rob would yell at David and sometimes hit him.

Understanding David's Problem

David's parents were very worried about David and his future, and wanted to do everything they could to help him overcome OCD. The first step involved the family and David learning more about OCD. The family learned that OCD in children is similar in many ways to OCD in adults. They learned that it was anxiety and fear that drove David's rituals and his reassurance-seeking. Figure 8.1 gives a very simple CBT model (a vicious circle) for understanding David's fears of being poisoned. It describes a typical situation in which David wanted to go to the toilet but was too fearful of doing so because of the smell of bleach or toilet cleaner. As soon as he smelled this, he would worry that he would somehow swallow the bleach, poisoning himself and ultimately dying. David would get a picture in his mind of himself lying dead on the ground outside his house and an evil-looking snake laughing at him. The picture was vivid and very upsetting. David would immediately seek

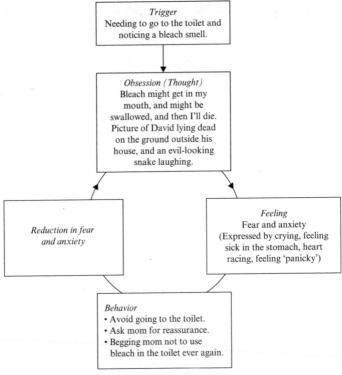

Figure 8.1   David's vicious circle of OCD

reassurance from his parents that he was OK, that he was not going to die, and he would avoid going near the toilet or bathroom. The reassurance alleviated his anxiety, but only temporarily, and, in fact, his avoidance and reassurance-seeking simply served to maintain the OCD.

Looking at the model in this way helped David and his parents to see the link between his thoughts and feelings and his behavior, and it helped them to see why the OCD persisted. It also helped David to understand a little about CBT and how CBT works to change both the thoughts and the behaviors associated with OCD.

Fighting Back Against the OCD

The next step for David and his parents was to begin to fight back against the OCD. In order to do this, David found it helpful to give OCD a name. He called it 'the snake', because of the vivid image that he had of an evil-looking snake. Giving OCD a name helped everyone in the family to separate David from the OCD. It helped them to develop a common language for talking about OCD (e.g. 'the snake is giving me a thought again that I am going to die') and it particularly helped David's brother to be critical of the 'snake' rather than being critical of David. Some children find it helpful and empowering to draw a picture of themselves fighting against the OCD (e.g. a picture of David fighting against an evil-looking snake).

David then learned the golden rules for fighting OCD:

- *Do what OCD doesn't want you to do*. This involved facing up to a feared object or situation, for example, deliberately going to the bathroom with toilet cleaner in the toilet.
- *Don't do what OCD wants you to do*. This involved fighting against the urge to use a compulsion, ritual, or safety behavior to alleviate the anxiety: for example, *not* arranging pencils or books when sitting down to complete class work or homework.

These exposure and response prevention rules *sound* simple, but actually they are very frightening and difficult for children to do. Children should never be pushed to do an exposure task that they do not feel ready for. Rather, fighting OCD needs to be done at the child's pace, and children need to feel confident that they have the support and encouragement of their family – like cheerleaders egging them on.

In order to make the task of fighting back against OCD a little easier, David and his parents developed a hierarchy of tasks. Each task involved exposure to a feared situation or object and prevention of the ritual, compulsion, or safety behavior usually associated with it. An example of David's hierarchy is presented in Table 8.1. The anxiety ratings correspond to how distressed or anxious David felt about facing up to the fear and *not doing* the associated compulsion.

In order to help him tackle these exposure steps, David learned about how anxiety works (for examples of 'anxiety curves', see Figures 3.1 and 3.2). He learned that although exposure would make him feel anxious, if he stuck with it and did not give in to the OCD by performing a ritual or avoiding, the anxiety would *go away anyway* (see Figure 3.1). He learned that each time he practiced fighting against the OCD, it would become a little bit easier (see Figure 3.2).

David agreed to try this out by doing the first step. He stood right beside his mother while she placed a dishwashing tablet into the dishwasher and he did not leave or turn away. He practiced this every day, morning and night, for four days. He was surprised but pleased to see that his feelings of anxiety decreased. David's parents were proud of him for trying so hard, and rewarded him with a small bar of chocolate. David felt con-

Table 8.1   **David's hierarchy to face his fear of being poisoned**

Exposure and response prevention steps	*Anxiety rating (1–100)*
1. Stand right next to Mom or Dad while they are putting a dishwashing tablet into the dishwasher (don't avoid)	20
2. Open the dishwashing tablet packet and hand the tablet to Mom or Dad (don't avoid)	40
3. Put the dishwashing tablet into the dishwasher, making sure to touch it with my hands	50
4. Touch the toilet cleaner bottle with my hands	60
5. Hold the toilet cleaner bottle and pour it in the toilet, and then go to the bathroom and not ask for reassurance	70
6. Pour bleach in the sink and then watch Mom clean and not ask for reassurance	75
7. Pour bleach into the sink myself and wipe the bench with a cloth dipped in the bleach and water and not ask for reassurance	100

fident enough to go up to the next step and, with hard work and practice every day, he progressed up the hierarchy.

David also learned to recognize that OCD thoughts were just thoughts. They could not hurt him or hurt anyone else. In fact, they were no different from a thought that he might have about riding his bicycle. To help him remember this, David wrote down a list of *fighting back* thoughts that he could use when he was not panicking.

- I see the snake, I know it's OCD.
- You're trying to upset me and trick me.
- I am not going to try to push you away.
- I am going to do something fun and not let you bother me.

At times, David found it really hard to fight against OCD, and he would still ask his parents for reassurance. In order to help David stop doing this, he and his parents together decided that it would be most helpful for them to stop giving reassurance, and instead to prompt David to fight against the OCD. They did this by saying:

- It's a snake thought again, David.
- It's trying to upset you.
- Use your fighting back thoughts instead.

The Key Role Played by David's Parents

David's parents played a crucial role in helping David overcome his OCD. They were David's co-therapists and his cheerleaders. They helped him to practice his exposure tasks by reminding him to do them each day. They reinforced his efforts by giving him lots of praise, and occasionally gave him small treats and rewards.

The key elements of the parents' role can be summarized as follows:

- Join together against OCD:
  – use a shared language;

– blame OCD, not the child;
– join with the child on the 'team' to fight against OCD.
- Don't punish.
- **Recognize OCD is an illness, not naughty behavior.**
- Pay attention to non-OCD behaviors.
- Praise children often and much for resisting OCD.
- Remember that a child can't 'just do it'. Fighting OCD must go at their own pace.
- Recognize how the family accommodates OCD, and work towards gradual withdrawal of the family's accommodation, with the child's consent.
- Agree on how to respond when child asks for help (this may involve a set answer, ignoring the child, or distracting them).

Keeping David's OCD at Bay

David worked very hard to overcome his OCD. It was not easy, and it took him about four months of really hard work, but he did it. To show OCD who was boss once and for all, David chose two *overlearning* tasks. These are tasks that children would not normally do in everyday life, but they are important to do as the final step in overcoming OCD. First, David decided to clean the whole house for his mother, using bleach on the bench tops and sinks, using toilet cleaner in the toilets, washing some dishes in the sink, and putting the rest into the dishwasher with a dishwashing tablet. Second, he decided to do his homework on the front room floor, and he threw the contents of his schoolbag all over the floor before beginning. Then he did his homework. Whenever he needed a particular pencil or pen, David would search for it around the floor, and when he had finished with it he would throw it back down in a different spot. David's parents were so pleased and proud of him that they cooked for him a special supper and then watched his new DVD with him as a special treat.

David and his parents recognized that although he was now free from OCD, it would be important to plan for any setbacks.

David decided that if he did experience any intrusive thoughts, he would boss back OCD right away using his fighting back thoughts. Whenever OCD tried to make him do something, David would remember his golden rules for fighting, and he would try not to do what OCD wanted him to do, or to do exactly what OCD did not want him to do (i.e. face the fear and fight the ritual). Sometimes, if this seemed really hard, David would break it down into smaller steps using a hierarchy, and work through the steps as quickly as he could. David's parents noticed that he had begun to go out to friend's houses again. He was excited about an upcoming school trip abroad, and he and Rob were getting along much better.

9

What Can Family and Friends Do to Help?

This chapter is addressed to anyone who has a relative, close friend, or partner with OCD. (We use the term 'relative' in this chapter as shorthand for all the possibilities.) Having OCD can play havoc with relationships and place an enormous burden on those who live with or love a person with OCD. This strain can lead to frequent conflicts and, occasionally, there can be violence on both sides. If you have OCD and are also reading this chapter, then the last thing we want to do is to cause you to feel yet more guilt, shame, or fear; but this is yet another example of how OCD can pretend to be keeping you or people you care about safe from harm, when the reality is far from it. Relationship stress and conflict are a consequence of this debilitating illness, and not the result of something defective in the person with the illness.

In this chapter we give examples of the sorts of conflicts that commonly occur and their consequences. We also raise some difficult ethical issues for which there are no easy answers. The chapter is rounded off with some general guidelines and solutions to the problems you may encounter.

Common Reactions of Caregivers to Someone with OCD

OCD can be a hidden disorder and even the closest members of the family may not be aware of the distress and handicap experienced by their relative. When you learn about the OCD, you may be shocked that your relative has chosen to keep it secret for so many years. Unfortunately, shame and fear are common reactions in someone with OCD and, as we have noted earlier in this book, on average a person with OCD struggles on for about ten years before seeking help.

Once the cat is out of the bag, and you know about the OCD, then there is a continuum of ways in which a family can respond. At one extreme, you may be excessively involved in the rituals or avoidance behavior. You may totally give in to ('accommodate') the OCD by taking responsibility for some of the rituals and going along with the demands in order to 'keep the peace'. It is tempting to take this option, because it reduces distress and prevents conflict. At the other end of the continuum, you may totally oppose your relative and be antagonistic. You might be extremely frustrated with the senselessness of OCD and may be critical, sarcastic, or aggressive to your relative. In this case, you are more likely to be someone who tends to be rather rigid, intolerant, and demanding, and you may sometimes shout or scream at your relative to stop a ritual. There is no evidence that either of these ways of responding causes OCD, but both can make OCD and life worse for everyone in the long term or set up a further vicious circle.

Family Roles in OCD

Very often, members of a family disagree on how best to respond, or take on different roles – for example, one person may become the main caregiver and be willing to accommodate the OCD, another may become frustrated and angry, and another try to use bribery to stop the rituals. Yet another may become emotionally detached and spend all their time trying to achieve great things outside the family to compensate for the misery within it. Nearly all these different responses are made in the effort to help someone they love, and it is very difficult for anyone to know how best to respond. However, when family members respond in different ways, discord is likely to result, with 'good' or 'bad' factions forming according to whether or not members are willing to accommodate the OCD. Your relative may respond by being aggressive to family members if they do not submit to the OCD, and the conflicts can build up in a vicious circle over many years. Over time, the main caregiver may become overprotective and feel like a martyr, building up resentment because their life is devoted to OCD.

Family therapy focusing on these roles is often helpful as an extra treatment. It is rarely of any benefit by itself unless the person with OCD is also getting help individually with a recognized treatment for that disorder, such as CBT or medication. We have observed that many who specialize in treating children and adolescents with OCD tend to focus excessively on the family roles, without providing adequate CBT. Providing adequate CBT often leads to a change in family roles without a need for additional therapy. However, each family is unique, and sometimes *extra* help for the family is very important.

Accommodating OCD

Because of the desperation they feel, individuals with OCD can be highly demanding or persuasive. As a family member you may find that you end up agreeing to participate in a ritual or avoidance behavior even if you would prefer not to. Thus, you are requested yet again for reassurance about whether the person with OCD had touched something contaminating, or whether they checked the front-door lock. You may be banned from using certain items, or parts of the home may be placed out of bounds to prevent an excessive time cleaning.

If you comply with the request it will stop the demand for a brief period and you relieve the person with OCD of anxiety. It seems such a small thing to do, and it gives you a break. It does, however, reinforce the likelihood that your relative will repeat the question as soon as they get anxious again – it worked once to reduce anxiety; it will work again: and so the vicious circle continues.

One of the most difficult decisions for you (and to a certain extent for professionals) is the degree to which you will accommodate rituals and avoidance behavior. Of course, the goal is not to do it at all, and this is often easier with new behaviors. However, in the short term you may agree to compromise as a step to recovery, and we discuss how to do this below.

Society's Response to OCD

We certainly know of many people with OCD who believe that everyone must adapt to meet their 'needs'. For example, Randy became very anxious because he had to register with a new family doctor after moving out of the area covered by his previous family doctor. He was obsessed with the new family doctor becoming dirty because his medical notes were contaminated. Randy demanded that the authorities scan his notes into an electronic format, transfer them by e-mail and destroy the paper originals. It was Randy's belief that all patients should have the right to keep their family doctor no matter where they move to, and to choose whichever family doctor they like regardless of location. Because of his obsession about contamination, Randy avoids urinating into anything associated with excrement, such as a toilet. He believes that all public toilets should have urinals as a matter of law, and that it should be unnecessary to touch any doors to get in or out of the urinal area. Another example is a woman who campaigned against dogs being allowed into public areas such as parks, because of her fears of becoming contaminated. Jack, who was afraid of knocking down a cyclist, began regularly shouting at cyclists on the road who he did not feel were sufficiently brightly dressed or illuminated. To what extent, then, should the family and society as a whole adapt to OCD?

Can OCD be regarded in the same way as a disease resulting in physical disability, like cerebral palsy, for which there is no treatment and which consigns those with the condition to a wheelchair? In such circumstances, you would obtain help to adapt the entrance to your home to include a ramp, and various modifications to be made within the home to allow you to live independently. It is rightly argued that wheelchair users are more disabled by the lack of wheelchair access in society than by their bodies. At a political level, disability rights campaigners are increasingly successful in changing society so that we are more accommodating and inclusive. Such moves are slow because change is expensive, but disability rights are correctly on the agenda. If the individuals with OCD who demand that their problems be accommodated are right, where should society begin? It would mean the whole community, from the family doctor to the plumber, having to do things differently or when the individual with OCD felt ready. Randy believes he needs modifications in order to live comfortably; but that does not mean that mental health professionals and society have to provide them. First, the defined needs may be prohibitively expensive; second, family members and health professionals also have 'rights', and can choose whether to participate in rituals and avoidance.

We are not denying that OCD can be extremely disabling and that individuals with mental health problems are extremely stigmatized. The critical difference with OCD is that, almost always, OCD will get worse the more it is accommodated (for a vivid example of this, think back to the final state of Howard Hughes, described in Chapter 1). Accommodating OCD is likely to lead to more, rather than less impairment. If we followed the imperative of accommodating emotional and behavioral problems, how far would we go? Should we remove spiders, snakes, birds, and cats from populated areas to protect people with phobias from feeling anxious?

Undoubtedly the greatest way in which society can and should assist people suffering from OCD is to destigmatize psychological problems, improve recognition of OCD and the severe impact it can have, and make effective treatments much more widely and easily available. In addition, society should continue to invest in research to improve our understanding and treatment of OCD so that more and more people can be helped.

Compromise as a Temporary Step in Recovery

Sometimes it may pay to compromise as a *temporary* step in recovery. However, it is important to be clear that any change in your behavior is contingent upon the person with OCD changing theirs. For example, a family member might agree to give reassurance about windows, only if the person with OCD has done exposure with doors. The following case illustrates how compromise may be used constructively to motivate someone with OCD.

> *Cynthia, aged fifteen, had OCD for two years. She lived at home with her mother and her younger brother, Michael (aged five). She had a number of obsessions and compulsions but two were particularly distressing, both for her and for her mother. Michael had an inflammatory bowel disease that resulted in frequent diarrhea and he would often defecate in the bath instead of using the toilet. Cynthia became fearful that the bath was contaminated, and she worried that if she used the bath she would become very ill. Although Cynthia's mother always cleaned the bath after Nick had soiled it, Cynthia would insist that her mother disinfect the bath morning and night using bleach and a scrubbing brush, and additionally disinfect and scrub the bath for fifteen minutes just before she had a bath. If Cynthia's mother did not clean the bath according to Cynthia's standards, Cynthia would become very angry and upset, shouting at her mother and refusing to bathe until the bath had been cleaned again. In addition, Cynthia had worries that someone was trying to poison her, and she would only eat food that had come directly from a newly opened packet. She would refuse to even eat a sandwich if the bread had been opened the day before.*
>
> *Understandably, Cynthia's mother was anxious that Cynthia overcome her OCD and change both of these behaviors as quickly as possible. However, she also felt that Cynthia needed to fight against the OCD at a pace that was comfortable for her. After discussing with her mother her goals for overcoming OCD, Cynthia made the decision that she would first try to fight her fears*

*that she would be poisoned. To help Cynthia feel that she was sup-
ported in her efforts, Cynthia's mother agreed that she would continue to disinfect and scrub the bath in accordance with the OCD
'rules' for three weeks while Cynthia worked on her hierarchy of
fears regarding being poisoned. After three weeks, they agreed,
they would review what progress had been made, and together
decide at that point whether changes could be made to the bath-
cleaning rituals.*

*By continuing with the bath-cleaning ritual, Cynthia's mother
was continuing to accommodate the OCD. However, this compromise was made explicit, and contingent upon Cynthia working
hard to overcome her ritualized eating. Also, it was agreed that
this compromise would be reviewed, and a date for that review
was set and agreed to by both parties.*

We have used compromise ourselves where appropriate. On
one occasion we wrote a supporting note to a university request-
ing a room with a separate bathroom for someone with OCD
with fears of contamination who was unable to use shared facil-
ities. We did this because the person concerned was engaged in
a treatment program. We agreed that it would be a short-term
measure for a month until the person could tackle more difficult levels in their hierarchy, such as using a public toilet.

Another example arose in connection with someone who
had severe problems with hoarding and with checking whether
she had lost any of her possessions. In this case, we became
extremely concerned about whether she was coping. In order
to get permission to enter her house and check on her safety,
we gave repeated reassurance that we would not interfere with
or remove her possessions; but (as we always do in such circumstances) we made it clear *why* we were accommodating her
OCD, and that this would not ultimately be a helpful approach.

Caution About Compromise

Collaborating in avoidance and rituals as part of a program of
overcoming OCD is a bit like providing an alcoholic with more

drink so that they can give it up – unlikely to be an effective solution. If the person with OCD believes they need the right conditions to exist so that they feel comfortable and in control, they have already been caught up by their OCD. To paraphrase Albert Einstein, 'You cannot solve a problem using the same attitude that keeps it going.' In short, don't accommodate OCD. Compromise if it is a means towards an end, but explain why you are compromising, for how long you will do so, and what the consequences of accommodating OCD are.

Hostility and Mockery

Some family members don't accommodate OCD but may be antagonistic by being sarcastic or critical of the person with OCD. They may be afraid of mental disorder and respond by being angry or making fun of a person with OCD. It is frustrating to watch someone you love wasting their life. However, the enemy is the OCD not the individual. It's very important to focus on this.

Frederick, age eighteen, had had OCD for six years and was living at home with his parents. Frederick was overconcerned about things catching fire in his home; he would frequently check electrical appliances, and insist that anything made of paper or wood was removed. His parents desperately wanted him to get well, go to university, and start to build his future. His mother was a very sensitive woman and, if anything, was overprotective. Frederick's father, however, was a very practical and down-to-earth man who had always believed that people who had emotional problems should pull themselves together. There was no doubt he loved his son, but he found Frederick's behavior confusing and very difficult to accept. He tended to feel that his wife was being too soft on Frederick, and their differing views on managing Frederick's behavior caused frequent arguments.

Frederick's father would complain that his son's problem was that he 'just didn't listen' and that they had told him hundreds of times not to worry. When he saw his son checking he would shout

*things like: 'Stop it! You know there's nothing to worry about,
you're acting like a crazy person.' Other times he would become
more sarcastic and mocking: 'Frightened Freddy's checking again
. . . why don't you stop it, son?'*

We understand that living with someone with OCD can be
very frustrating, but being critical or sarcastic or just telling
someone to stop makes things worse, as your relative cannot
just comply with your demand. Your attack will make it harder
to resist the compulsion. Attacking them will exacerbate their
shame and intensify rituals. A person with OCD is likely to
have been born with a predisposition to the condition in the
same way that someone is born with a predisposition to dia-
betes. You've done well not to participate in the person's OCD,
but the next step will be to be as calm, compassionate, and
caring as possible, and not engage in any judgment or criticism.
If necessary, walk away from the ritual. If it is impinging on
family life, then discuss it as a family. You might decide,
together, that you should seek help independently through
your family doctor and therapist, or attend a family support
group for OCD. Try to make a plan of action *as a family* on how
to respond that does not accommodate and does not involve
sarcasm or aggression.

Couples

Many people with OCD have never had any lasting relationships and can become estranged from their family and isolated
within the community. In couples where one partner has OCD,
the rate of separation and divorce is higher than normal. The
break-up may come because the partner feels that the person
with OCD is no longer the person they married, or simply
because they feel they cannot cope any longer with incessant
questioning and demands. Sex may be avoided because of fears
of contamination or worries about passing on HIV.
Alternatively, a person's libido may be reduced because of the
emotional consequences of OCD or the medication they are

taking for OCD. It may be helpful to get help as a couple, but again, this should be as an *extra* to standard treatments for OCD such as CBT or medication, not instead of it.

Children of Parents with OCD

Very little research has been done on the children of individuals with OCD and the effect that OCD has on their upbringing. However, it is clear that all sorts of problems can arise when one parent has OCD and the children have to comply with their demands.

> *Lynne has an obsession about contamination from dirt coming into her house. Anyone entering the home, including her husband and children, has to be 'decontaminated'. When her sons return from school they are made to bathe immediately on entering the house. Without question, the children go straight upstairs to the bathroom and undress. Their clothes are put directly into a laundry basket (if the clothing or child were to touch any other area, it would have to be cleaned). Once the children have had their bath and are wearing 'indoor clothes' they're restricted to certain areas of the house. They're not allowed to bring their schoolbooks into the home but must have completed their work at school. Any belongings that have been brought from the outside world are restricted to the kitchen so as to minimize cleaning. The children are rarely allowed to play in the garden unless they first change into 'outdoor clothes'; then on re-entering the house they have to have a bath and change into 'indoor clothes'. They're rarely allowed to bring friends to play at home; and they are not allowed to help themselves to items from the refrigerator or prepare their own food because of the number of rituals involved. For instance, if one of the boys gets cereal from the cupboard he has to wash his hands before Lynne can pour the milk because he has touched the outside of the cereal box which in her mother's mind is contaminated. Once the milk has been poured she has to wash her hands again before putting the cereal away because she has touched the outside of the milk carton which she feels is contaminated. As long as she washes her*

hands in between tasks she believes that the contamination will not spread.

An independent observer would see that in the long term this could amount to emotional abuse of the children, and that help is required that will first focus on allowing the children to have a normal lifestyle. Lynne's husband may choose to comply with OCD to keep the peace, and Lynne has the right to choose not to change, but the children do not have an option and need to be protected. A parent may be doing what they believe is best for a child – a parent with OCD often feels they are making sure that neither of them is harmed – but it is another example of trying too hard: the attempt to prevent harm is actually causing a different sort of harm, namely to the emotional well-being of the child.

The long-term consequences in the relationship between a parent with OCD and their children can be very damaging.

Fugen wrote to tell us about her mother, who had OCD with fears of contamination and compulsive washing. Her parents' relationship was always very volatile. Somehow they remained together because her father accommodated her mother's OCD, despite the frequent arguments. As a child, Fugen did as she was told and wanted to please her mother, so she helped her to carry out her cleaning compulsions. These ranged from simple things such as washing her hands whenever told to do so to bending over to allow her mother to clean her bottom with soap and water after opening her bowels. After the age of about ten her mother stopped cleaning her bottom, but in many ways she felt that the restrictions imposed by her mother were more humiliating. For example, she wasn't allowed to have friends visit her at home, ride a bike, or do any gardening with her father. She blamed herself for accommodating her mother's OCD as a child and felt that she had been robbed of her childhood.

There is no doubt that it will take Fugen a long time to reach a state of any compassionate understanding of her mother's

OCD. If you are in a similar position, it is possible to seek help and in time achieve a sense of forgiveness. For Fugen, we would recommend she see her family doctor for a referral or go direct to a cognitive behaviour therapist for an assessment (see Appendix 3).

If you have OCD yourself and worry about the effect your OCD is having on your children, please understand: we are not trying to make you condemn yourself as bad and make you feel guilty. However, you do need to take responsibility for your OCD and concentrate on changing your behavior with your children. Consider the consequences of your OCD for them, and at least contain it if you can and do not expect your children to participate. An adult partner of someone with OCD has more of a choice whether to accommodate OCD, but children don't. Children need to be protected and you need to seek help. OCD is treatable and you can function normally again as a family.

Another problem may arise in divorce proceedings, where one parent, usually the father, may argue that a mother with OCD is not fit to look after their children. In our experience it is very difficult to obtain objective information about this, but it is rare for a mother with OCD not to be able to care effectively for her children. Although having a child may precipitate OCD or make it worse, it is also a powerful motivating factor for individuals to seek help. Most parents do not want to involve their children in their OCD and desperately worry about teaching them their 'habits'. Every case is different, but OCD is rarely bad enough to prevent a person being an effective mother. Much depends on the severity and nature of the condition. OCD in itself does not make one an 'unfit' parent but a severe form might do. Remember, even a severe form of OCD, is a product of good intention and trying too hard to protect one's children.

The Difficulties for Parents of Children with OCD

We covered the experience of a parent with a younger child with OCD in Chapter 8; here we look at what is involved in dealing with OCD in a teenager or young adult. When a child is sixteen or under and living with you, then it is usually possible at least to get them to an assessment. Whether they will then fully participate in a treatment program is a different matter, and that problem can be more acute with an older child.

A big issue for parents is trying to decide when behavior is evidence of OCD and when it is simply part of being an angry adolescent. 'Bad behavior' usually occurs when a ritual is threatened, when there is accidental exposure, or when the person is feeling very hurt, rejected, and criticized.

The most important thing is to have a calm discussion about any changes that will take place (e.g. if you as a parent are now going to change your behavior and stop accommodating the OCD, or negotiate a short-term compromise.) Discuss your child's likely reactions and how you will respond. If foul language and throwing objects or violence is anticipated, it's important for the family to plan what to do. If safety is an issue, it may be necessary for one or more family members to leave the house to go for a walk and return half an hour or an hour later when things have calmed down. For foul language and aggression, you should have a discipline that is appropriate for a teenager, and apply it consistently. For example, an adolescent may be grounded for a set period, and have to clean up or pay for any damage.

What if your child is now an adult? This can be a very trying situation.

One of us had a telephone call from Padmal. He told us that he and his wife were desperate for help for their son, who was now aged twenty-seven and still living with his parents. He had suffered from OCD since the age of about twelve but it had become worse when he was at college. He had dropped out of his degree course and now rarely went out. He had refused any help from his family doctor or local mental health services. He spent several hours a day in various rituals, including checking and mental reviewing, until he felt comfortable. He avoided going out of the house because of the risk of contamination. When his OCD was bad, he tended to neglect himself. His sleep/wake cycle was reversed so that he would spend much of the night awake watching TV or playing on the computer. At night, his parents could hear their son pacing up and down. Their son accepted that he had OCD but believed that he had it under control and that he didn't have a problem that needed help; he would get a job when he felt right.

Padmal and his wife understandably felt helpless and desperate in the face of their son's plight. They found some benefit in attending a local support group for relatives of people with mental health problems, which gave them a welcome opportunity to get some support and stop blaming themselves. They began to realize that they couldn't take responsibility for their son's behavior. They also came to realize that their son's OCD was dominating their household and that they were talking about little else. They continued to encourage him to seek help and reduce his avoidance and rituals, but also began to try harder to talk to Padmal about things that weren't related to his OCD.

There is a significant minority of individuals with severe and chronic OCD who are hidden in the community. Many are cared for by aging parents who become increasingly concerned at the effect OCD is having on their son or daughter. As professionals, we find this is one of the most difficult situations in which to help. We recognize the limited influence we have on someone with OCD. No one can 'control' OCD or make someone with OCD change. When you have an adult child with chronic OCD in your home, trying to get them to get help is difficult. The road ahead may be a long and difficult one and you'll need to also look after yourself; we discuss how to do this in the general guidelines at the end of this chapter.

Dealing with 'Minimizing'

If your family member is minimizing the effect of OCD on their life, try to find out what their feelings are about having such a problem (shame, for example), what they fear, or what doubts they have about therapy or change. Ensure that as a family, or if possible as a wider group, including friends, you take a consistent approach, and that nobody is accommodating the OCD. Agree upon your message, and if necessary talk to the individual both within the family group and with a mental health professional. Someone might draw up, with your family member, a list of costs (or disadvantages) and benefits (advantages) of (a) staying the way they are, and (b) engaging in a program of therapy (see Appendix 5 for the blank form). Each of the costs and benefits may be divided into those for the 'self' and those for 'others'. Even if your relative sees few disadvantages in staying the same way, you can emphasize the costs of OCD to others in the family and the benefits to the person in the long term. Continue to emphasize that you will still provide support and help during therapy. If your relative finally agrees to seek help, discuss the time-frame within which this can be done, and the process it will involve.

What If a Relative Refuses to Seek Help?

If your relative continues to refuse help and you decide that the status quo is no longer tenable, you will need to explore your own options, such as finding your relative independent living arrangements by getting help from the local mental health services. We know that local mental health services do not always respond positively to requests for medical help for a relative with OCD who does not want help. The main priority for a psychiatrist in public health services is patients with 'severe mental illness', which is usually interpreted to mean those who suffer from schizophrenia or bipolar disorder, especially those who may be suicidal or a danger to the community. UK and USA mental health law allows a patient to be detained in hospital against their will in certain circumstances, but this is usually too blunt an instrument for individuals with chronic and severe OCD. In the absence of a risk to themselves or self-neglect, patients with OCD are unlikely to be admitted to a hospital and would, in any case, experience limited benefit from admission to the average acute psychiatric ward. Short-term in-patient care in a specialist unit where the staff are used to dealing with OCD patients and CBT is available may, however, be helpful in some cases.

Under UK mental health legislation, in severe cases of OCD patients may be admitted against their will for a trial of medication. A full such trial may take a few months, and at discharge a patient would need to continue with it in the absence of any CBT (see Appendix 1 for a discussion on medication). CBT is, however, *powerless* without the cooperation of a person with OCD. It is both unethical and counterproductive to coerce exposure to feared situations or activities. Therapists may encourage and challenge a patient, but would *never* force exposure and spring something on their patient unannounced. Nor should you ever do this to a relative with OCD. A program of CBT has to be done voluntarily, and the motivation has to come from the patient, if it is to be ethical and effective.

In Padmal's case, we would recommend trying to engage his son in therapy by several visits to the home. We would want to focus on what he really wants to do in life and his real values that are being obscured by his OCD. If this were not possible, we would try to engage him over the telephone. Slowly, over time, it may be possible to engage a person if enough trust is built up and they can envisage reaching goals over a longer period. An exceptional mental health team with therapists familiar with OCD may provide this service. However, the success of any treatment will still depend on the cooperation of the person with OCD, and ultimately on their willingness to see a therapist and do the homework.

The Notion of Being 'Untreatable'

Are there special cases of OCD who are ultimately unable to engage in treatment or whose problems are unresponsive to treatment? Here again there are difficulties. Many of the people we have seen successfully overcome their OCD have made previous unsuccessful attempts, and have even been diagnosed as 'untreatable'. A full debate on the practical and ethical aspects of deciding under what circumstances a person should be considered unable to recover from OCD lies outside of the scope of this book. However, it is clear that many people with OCD (and some less well-informed health-care practitioners) arrive at the 'untreatable' conclusion much too quickly. On the whole, the best advice you can give to your relative with OCD is to keep fighting to change the OCD rather than fighting to get the world to go along with it.

A very small number of individuals with OCD are beyond the skills of mental health professionals or mental health law and cannot be engaged in treatment. Such individuals often have what are termed 'overvalued ideas'. These are, as discussed earlier, values that have become idealized and central to the person's identity. Such values are more likely to be seen in someone with hoarding or who is housebound, and those who cannot bear anxiety and strenuously avoid situations that may provoke any distress. They feel that they must have a high degree of control so that everything has to be done their way and at a time and speed that suits them. In this case, as a relative, we would advise you to seek help for yourself from your family doctor. It's perfectly acceptable for your mental health, if you decide you can't carry on caring for your relative, to ask local services to find suitable independent living arrangements for them.

If the person with OCD cannot cope on their own or demands that all the local services adapt to their disorder, then in general we would not as professionals support their 'needs' but try to compromise in some areas as part of a process of change. In our *ideal* world, we would try to engage the person in therapy and admit them to a home for individuals with chronic and severe OCD who need long-term therapy (over a year or more). However, while there are houses for people with problems resulting from alcohol and drug abuse and community homes for individuals with severe mental illness, there is rarely any similar facility suitable for individuals with chronic and severe OCD. For someone with this condition there are so many problems with shared bathrooms and other aspects of community living that the accommodation would have to be sufficiently self-contained and yet still have access to therapeutic community. We think that there is a pressing need for a home with a focus on overcoming OCD and improving life skills for independent living, to which individuals with severe and chronic OCD could be admitted for long-term therapy.

Being an Ally in Overcoming OCD

One of the practical things a relative can do is become an ally for the individual in overcoming their OCD, *if* he or she wishes you to. In children, parents have to be involved in therapy, but teenagers should be given the option of asking their parent to be involved. In CBT, the person who acts as an aid to the process of therapy in this way is called a 'co-therapist'. Such allies can be of enormous value and can help in numerous ways, as set out in Chapter 6.

It makes sense for both you, as ally/co-therapist, and your relative with OCD to work through this book together, and review it together as things progress. However, be aware that your relative may feel that you are overinvolved with monitoring their homework or progress. In such situations, you'll need to negotiate your degree of involvement. If your relative is in therapy and you think they are not being honest with the therapist, it is usually possible to inform the therapist of your observations without the therapist breaching confidentiality. Ultimately, it's the responsibility of the person with OCD to do their homework and to be honest with their therapist about their difficulties – and, as their ally, you can gently remind them that having setbacks is part of overcoming OCD.

General Guidelines for Relatives

OCD is Not a Sign of Madness or Badness

If you are a relative or a friend of someone with OCD, and especially if you are parent of a child with OCD, familiarize yourself with the condition: get to know your enemy by reading books like this one, and learn as much as you can about the symptoms and treatment. The first step is to accept that, however bizarre the symptoms seem, they are just part of OCD. OCD is not a sign of madness or psychosis – it's simply a disorder, and part of the rich diversity of human life. It's not something that can be easily stopped. It will take time, commitment, and the right guidance to improve everyone's quality of life.

Furthermore, OCD is not 'bad' behavior done to annoy you. If you have a child with OCD, it's still important to set consistent boundaries with behaviors that are unrelated to OCD and to problem-solve OCD behavior where it impinges on your family life (e.g. the length of time the person spends in the bathroom when everyone is getting ready in the morning). Each person needs to overcome their problems at their own pace, even though this may be a lengthy process. Avoid comparing your relative with other individuals with OCD or indeed without it.

Avoid the Blame Game

No one should be blamed for causing OCD – it's not the fault of the person with OCD or of you as a relative. Hence there is no need to feel guilty for 'causing' OCD even if there is a possible genetic link. If you start blaming your genes then you can go all the way back to Adam and Eve!

Encourage Your Relative to Seek Help

Encourage your relative with OCD to try out the principles in this book, and to seek professional help with therapy or medication if they need it. Be supportive of that decision and do everything you can to help them change. That means helping them to assess and define their problems clearly and, if they wish, being an ally as described above. Encourage them to persist with their treatment and praise improvement, however small.

Keep Your Home as Normal as Possible

Families should *not* try to adapt their ways of doing things to accommodate the person's obsessions and compulsions. Don't put family life on hold; accept that OCD may complicate family life, but do it anyway.

Don't Participate in OCD

At home, your relative should be encouraged to maintain as normal a lifestyle as possible. Don't take on their responsibilities (unless of course you are a parent of a child). Don't make excuses for them, for example about their being late for work or for an appointment. If necessary, compromise in the short term in the way we have described, but draw the line when new avoidance behaviors and compulsions are announced. If the person is in therapy, ask to see the therapist with your relative and discuss a program of reducing your involvement in your relative's OCD. If the person is not in therapy, try to negotiate a program of gradual withdrawal from the person's rituals and avoidance behavior before you implement it. Make sure that you communicate that you are changing your involvement in order to help rather than punish. Practice saying 'No' or 'No, thank you' to requests for reassurance or participation in rituals. (Children may use a nickname for 'OCD', like David's 'snake': see Chapter 8.) Alternatively, discuss in advance and negotiate it if you are going to provide exposure in response to requests for reassurance. For example, if you are being asked by your family member if he or she has just run someone over, then you could say yes, several small children were run over and are now lying dead in the gutter. You can joke like this; but be careful, because your response *may* be interpreted as reassurance – it can get very complicated! In general, we would encourage just saying 'No' or 'No, thank you' to requests for avoidance, reassurance, or rituals.

Anticipate how you will deal with your relative becoming stressed or irritated by your new way of responding and have a plan that you can both agree upon if he or she becomes aggressive or angry. Where aggression is a problem, discuss it with the therapist involved and always ensure your safety, if necessary by calling the police. You may have to be very persistent until requests for reassurance or rituals stop happening, because if you respond just once, it immediately becomes more likely that they will involve you again. Individuals with OCD will not come to any harm as a result of anxiety, though they may be distressed in the short term. Accommodating rituals and avoidance means that you are helping to fuel OCD in the long term – and you are not taking care of yourself. It may feel as if you're protecting yourself from stress and helping someone with OCD, but the effect is the opposite. What is good for the family is good for the person with OCD, and this can only occur when no one else engages in the OCD. A family that is all pulling together can provide better support for your relative with OCD. Its members can also better support each other and solve problems more efficiently.

Be a Coach and Cheerleader

You and your relative both need to see OCD, and not the individual experiencing it, as your shared enemy. Approach the problem as a team, working together, and as your relative improves see yourself as a coach shouting encouragement from the sidelines, or cheerleading, as you become less involved. Enthusiasm, understanding, and general support are the best help you can provide.

Look After Your Own Needs

You need to follow your own interests and have your own sources of support. At times you may need time out (or respite care). When you need time away from OCD, tell the person with OCD that you need a break but that you have not given up on them, and try to get others to help. Feelings such as guilt, sadness, or anger are normal in caregivers of those with any long-term disability. Try not to engage in self-pitying thoughts such as 'Why me?' or 'Poor me, I don't deserve to have OCD in the family,' which will make you more depressed and feed another vicious circle. Try to detach yourself emotionally from your relative's OCD and take it less personally. If you're not coping emotionally or it is affecting other areas of your life, seek help. There may be a local caregivers' group or, even better, a group for caregivers of individuals with OCD. Alternatively, see your family doctor for a referral or go directly to a therapist.

If withdrawal from participating in a ritual provokes extreme temper or violence, then you must seek help for yourself. If you think violence could be a problem, then plan a response in advance. Try to respond calmly. In extreme cases you may need to telephone the police for everyone's safety.

De-Catastrophize Anxiety and Discomfort

We've met many family members who seem to share the view that anxiety and discomfort should be avoided, and have even been critical of CBT because it requires the tolerance of discomfort. In some cases this is entirely understandable, given the profound distress that the individual with OCD, whom they care about, experiences as they wrestle with a doubt or intrusive thought. Some families share 'rules' about emotions that can be unhelpful in overcoming OCD. For example:

- Emotions are a sign of weakness and should be controlled.
- If something upsets you, don't think about it.
- Being upset is terrible, and it's important to do something to make yourself feel better as soon as possible.
- If something bothers you, do something to take your mind off it.
- Be careful about showing that you feel upset to other people, or they might use it against you.
- If you get too upset it could make you ill, so it's best to avoid intense emotions.

These rules are sometimes explicitly taught; at other times they are taught by the way a family or person within that family behaves. If you think you or your family shares any rules like these which might make experiencing emotions even harder, try to make sure that you communicate the message that you are confident that feeling short-term distress is a sensible and helpful thing to do when overcoming OCD.

Individuals with OCD will not come to any harm as a result of anxiety. They may be distressed in the short term, but 'sticking with it' is one of the most crucial aspects of overcoming OCD. Do not participate in any of your relative's rituals or avoidance. Support them in seeking help and encourage them when they are in therapy. If you are worried about the effects, ask to see the mental health professional who is treating your relative. At the very least, you will have your questions answered.

Be Prepared for Setbacks

It's likely that on some days your relative will be better able to deal with symptoms than on others. It will be harder for both of you at certain times – for example, when either of you is feeling tired or stressed by other problems. Setbacks are expected and predictable, and to a certain extent can be planned for. Taking time out can be helpful at these points. Each person with OCD will need to overcome their problems at their own pace, even though this may be a lengthy process. It's entirely normal to experience setbacks along the road to recovery. Don't lose heart. You can help by staying optimistic and encouraging them to keep trying. You probably won't see the hundred times that OCD doesn't get in the way, but are bound to notice the time that it does!

Keep a Sense of Humour

People with OCD are often aware of the humorous aspects of their obsessions and compulsions. OCD treatment groups are frequently filled with laughter, and many people are relieved at not having to take things too seriously. Such mirth can be used to help people with OCD distance themselves from the condition and their catastrophic thoughts. However, it is very important to resist mocking the person for their symptoms, as this may cause additional stress, shame, and embarrassment.

Keep Communicating

Make sure that you communicate, both with your relative who has OCD and with everyone in your family. Remember that you may need help and support yourself. Make sure that you continue to do things you enjoy and have people to talk to about your own feelings and concerns. Eventually, you may decide that, for the sake of your own mental health, you can't carry on caring for your relative with OCD. In that case you'll need to communicate as a family and get help from the local services.

Remember: Recovery From OCD Is a Process

When your relative is recovering, you may expect everything to go back to how it used to be. This may not be how it happens at all, and the family may need to go through various stages of adjustment. This is a normal process. Each person will adjust and recover at a different rate. You may want to see OCD as something that is 'over' or 'finished', but remember that setbacks are part of the process.

In summary, OCD can have a profound effect on the person with OCD or their caregiver. However, it is not hopeless, and there is a lot that you can both do as a team to help each other.

Medication for Obsessive Compulsive Disorder

Should I Take Medication?

This chapter aims to help you make an informed choice about whether you wish to take medication for OCD by looking at the potential benefits and disadvantages. We cover the possible side effects and what you can do to minimize them. We also look at some of the medications used for OCD when standard drugs do not work.

There are two main treatment paths for helping someone to overcome OCD: cognitive behavior therapy (CBT) and medication. Both have a substantial amount of evidence to recommend them. CBT and medication can be used alone or in combination. However, because CBT lasts longer and tends to have fewer side effects, it is the preferred initial treatment. We usually recommend medication as an *additional* treatment for those who fail to make progress with CBT, whose OCD is more severe, or who are also significantly depressed.

Wherever you live, you may find it difficult to obtain CBT because of long waiting lists or other restrictions in public medicine. As a result, you may be offered medication before you receive CBT. Research suggests that CBT and medication are just as effective as one another and it is very important, therefore, that you have a real choice; but this is a political problem. Research suggests that, in the short term, combining the two kinds of treatment may be beneficial. *Some* individuals do better on a combination of CBT and medication. Unfortunately, research does not yet tell us who is more likely to benefit from adding medication to CBT.

Whatever treatment path you decide to take, make sure you monitor your progress using the rating scales in this book.

First Choice: SSRI Medication

Evidence suggests that the most effective medication for OCD is a class of antidepressants called 'selective serotonin reuptake inhibitors' (or SSRIs for short; see Table A1.1). These drugs are serotonergic, which means that they act on serotonin nerve endings in the brain. 'Selective' refers to the fact that they act on serotonin nerve endings rather than others such as noradrenaline or histamine nerve endings. 'Reuptake inhibitor' refers to the way the drug acts: it helps to increase the concentration of serotonin in the nerve cells. This, in turn, helps to increase the messages passing along certain pathways in the brain and reduce anxiety. You may recall that in Chapter 2, describing the causes of OCD, it was suggested that certain modules in the brain may be failing because there is an excessive load placed on the system as they desperately try to reduce anxiety. SSRIs enhance this *normal* activity of the brain and improve its ability to dampen down anxiety.

SSRIs are widely used in the treatment of depression, and to a lesser extent, of panic attacks and eating disorders. A family doctor may prescribe the drug or may refer you to a psychiatrist who will be more aware of the doses required and can give you an opportunity to discuss your experience and circumstances in more detail.

In controlled trials, in which an SSRI is compared with a placebo (a 'dummy pill'), about 60 per cent of OCD patients who receive an SSRI will substantially improve compared with about 10 per cent of patients who receive a placebo. This means, of course, that about 40 per cent of patients do not experience any significant improvement. On average, symptoms reduce by half for everyone so some patients may get no

Table A1.1 **Serotonin Reuptake Inhibitors**

Chemical name	UK trade name	USA trade name	Manufacturer	Usual daily starting dose (mg)	Target daily dose (mg)	Liquid preparation
Citalopram	Cipramil	Celexa	Lundbeck	20	50	Yes
Clomipramine	Anafranil	Anafranil	Ciba-Geigy	50	225	Yes
Escitalopram	Cipralex	Lexapro	Lundbeck	10	30	Yes
Fluoxetine	Prozac	Prozac	Eli Lilly	20	60	Yes
Fluvoxamine	Faverin	Luvox	Solvay	50	200	No
Paroxetine	Seroxat	Paxil	GSK	20	40	Yes
Sertraline	Lustral	Zoloft	Pfizer	50	200	No

benefit, whereas others may become symptom-free. Some people with OCD do not do well on SSRIs, including those without much insight into the nature of their OCD, those who hoard, and those whose anxiety levels are low. Even if the medication is beneficial, it will not work right away. Most people notice some improvement in their symptoms by four weeks, and maximum benefit should occur within twelve weeks. It is important to continue to take your medication at the highest dose you can tolerate for this period before judging how effective it has been.

All the SSRIs are equally effective for OCD overall, but any one person may respond better to one SSRI rather than another. The initial choice will depend upon various factors. The prescribing doctor may have a personal preference; also, if you or someone in your family did well or poorly with a particular medication in the past, this may influence the choice. Side effects will be taken into account; if you have other problems (e.g. difficulty sleeping) or are taking another medication, these factors may influence your doctor's choice so that side effects and possible drug interactions are minimized. For example, citalopram and its newer version, escitalopram, are usually better choices if you are on other drugs that might interact with an SSRI. Citalopram is a mixture of two molecules which are mirror images of each other; escitalopram is the molecule that has the serotonin action and is available without a redundant molecule that has no serotonin action. The result is the same, but escitalopram may have slightly fewer side effects.

There are some differences between the other SSRIs. For example, fluoxetine takes longer to be metabolized by the body. Thus if you forget a dose one day, you can get away with it because fluoxetine does not vanish from the blood when you stop taking it. It also tends to be easier to stop taking.

In general, most SSRIs do not interact with small amounts of alcohol and you may drink safely as long as you do so in moderation! However, people's reactions to alcohol do vary when taking an SSRI: some individuals can become more aggressive or sedated. Of the SSRIs, fluvoxamine and sertraline are known not to mix very well with alcohol, so be aware that this mix may impair your judgment. You should not drive, for example, if you have taken either of these medications and had a drink. Excessive alcohol can also be a factor in depression and will interfere in any therapy program.

Compared with the older antidepressants, SSRIs are generally safe. An overdose will not kill you.

What Dose of an SSRI Should I Be Prescribed?

The normal starting and target daily doses of the medication are listed in Table A1.1. You may be recommended a higher dose for various reasons. When progress is slow, some experts advise that increasing the dose above the target level often gives better results; if you are metabolizing the drug excessively fast you may need a higher dose than is normally recommended. Occasionally, your doctor may want to measure the level of the drug in your blood to see whether enough is circulating. If you experience significant side effects, then you can always start on a lower dose and build it up slowly.

What About SSRIs for a Child or an Adolescent?

SSRIs have been reasonably well studied for children with OCD and seem to be both effective and safe. It's true that we don't yet know the long-term effects of such drugs on the immature brain of a child, but this theoretical risk needs to be judged against the risk in some cases of *not* using medication in a young person who has not responded to CBT (or has difficulty accessing it) and is continuing with OCD symptoms, which may have a major impact on their development and education.

The dose for a young person is similar to that for an adult, although younger or smaller children usually start at a lower dose that is increased gradually. Sertraline and fluvoxamine are licensed for use in young people with OCD in the UK, and sertraline and fluoxetine are licensed for young people in the

USA. Licensing of a drug only means that the manufacturer may promote the drug for a particular condition. Others may be licensed before very long, and they all seem effective, so your doctor may choose an unlicensed one if he/she thinks it may suit the child better.

In general, the use of SSRIs for children should be supervised by a psychiatrist, especially as concerns have been raised about the use of such drugs for young people with depression. In the UK, the authorities have advised against the use of SSRIs (except fluoxetine) for children under eighteen *with depression*. Only fluoxetine has been shown in clinical trials to have a good balance of risks and benefits for the treatment of *depression* in children under eighteen.

In summary, the authorities continue to recommend SSRIs for young people with OCD. The side effects listed below occur in children as they do in adults. In addition, children may become over-excited, irritable, or silly; if these responses are very marked, it may be a reason to stop the medication.

Will SSRI Medication Have Side Effects?

The side effects SSRIs are likely to have depend on the dose of your medication and for how long you have been taking it. Most people find side effects are minor irritations that decrease after a few weeks, and they are not usually a problem for people who need to take a drug in the long term. The worst side effects usually occur in the first few days or weeks after commencing the drug. This is the time when you are most likely to stop taking the drug because you have not experienced any improvement in symptoms of your OCD. (Remember, it takes up to twelve weeks for the full benefits of the medication to become evident.) There is one side effect that does not tend to improve over time: sexual difficulties. We discuss below how these can be relieved. Side effects that persist, including those of a sexual nature, will decrease when you stop taking the medication.

You are more likely to experience side effects if you are on a higher dose or if your dose has been rapidly increased. If you are unable to tolerate the medication, you can try reducing the dose and then increasing it to the previous level more slowly. For example, if you find that you are feeling nauseous after a few days of taking paroxetine 20 mg, you can reduce the dose to 10 mg for a week or two and then increase it to 20 mg again when your body has become more accustomed to the drug. If you are very sensitive to side effects your doctor may start you on a lower dose as a liquid and increase it very slowly. You might start on 2 mg of fluoxetine and increase by 2 mg per week. Another alternative is to switch to a different SSRI altogether.

We have listed below the most common side effects of SSRIs and how to deal with them. All will stop if you discontinue the drug under guidance from your doctor.

Nausea
Nausea (feeling sick) is the most common, but transitory, side effect of an SSRI and affects about 25 per cent of patients taking an SSRI compared with about 10 per cent of those on a placebo. Citalopram and fluvoxamine are slightly more likely than the other SSRIs to cause nausea. The nausea can be minimized by taking the drug after food. Alternatively, halve the dose for a couple of weeks and then increase it slowly back to the normal dose. If the nausea still persists then an anti-nausea drug (e.g. metoclobemide) may help.

Diarrhea or constipation
SSRIs can cause diarrhea in up to 15 per cent of patients on an SSRI compared with about 5 per cent taking a placebo. Diarrhea can be minimized by drinking plenty of apple juice (which contains pectin) or the use of a drug such as bismuth subsalicylate (Kaopectate). Constipation occurs in another 5 per cent of patients taking an SSRI. Diarrhea or constipation may be improved by taking bulking agents such as Fybogel or psyllium seed husk and eating plenty of bran and roughage. If you experience either diarrhea or constipation, you should drink at least two litres (1.8 quarts) of water a day.

Headache
Up to 20 per cent of patients taking an SSRI find that they develop headaches. Headache is also a common symptom of tension and occurs in about 15 per cent of patients taking a placebo. Symptoms of headache can usually be helped by simple painkillers such as paracetamol, and should decrease after a few weeks of taking an SSRI.

Excessive sweating
Excessive sweating occurs in about 10 per cent of patients taking an SSRI compared with 5 per cent taking a placebo. There is no easy solution to this problem, although like most side effects it should decrease over time.

Dry mouth
Dry mouth affects about 10 per cent of patients taking an SSRI compared with 5 per cent taking a placebo. Sucking on sugar-less gum may stimulate the production of saliva, or you could try a spray that can be bought over the counter that provides artificial saliva. Again the symptoms usually decrease over time.

Tremor
Shakiness or tremor occurs in about 10 per cent of patients taking an SSRI and 3 per cent of those taking a placebo. If it is severe, a beta-blocker (e.g. propranolol) may help to reduce it.

Sedation or insomnia
About 10–20 per cent of patients on an SSRI feel sedated and another 5–15 per cent cannot sleep. The problem can sometimes be resolved by changing the time of day you take your medication (take it at night, for example, if it makes you drowsy) or taking a different SSRI altogether. Fluvoxamine is more likely to cause sleepiness and is often best taken at night.

Sexual problems
Sexual side effects can take the form of delayed ejaculation in men and an inability to reach orgasm in women. They can also

occasionally cause both men and women to lose libido, although this is complicated to assess in the presence of depression. However, there is one case report of an SSRI causing orgasms with yawning!

Sometimes the problem can be solved with a lower dose of medication, although this may make the OCD worse. Another possible solution is ginkgo biloba. This is a herbal extract of the maidenhead hair tree and is sometimes used to enhance memory, particularly in the elderly. It can be purchased in health food shops. Ginkgo biloba has been used to treat sexual problems caused by antidepressant drugs in a series of fourteen patients. They had a variety of difficulties including erectile problems, delayed ejaculation, loss of libido, and inability to reach orgasm. Patients took a daily dose of 240 mg for six weeks. The only side effect was gastric irritation (reported by two patients). Overall the group reported improvements. Two of the fourteen patients reported no improvements and two reported that sexual functioning was completely restored. The study needs to be repeated as a controlled trial, but in the meantime, it suggests that gingko biloba may be worth trying.

There are also reports concerning the use of Viagra or Cialis for men and women. Viagra has been reported as successful in reversing the sexual side effects of an SSRI. Again these studies need to be done as a controlled trial. The dose of Viagra is 50 mg, to be taken one hour before sexual activity. If this does not improve things or gives only a partial response, you could try increasing it to 100 mg. Some patients with heart conditions will not be able to take it. The possible side effects of Viagra include headache, flushing, and dizziness.

Loss of appetite
Loss of appetite and weight loss occur in about 5–10 per cent of patients taking SSRIs. Reducing the dose can halt this effect, though it usually improves over time anyway. Some SSRIs can also cause mild weight gain in the long term and you may need to adjust your diet and exercise program to compensate for this.

However, depression and inactivity will also contribute to weight gain.

Nervousness or agitation

Some people feel more anxious or 'wired', especially when starting an SSRI. It is always difficult to tell the difference between the anxiety that comes from the OCD and what might be caused by the drug. If the anxiety is caused by the drug it may be solved by (a) switching to a different SSRI, (b) trying a lower dose, or (c) adding a different drug. The feeling of increased anxiety is usually temporary and will subside over time.

Whenever side effects are a problem, always discuss it with your doctor. The doctor may advise you to (a) reduce the dose, (b) try a different SSRI, (c) add another medication to counteract side effects such as insomnia or sexual problems, or (d) wait and see, as many of the side effects improve over time.

Use of an SSRI During Pregnancy and Breastfeeding

SSRIs are generally considered to be safe for pregnant women. However, because no manufacturer wants to be sued, they all recommend 'caution' and say that their product should not be used during pregnancy or breastfeeding. No mother (and especially one with OCD) wants to cause harm to her baby, but so far no significant problems have emerged. Fluoxetine has been around the longest and is the most studied in pregnancy and breastfeeding, so this is the most widely prescribed SSRI for pregnant women. Most experts prefer to treat OCD with CBT alone where pregnancy is possible or planned. However, if you and your doctor believe that medication is necessary (and OCD commonly gets worse during pregnancy), then it is nearly always better for you to be functioning as a mother than suffering from OCD. You should discuss this in detail with your doctor.

SSRIs for Vegans

Some SSRIs are free of animal products. The manufacturers have informed us that citalopram elixir, fluoxetine elixir, clomipramine elixir, sertraline tablets, and paroxetine tablets or liquid do not contain any animal products.

If SSRI Medication Doesn't Work, Is There Anything Else I Can Try?

All SSRIs are equally effective overall, but one person may get a better response from one than another. If one SSRI does not work then best practice is to try a different SSRI in the highest dose you can tolerate for at least twelve weeks. Sometimes it is necessary to check the level of the drug in your blood to ensure that you are not metabolizing it too quickly.

If you have tried two or three SSRIs at the highest tolerated dose and for at least twelve weeks, but your symptoms are not improving, the advice would be to try clomipramine instead. This is an older drug in a class called the tricyclics (the name describes the structure of the chemical), which were first developed for the treatment of depression in the 1960s. Clomipramine is not strictly classified as an SSRI because although it has a potent effect on serotonin receptors it also enhances other chemicals, which is why it has more side effects. As with other antiobsessional drugs, the response to medication will depend on the dose. This means that, for many people, the higher the dose, the greater the effect in reducing obsessional symptoms. However, higher doses also lead to increasing side effects. These side effects are usually mild and can often be minimized by reducing the dose. Most of the side effects are related to the dose and tend to reduce over time, but some may persist. They will cease if the drug is discontinued.

What Dose of Clomipramine Should I Be Prescribed?

The dose of clomipramine is normally started low (50–75 mg) and gradually increased to the maximum that you can tolerate.

It is usually prescribed to be taken at night so that the sedative side effects have worn off by the morning. Some people metabolize clomipramine very quickly and so, even when they are taking a high dose, may have a relatively low level of the drug in the bloodstream. If necessary the level of clomipramine and its metabolite can be checked by a blood test to determine if it is safe to increase the dose to a higher level. In severe cases, it is possible to have clomipramine administered intravenously for two weeks before starting on a high oral dose. Intravenous clomipramine, however, is no longer available in some countries and has to be specially obtained. It is not suitable for people with heart disease.

What are the Common Side Effects of Clomipramine?

Dry Mouth

At least two thirds of patients taking clomipramine experience a dry mouth. You get a dry mouth when you produce less saliva than normal. Sucking on sugarless gum may stimulate the production of saliva or you could try a spray that can be bought over the counter that provides artificial saliva. Good mouth hygiene is important, as are regular visits to your dentist.

Dizziness

Dizziness on standing is a common side effect for about 25 per cent of patients taking clomipramine. It rarely occurs with SSRIs. You can minimize dizziness by rising slowly or first sitting on the side of the bed and then squeezing the muscles in your calf as you stand up.

Tremor

About 15 per cent of patients taking clomipramine develop shakiness or tremor in their arms. There are no simple remedies for tremor, although a beta-blocker such as propranolol may reduce it if it is severe.

Weight gain

Weight gain can be a problem with clomipramine and you should therefore be especially careful to eat healthily.

Constipation

You have a one in four chance of becoming constipated if you take clomipramine. A diet with lots of roughage from vegetables or bran and prunes, or a bulking agent such as Fybogel or psyllium husks, will help. Always remember to drink plenty of water. Laxatives that stimulate the bowel should be used only occasionally.

Drowsiness or fatigue

Clomipramine can cause daytime drowsiness, which can be minimized by taking the dosage at night. Some people may still experience residual sleepiness in the morning: in that case, spread the dose over the day.

Blurred vision, headache

Clomipramine can also cause blurring of vision or headache. There is no good solution to this, apart from switching to an SSRI.

Sexual problems

Clomipramine can be a reason for delayed ejaculation or, less commonly, impotence in men. It can also cause women difficulties in reaching orgasm. For suggested solutions see above under side effects of SSRIs.

Increased sweating

People taking clomipramine sometimes complain that they sweat more or, if they are menopausal, that their hot flushes have increased. There is no easy solution to this but it should improve over time.

Epileptic fit
There is a small risk of having an epileptic fit for about 0.5 per cent of individuals taking clomipramine. In this case, the drug will need to be discontinued or the dose significantly reduced. The majority of fits, however, occur in patients taking clomipramine in doses above 250 mg.

Urinary problems
Occasionally, clomipramine can cause urinary retention or hesitancy in the elderly, in which case the drug will need to be discontinued.

Heart problems
Individuals with pre-existing heart disease should have an ECG (electrocardiogram) before beginning treatment with clomipramine, and at regular intervals during treatment, as the drug may cause some individuals to develop an irregular heartbeat.

Stopping an SSRI or clomipramine

When you stop taking an SSRI or clomipramine, you may experience discontinuation symptoms for a few days or weeks. These can include dizziness, sleep disturbances, agitation or anxiety, nausea, excessive sweating, and numbness. These are not the same as the withdrawal symptoms which can occur with tranquillizers, in which symptoms of rebound anxiety may persist over many months. It is, however, sensible to reduce gradually over several weeks when you have decided to stop taking medication. This will also help to reduce the risk of relapse. When the standard dose of the drug is reached, then it may be a good idea to halve it before stopping it completely. Fluoxetine lasts longer in the body than other SSRIs before it is metabolized. One way of reducing intake of the drug gently is to take it on alternate days.

Fluoxetine is the least likely SSRI to cause discontinuation symptoms and paroxetine the most likely, because of the different rates of breakdown in the body. For example, fluoxetine reduces very slowly and remains in your body for up to five weeks after your last dose. Paroxetine breaks down very quickly and is out of your system by the next day. Most discontinuation symptoms can be minimized by reducing the drugs slowly, and this should be done under the guidance of your doctor. If you are on a high dose, the usual advice is to reduce it by about 25 per cent every month.

How Long Do I Need to Take Medication For?

Relapse in OCD is very common when you stop taking medication *and* have had no CBT. The risk of relapse will partly depend on the natural pattern of your OCD without treatment. For example, if you are lucky enough to have had just a single episode of OCD, then it is unlikely to recur whether you are on the medication or not. If you have chronic OCD, for which medication was providing some benefit, then when you stop taking it you are very likely to relapse into your previous pattern. If, however, you are someone whose OCD comes and goes, then when you stop medication you may have a much longer period symptom-free. For some people (and it is very difficult to predict which ones), the risk of relapse can be minimized by combining the medication with CBT. This can, however, be a double-edged sword. If medication has been very successful in decreasing symptoms of OCD, it is quite difficult to learn and practice CBT when you are symptom-free!

If you are planning to stop medication, ensure that you do it after discussion with your doctor and within an agreed time frame. Be aware that your OCD symptoms may start to return within a few weeks or months. If therapy without medication has been unavailable or unsuccessful, then you may need to take medication in the long term. As SSRIs have been taken for many years without any untoward side effects, this is regarded as safe by experts.

Liquid Preparations

If you have to start your medication at a low dose, then it is usually easier to measure a liquid rather than break a tablet into smaller pieces. Also, if you are simply unable to tolerate a tablet, then you may find it easier to swallow your medication as an elixir. The last column of Table A1.1 shows which drugs are available in elixir form.

What Can I Take if SSRIs and Clomipramine Fail?

There are other options if you have tried two or more SSRIs or clomipramine and still seen no improvement. The next step is best discussed with a psychiatrist experienced in the treatment of OCD. For example, there is some evidence for the benefits of combining the SSRI citalopram with clomipramine (although it may be better to just take a much higher dose of the citalopram first rather than combining the two). There is also some evidence for the benefits of combining an SSRI with certain drugs that block dopamine receptors as an additional treatment to a SSRI (these are listed in Table A1.2). Any benefit is likely to become apparent within one to four weeks of starting the medication. Such drugs are more helpful in those who have tics or Tourette's syndrome, and perhaps a need for order and symmetry. Dopamine-blocking drugs are normally used for treating psychosis; however, the dose is usually lower when used for treating OCD. They are not helpful for OCD if used alone (without an SSRI). Not all of the dopamine-blocking drugs have been shown to be of benefit with an SSRI – for example, one study has shown no benefit from adding olanzapine.

What are the Side Effects of Dopamine-Blocking Drugs?

In the lower doses recommended for OCD, dopamine-blocking drugs help to reduce anxiety and rarely cause problems. The main side effect may be fatigue. Some anti-dopamine drugs may

Table A1.2 **Anti-dopamine drugs used in OCD**

Chemical name	UK trade name	USA trade name	Manufacturer	Starting daily dose (mg)	High daily dose (mg)	Liquid preparation
Haloperidol	Haldol	Haldol	Jannsen	0.25–0.5	2–4	Yes
Olanzapine	Zyprexa	Zyprexa	Eli Lilly	2.5	5–10	No
Quetiapine	Seroquel	Seroquel	Astra Zeneca	25	100	No
Risperidone	Risperidal	Risperidal	Jannsen	0.25–0.5	2–3	Yes
Sulpiride	Dolmatil, Sulpor or Sulpitil	Not available	Solian	200	800	Yes

be more likely to cause weight gain, especially at higher doses. When dopamine blockers are prescribed in higher doses, they can have side effects such as stiffness in the limbs or slurred speech that can be countered by other medication such as pro-cyclidine. However, at the lower doses usually used in OCD this should not occur. A small minority of women may experience hormonal changes, such as stimulation of prolactin, which stops menstrual periods. There are some case reports of dopamine-blocking drugs making OCD worse.

What If I Want to Stop Taking My Medication?

If you are already taking medication, then please don't stop or change the dose on your own. The reason is that you may experience some discontinuation symptoms from an SSRI and it's best to reduce such medication slowly. Always discuss your wishes with your doctor and plan things together. Do not be afraid to ask for a second opinion where necessary. Visiting a specialized centre for the treatment of OCD may be the most effective solution.

What About Electroconvulsive Therapy (ECT) for OCD?

There is no evidence that ECT helps in OCD. It might very occasionally be recommended, however, where the person with OCD has very severe depression that has not responded to medication or a psychological treatment.

What About Brain Surgery?

Very rarely, in people with extremely severe and incapacitating OCD for whom, after several years, both medication and therapy have proved ineffective, is psychosurgery considered an option. Unfortunately, this is too complex a topic to discuss in this book! Professionals do not generally agree on the benefits of neurosurgery for OCD, as it is under-researched.

A significant number of cases of improvement have been reported but there is one (unpublished) trial, comparing surgery against a sham operation, that showed no benefit. In this study, the researchers decided they had not performed a big enough lesion. It is also difficult to interpret older case descriptions of neurosurgery, as it might never have been considered for many of these patients had modern psychological treatments been available.

Neurosurgery is generally safe, but can be followed by some rare complications such as epilepsy, hemorrhage, persistent headaches, or infections. Before even being considered for surgery, you would have to have tried several different SSRIs and clomipramine in the highest doses you could tolerate for at least twelve weeks and in combination with other medications. You would also need to have had two or more trials of intensive CBT at a specialist unit. After surgery you would need further CBT and improvements might then occur over several months. Our personal experience of one patient, with very severe OCD, following neurosurgery was that no benefit resulted. We may be biased, but we would not generally recommend neurosurgery until more and better research has been done. We are not saying that neurosurgery for severe incapacitating OCD should not be investigated as a possibility, but that the evidence so far is difficult to interpret.

Other techniques involving direct stimulation of the brain are also being researched, but these are still experimental. One, known as deep brain stimulation, passes an electric current to electrodes implanted in the brain. Because the stimulator can be switched on and off, the effects are reversible.

In our experience, individuals with OCD raise the possibility of neurosurgery and deep brain stimulation when they are *avoiding* a great deal, and this needs to be the focus of the therapy.

Finding Professional Help

Self-help books may be all that is required for some people with OCD. However, for many individuals we would recommend seeking professional help as well, as this is usually the most effective approach. This involves working with a psychologist, psychiatrist, or nurse therapist who has experience of treating OCD. Treatment helps most people and it rarely makes symptoms worse.

If you are prescribed a dose of medication for OCD, for example fluoxetine, you can virtually guarantee that you will receive that dose of fluoxetine and it will be the same quality whichever pharmacist you go to. Unfortunately, the same cannot always be said for psychological therapy for OCD. This is not meant to scare you, as most people with OCD will obtain excellent therapy. However, many individuals have told us about their experience of therapy, and we know that, sadly, it can be ineffective or even counterproductive. So the first thing to understand is that only one specific type of psychological therapy has been shown to work for OCD: it is called cognitive behavior therapy or CBT.

In choosing a suitable therapist for you, the major danger signs to watch out for are therapists who:

- do not tell you what type of therapy you are receiving;
- keep asking 'How does that make you feel?';
- spend most of the time wanting you to discuss your childhood and the cause of your symptoms;

- do not share their understanding of what maintains your OCD;
- do not problem-solve with you;
- teach you 'better' mental rituals;
- focus only on gradually reducing rituals, without exposure;
- do not negotiate relevant homework between sessions;
- do not monitor your progress in overcoming your symptoms

If you are not sure, ask what type of therapy or counseling you are receiving. There is no evidence that general counseling, psychodynamic therapy, psychoanalytical therapy, hypnotherapy, or transactional analysis are of any benefit in OCD. People may have found such approaches supportive or helpful for other issues, but they are rarely helpful for overcoming OCD. Similarly, beware of a doctor who offers only medication without referring you for CBT, unless there is a very good reason such as severe depression and/or suicidal tendencies.

Fears About Seeking Help

You may have a number of worries about seeking help, such as:

- 'They'll be disgusted by my intrusive thoughts.'
- 'What if it doesn't help?'
- 'It will be too embarrassing to tell them about my rituals.'
- 'They'll think I'm crazy and want to keep me in the hospital.'
- 'What if they pass the information on to social services or my employer?'

If you find it difficult to talk about some of your intrusive thoughts and compulsions, it's usually helpful to say you are embarrassed or ashamed. Remember that intrusive thoughts are normal and any health professional with the slightest experience in OCD will be sensitive to your difficulties. They will not consider you crazy or want to keep you in hospital against your will. Individuals are only assessed for detention in extreme circumstances: if you are a danger to others, for example, or if you are actively suicidal or neglecting yourself badly. The information you give your therapist is kept confidential and cannot be shared with other agencies or your employer without your permission. It does not go on any employment records or to social services. Only in extreme circumstances would a therapist ask someone to assess the impact of OCD on children (see Chapter 8).

Treatment may not help initially, but if nothing is risked, nothing is gained, and your OCD will persist. Furthermore, CBT or medication very rarely makes OCD worse. In teaching centres, you may be asked if a student or trainee may sit in. It is important to continue training others in OCD but you are entitled to refuse without it affecting your treatment.

Getting the Most from CBT

You will get most from CBT if you:

- keep your appointments;
- are honest and open with your therapist;
- tell your therapist if you feel very embarrassed or ashamed about your symptoms;
- attempt the homework agreed between you and your therapist during therapy sessions (having a good relationship with your therapist is important, but adherence to daily homework is the single best predictor of success in therapy);
- act as if the problem is a thinking problem, act against the way you feel, and do the homework you negotiate daily;
- do the homework unconfidently and uncomfortably, tolerate the uncertainty, and continue for long enough – you can never have too much exposure;
- have clear goals that you want to achieve and on which you can agree with your therapist;
- regularly monitor your progress with the therapist using rating scales;

- tape-record the sessions so you can listen to them again;
- give the therapist feedback

Sometimes you may not be ready for CBT, in which case it may be better to return when you feel more committed to change and able to do the homework regularly. Don't believe you are a 'hopeless case' – change, however small, is nearly always possible. You can then build on it. Don't be afraid to seek a second opinion or a referral to a specialist OCD centre.

Types of Professionals Offering Help

A range of mental health professionals will offer help for OCD. Most mental health teams are multidisciplinary, which means that they include people from different professional backgrounds.

- Psychiatrists are medical doctors who specialize in mental disorder. Psychiatrists can prescribe medication for OCD and will probably be more aware of the doses and duration required in OCD than your family doctor. Only some psychiatrists are trained in CBT for OCD.
- Clinical psychologists have a basic training in psychology and have then trained in the clinical application of psychological assessment and therapies. They do not prescribe medication. Many will offer CBT but may not have had specialist training or be experienced in OCD.
- Counseling psychologists have a basic training in psychology and are then trained in counseling. They do not prescribe medication. Some may offer CBT but they have not usually had specialist training or experience in treating OCD.
- Nurse therapists in the UK are originally trained in psychiatric nursing but have specialized in CBT and most will be experienced in treating OCD.
- Psychotherapists and counselors come from a broad range of therapies. Most will listen to you and help you to work

through issues in your life. They do not prescribe medication. They are not usually trained in CBT or experienced with OCD.

It is important to realize that there is nothing to stop anyone calling themselves a counselor or psychotherapist, whether they are properly trained or not. No therapist with a recognized professional qualification is going to mind you asking about their relevant training and qualifications. It is very important that you satisfy yourself about these things, as well as the type of therapy they use and how they learnt about OCD treatment. Ask what experience they have had of treating OCD: for example, the number of patients or clients they have treated. Are they willing to get their hands dirty in exposure tasks? Will they leave their clinic, if necessary, to see you in your home or other relevant location? What proportion of their clients/ patients have OCD and related disorders? What are their expectations for change at the end of therapy, and do these expectations match your goals? Do you get on with the therapist? Of course, you will want someone who is experienced in OCD, but if they are not, then try to judge whether they are willing to learn more.

Complaining

If you want to complain to any professional, think clearly about the nature of the problem – for example, is it the type of treatment, the therapist, the location, or something else?

Are there contributing factors – for example, the personality of your therapist, or are you feeling more depressed? Can you solve it with the therapist or another member of the team? Can you think of possible solutions to discuss with the professional? If the professional is refusing further therapy, listen to their reasoning and write down their explanation. If the reasons are financial (e.g. it costs too much), then don't give up as you may have to persist to get further funding.

Appendix 2

Finding Professional Help in the UK

If you would like professional treatment in the UK, the best place to start is with your family doctor. They may not be highly knowledgeable about OCD but will usually be aware of what services are available locally and will want to help you get better. If you are worried about seeing your family doctor, you can take a relative or friend with you. If you find it difficult to talk to your family doctor, then write a letter. If you think that your doctor does not know about OCD, you can always take along an information leaflet. At your consultation, write down the key points that you want answered. If you have a significant problem, you can always change your family doctor.

The information that you tell your family doctor is confidential and cannot be shared without your permission. If your local service is unable to assist, they may refer you to a national service. Getting referred to a specialist service usually depends upon the support of your local mental health team. Communicate clearly that you need CBT from a practitioner experienced in OCD. Unfortunately, for many public services, you can only be referred to a department and not to a particular individual. Despite this, you may find it helpful to do your own research and find out the names of recommended therapists from your local OCD support group or national charity.

In the UK it is usually quicker to obtain help privately, but private treatment does not mean better treatment. Good and bad treatment can occur in both the public and private sectors. It is best to do your homework and to ask for recommendations from your local OCD support group or national charity (see Appendix 3), which may keep a directory of practitioners. In the UK, you can also try searching for an accredited therapist on the website of the British Association of Behavioral and Cognitive Psychotherapists (www.babcp.com) under 'Find a Therapist'. If you don't have access to the internet, you can buy a copy of their directory (for contact details, see Appendix 3). Not all cognitive behavior therapists bother to become accredited and there are many from psychiatry, psychology, or nursing backgrounds who are excellent therapists. There are also other options such as therapy via a computer such as BT Steps. This is a self-help behavior therapy package which may become more widely available.

Finding Help in the USA

In the USA, too, finding a cognitive behavior therapist experienced in OCD may be difficult and depend on where you live. You could ask for a referral from your family doctor or recommendation from an academic psychiatry or psychology department. The best recommendation may come from your local OCD support group or charities such as the Obsessive Compulsive Foundation or the Anxiety Disorders Association of America. Cognitive behavior therapists are usually members of the Association for the Advancement of Behavior Therapy, which maintains a directory of therapists who can be contacted on their website (see Appendix 3). As in the UK, it is usually quicker to obtain help privately but this does not mean that you will necessarily get better treatment. Good and bad treatment can occur in both the public and private sectors.

Finding Help in the Rest of the World

We have included in Appendix 3 contact details of other national OCD charities around the world, which may be valuable resources in looking for recommended professionals dealing in OCD.

Charities and Support Groups

In addition to professional help, national charities and local support groups can be invaluable. In the UK, for example, support can be obtained from OCD Action, and in the USA from the Obsessive Compulsive Foundation. If you join OCD Action or the OC Foundation, you will receive a newsletter and help put OCD on the national agenda. These national groups also have information on local resources and support groups. Support groups provide a forum for mutual acceptance, understanding, and setting of goals. They will also be able to recommend local therapists or psychiatrists. People new to OCD can talk to others who have learned successful ways of coping. Reading books about OCD and looking at sites on the internet are useful ways of getting further information or support; for some suggested websites see Appendix 3.

The more you know about OCD and the more you can become your own therapist, then the better equipped you will be to overcome it. And if you join one or more of these charities, when you recover from OCD, you can help raise funds for research into better treatments for OCD and campaign for better services and the training of more cognitive behavior therapists in public medicine! Unfortunately, at present many of the charities in OCD are too small to focus enough energy on raising funds for research compared with the big charities in cancer or heart disease; so they need all the new members they can get.

Support Groups, Charities, and Other Resources for Obsessive Compulsive Disorder

Support Groups and Charities

Australia

Anxiety Recovery Centre Victoria
Obsessive Compulsive and Anxiety Disorders Foundation of Victoria (Inc)
42 High Street Road
Ashwood, VIC 3147
Australia
Tel.: OCD and Anxiety Helpline: 03 9886 9377
Tel.: Office Line: 03 9886 9233
Fax: 03 9886 9411
E-mail: arcmail@arcvic.com.au

Obsessive Compulsive Disorders Support Service Inc.
Room 318, Epworth Building
33 Pirie Street
Adelaide, SA 5000
Australia
Tel.: 08 8231 1588
Fax: 08 8221 5159
Website: http://www.givewell.com.au/details_name.asp?txt
Organisation=OCD

Appendix 3

Canada

Obsessive Compulsive Information and Support Centre, Inc.
204–825 Sherbrook Street
Winnipeg
Manitoba R3A 1M5
Canada
Tel.: (204) 942 3331
Fax: (204) 975 3027
E-mail: occmanitoba@shaw.ca
Website: http://www.members.shaw.ca/occmanitoba/

New Zealand

OCD Support Group
PO Box 13
167 Christchurch
New Zealand
E-mail: info@ocd.org.nz
Website: http://www.ocd.org.nz/

South Africa

The South African Depression and Anxiety Group
Suite 219, 2nd Floor
Benmore Gardens
Greystone Drive
Benmore 2010
South Africa
National Helpline: (011) 783 1474/76
E-mail: anxiety@iafrica.com

Mental Health Information Centre
(and MRC Unit on Anxiety Disorders)
PO Box 19063
Tygerberg 7505
South Africa
Tel.: (021) 938 9229
Fax: (021) 931 4172
E-mail: mhic@sun.ac.za
Website: www.mentalhealthsa.co.za

OCD Association of South Africa
PO Box 87127
Houghton 2041
South Africa
Tel.: (011) 786 7030
E-mail: pserebro@iafrica.com

United Kingdom

Anxiety Disorders Conference
Zion Community Resource Centre
339 Stretford Road
Hulme
Manchester M15 4ZY
UK
Tel.: 0161 232 0163
E-mail: registration@anxietyconference.org.uk
Website: http://www.anxietyconference.org.uk

First Steps to Freedom
1 Taylor Close
Kenilworth CV8 2LW
UK
Tel.: 0845 120 2916 (freephone helpline 10 a.m.–10 p.m.)
E-mail: info@first-steps.org
Website: http://www.first-steps.org/

National Phobics Society
Zion Community Resource Centre
339 Stretford Road
Hulme
Manchester M15 4ZY
UK
Tel.: 0870 7700 456
Fax: 0161 227 9862
E-mail: nationalphobic@btconnect.com
Website: http://www.phobics-society.org.uk/contact.php

No Panic
93 Brands Farm Way
Telford TF3 2JQ
UK
Tel.: 01952 590005
Freephone helpline: 0808 808 0545 (10 a.m.–10 p.m.)
E-mail: ceo@nopanic.org.uk
Website: http://www.nopanic.org.uk/

OCD Action
Aberdeen Centre
22–24 Highbury Grove
London N5 2EA
UK
Tel.: 0207 226 4000
Fax: 0207 288 0828
E-mail: info@ocdaction.org.uk
Website: http://www.ocdaction.org.uk/

OCD UK
PO Box 8115
Nottingham NG7 1YT
UK
E-mail: admin@ocduk.org
Website: http://www.ocduk.org/

Triumph over Phobia UK
PO Box 3760
Bath BA2 3WY
UK
Tel.: 0845 600 9601
E-mail: info@triumphoverphobia.org.uk
Website: www.triumphoverphobia.com

United States of America

Anxiety Disorders Association of America
8730 Georgia Avenue, Suite 600
Silver Spring, MD 20910
USA
Tel.: 240 485-1001
Fax: 240 485-1035
Website: http://www.adaa.org/Public/index.cfm

Obsessive Compulsive Foundation
676 State Street
New Haven, CT 06511
USA
Tel.: 203 401 2070
Fax: 203 401 2076
E-mail: info@ocfoundation.org
Website: http://www.ocfoundation.org/

Professional Groups

Association for Advancement of Behavior Therapy
305 7th Avenue
16th Floor
New York, NY 10001
USA
Tel.: 212 647 1890
Fax: 212 647 1865
Website: http://www.aabt.org

The Australian Association for Cognitive and Behavior Therapy
Website: http://www.aacbt.org/

British Association for Behavioural and Cognitive Psychotherapies (BABCP)
BABCP General Office
The Globe Centre
PO Box 9
Accrington BB5 OXB
UK
Tel.: 01254 875 277
Fax: 01254 239 114
E-mail: babcp@babcp.com
Website: http://www.babcp.org.uk/

The European Association for Behavioral and Cognitive Therapists has a list of member associations
Website: http://www.eabct.com

Websites and Bulletin Boards for OCD Sufferers

http://www.angelfire.com/il/TeenOCD/
http://www.ocdaction.org.uk/forum/
http://www.ocduk.org/forums/
http://www.geonius.com/ocd/
http://groups.google.com/groups?oi=djq&as_ugroup=alt.support.ocd
http://www.healthyplace.com/Communities/ocd/sandra/
http://understanding_ocd.tripod.com/index.html

Self-Assessment Forms

Obsessive Compulsive Inventory (OCI)

This questionnaire has been reproduced by kind permission of Paul Salkovskis. It was first published in Foa, E.B., Kozak, M.J., Salkovskis, P., Coles, M.E. & Amir, N. 'The Obsessive Compulsive Inventory', *Psychological Assessment*, 10, (1998), 206–14.

The following statements refer to experiences that many people have in their everyday lives. Circle the number that best describes **HOW MUCH** that experience has **DISTRESSED** or **BOTHERED you during the PAST MONTH**. The numbers refer to the following verbal labels:

0	1	2	3	4
Not at all	A little	Moderately	A lot	Extremely

1. I think contact with bodily secretions (perspiration, saliva, blood, urine, etc.) may contaminate my clothes or somehow harm me.   0 1 2 3 4

2. I ask people to repeat things to me several times, even though I understood them the first time.   0 1 2 3 4

3. I need things to be arranged in a particular order.   0   1   2   3   4

4. After doing something carefully, I still have the impression that I have not finished it.   0   1   2   3   4

5. Before going to sleep I have to do certain things in a certain way.   0   1   2   3   4

6. I am upset by unpleasant thoughts that come into my mind against my will.   0   1   2   3   4

7. I collect things I don't need.   0   1   2   3   4

8. I feel that I must repeat certain words or phrases in my mind in order to wipe out bad thoughts, feelings, or actions.   0   1   2   3   4

9. I wash and clean obsessively.   0   1   2   3   4

10. I check things more often than necessary.   0   1   2   3   4

11. I feel that there are good and bad numbers.   0   1   2   3   4

12. I am afraid of impulsively doing embarrassing or harmful things.   0   1   2   3   4

13. I repeatedly check anything which might cause a fire.   0   1   2   3   4

14. I have thoughts of hurting someone and not knowing it.   0   1   2   3   4

15. I repeatedly check doors, windows, drawers, etc.   0   1   2   3   4

16. I have saved up so many things that they get in the way.   0   1   2   3   4

17. I get upset at the sight of knives, scissors, and other sharp objects in case I lose control with them.   0   1   2   3   4

18. I avoid using public toilets because I am afraid of disease or contamination.   0   1   2   3   4

19.	After I have done things, I have persistent doubts about whether I really did them.	0	1	2	3	4
20.	I repeatedly check gas and water taps and light switches after turning them off.	0	1	2	3	4
21.	I am excessively concerned with cleanliness.	0	1	2	3	4
22.	I get upset if objects are not arranged properly.	0	1	2	3	4
23.	I feel I have to repeat certain numbers.	0	1	2	3	4
24.	Even when I do something very carefully I feel that it is not quite right.	0	1	2	3	4
25.	I frequently get nasty thoughts and have difficulty in getting rid of them.	0	1	2	3	4
26.	I find it difficult to touch an object when I know it has been touched by strangers or certain people.	0	1	2	3	4
27.	I get upset if others change the way I have arranged things.	0	1	2	3	4
28.	I keep on checking forms or other things I have written.	0	1	2	3	4
29.	I feel compelled to count while I am doing things.	0	1	2	3	4
30.	I go back to places to make sure that I have not harmed anyone.	0	1	2	3	4
31.	I feel obliged to follow a particular order in dressing, undressing, and washing myself.	0	1	2	3	4
32.	I find it difficult to control my own thoughts.	0	1	2	3	4

33. I have to mentally review past events, conversations, and actions to make sure that I didn't do something wrong.   0 1 2 3 4

34. I find it difficult to touch waste or dirty things.   0 1 2 3 4

35. Unpleasant thoughts come into my mind against my will and I cannot get rid of them.   0 1 2 3 4

36. I avoid throwing things away because I am afraid I might need them later.   0 1 2 3 4

37. I sometimes have to wash or clean myself simply because I feel contaminated.   0 1 2 3 4

38. I have thoughts that I might want to harm myself or others.   0 1 2 3 4

39. I need to pray to cancel bad thoughts or feelings.   0 1 2 3 4

40. I get behind in my work because I repeat things over and over again.   0 1 2 3 4

41. I have to do things over and over again until it feels right.   0 1 2 3 4

42. I wash my hands more often and longer than necessary.   0 1 2 3 4

Appendix 4

Scoring Instructions

The OCI, contains forty-two statements and seven subscales. Statements are summed to produce a total score and seven subscale scores. If you score 21 or above then you are probably suffering from OCD.

Subscales

Factor 1 (Washing)
Statement 1
Statement 9
Statement 18
Statement 21
Statement 26
Statement 34
Statement 37
Statement 42

Factor 2 (Checking)
Statement 2
Statement 5
Statement 10
Statement 13
Statement 15
Statement 20
Statement 28
Statement 30
Statement 40

Factor 3 (Doubting)
Statement 4
Statement 19
Statement 24

Factor 4 (Ordering)
Statement 3
Statement 22
Statement 27
Statement 31
Statement 41

Factor 5 (Obsessing)
Statement 6
Statement 12
Statement 14
Statement 17
Statement 25
Statement 32
Statement 35
Statement 38

Factor 6 (Hoarding)
Statement 7
Statement 16
Statement 36

Factor 7 (Neutralizing)
Statement 8
Statement 11
Statement 23
Statement 29
Statement 33
Statement 39

Grand Total = _____

Appendix 4

Disability Ratings

Please rate how far your problems have impaired you in various areas of your life *in the past week*. Circle the number that best describes your impairment.

(a) Because of the problems, my *ability* to **WORK** or **STUDY** or my role as a **HOMEMAKER** is impaired. (Note: please rate this even if you are not currently working; you are rating your *ability* to work or study):

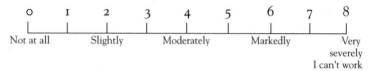

(b) Because of the problems, my **HOME MANAGEMENT** (e.g. cleaning, shopping, cooking, looking after my home or children, paying bills, etc.) is impaired:

(c) Because of the problems, my **SOCIAL LIFE** activities (*with other people*, e.g. parties, bars, outings, visits, dating, home entertainment, etc.) are impaired:

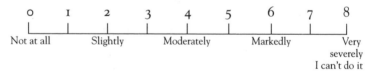

(d) Because of the problems, my **PRIVATE LEISURE** activities (*done alone*, e.g. reading, gardening, hobbies, walking alone, etc.) are impaired:

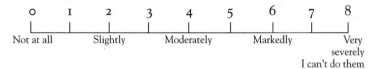

| 0 | 1 | 2 | 3 | 4 | 5 | 6 | 7 | 8 |

Not at all   Slightly   Moderately   Markedly   Very severely
I can't do them

(e) Because of the problems, my **GENERAL RELATION-SHIP WITH MY PARTNER** (e.g. affectionate feelings, number of arguments, enjoyment of activities together, etc.) is impaired:

| 0 | 1 | 2 | 3 | 4 | 5 | 6 | 7 | 8 |

Not at all   Slightly   Moderately   Markedly   Very severely

(f) Because of the problems, my **SEXUAL RELATIONSHIP** (enjoyment of sex, frequency of sexual activity, etc.) is impaired:

| 0 | 1 | 2 | 3 | 4 | 5 | 6 | 7 | 8 |

Not at all   Slightly   Moderately   Markedly   Very severely

Appendix 4

Saving Inventory Revised

Copied with permission from R. O. Frost, G. Steketee, and J. Grisham, 'Measurement of Compulsive Hoarding: Saving Inventory Revised', *Behaviour Research and Therapy*, 42, (2004) 1163–82.

This inventory is for anyone who has OCD hoarding. Circle the response that is most appropriate for each of the following questions.

1 **To what extent do you have difficulty throwing things away?**
   0 = Not at all
   1 = To a mild extent
   2 = To a moderate extent
   3 = To a considerable extent
   4 = Very much so
2 **How distressing do you find the task of throwing things away?**
   0 = No distress
   1 = Mild distress
   2 = Moderate distress
   3 = Severe distress
   4 = Extreme distress
3 **To what extent do you have so many things that your room(s) are cluttered?**
   0 = Not at all
   1 = To a mild extent
   2 = To a moderate extent
   3 = To a considerable extent
   4 = Very much so
4 **How often do you avoid trying to discard possessions because it is too stressful or time-consuming?**
   0 = Never avoid, easily able to discard items
   1 = Rarely avoid, can discard with little difficulty
   2 = Sometimes avoid

3 = Frequently avoid, can discard items occasionally

4 = Almost always avoid, rarely able to discard items

5 **How distressed or uncomfortable would you feel if you could not acquire something you wanted?**

0 = Not at all

1 = Mild, only slightly anxious

2 = Moderate, distress would mount but remain manageable

3 = Severe, prominent and very disturbing increase in distress

4 = Extreme, incapacitating discomfort from any such effort

6 **How much of the living area in your home is cluttered with possessions? (Consider the amount of clutter in your kitchen, living room, dining room, hallways, bedrooms, bathrooms, or other rooms.)**

0 = None of the living area is cluttered

1 = Some of the living area is cluttered

2 = Much of the living area is cluttered

3 = Most of the living area is cluttered

4 = All or almost all of the living area is cluttered

7 **How much does the clutter in your home interfere with your social, work, or everyday functioning? Think about things that you don't do because of clutter.**

0 = Not at all

1 = Mild, slight interference, but overall functioning not impaired

2 = Moderate, definite interference, but still manageable

3 = Severe, causes substantial interference

4 = Extreme, incapacitating

8 **How often do you feel compelled to acquire something you see (e.g. when shopping or offered free things)?**

0 = Never feel compelled

1 = Rarely feel compelled

2 = Sometimes feel compelled

3 = Frequently feel compelled

4 = Almost always feel compelled

9 **How strong is your urge to buy or acquire free things for which you have no immediate use?**
   0 = Urge is not at all strong
   1 = Mild urge
   2 = Moderate urge
   3 = Strong urge
   4 = Very strong urge

10 **How much control do you have over your urges to acquire possessions?**
   0 = Complete control
   1 = Much control, usually able to control urges to acquire
   2 = Some control, can control urges to acquire only with difficulty
   3 = Little control, can only delay urges to acquire only with great difficulty
   4 = No control, unable to stop urges to acquire possessions

11 **How often do you decide to keep things you do not need and have little space for?**
   0 = Never keep such things
   1 = Rarely keep such things
   2 = Occasionally keep such things
   3 = Frequently keep such things
   4 = Almost always keep such things

12 **To what extent does clutter prevent you from using parts of your home?**
   0 = All parts of the home are usable
   1 = A few parts of the home are not usable
   2 = Some parts of the home are not usable
   3 = Many parts of the home are not usable
   4 = Nearly all parts of the home are not usable

13 **To what extent does the clutter in your home cause you distress?**
   0 = No feelings of distress or discomfort
   1 = Mild feelings of distress or discomfort
   2 = Moderate feelings of distress or discomfort
   3 = Severe feelings of distress or discomfort
   4 = Extreme feelings of distress or discomfort

14 **How frequently does the clutter in your home prevent you from inviting people to visit?**
   0 = Not at all
   1 = Rarely
   2 = Sometimes
   3 = Frequently
   4 = Very often or nearly always

15 **How often do you actually buy (or acquire for free) things for which you have no immediate use or need?**
   0 = Never
   1 = Rarely
   2 = Sometimes
   3 = Frequently
   4 = Almost always

16 **How strong is your urge to save something you may never use?**
   0 = Not at all strong
   1 = Mild urge
   2 = Moderate urge
   3 = Strong urge
   4 = Very strong urge

17 **How much control do you have over your urges to save possessions?**
   0 = Complete control
   1 = Much control, usually able to control urges to save
   2 = Some control, can control urges to save only with difficulty
   3 = Little control, can only stop urges with great difficulty
   4 = No control, unable to stop urges to save possessions

18 **How much of your home is difficult to walk through because of clutter?**
   0 = None of it is difficult to walk through
   1 = Some of it is difficult to walk through
   2 = Much of it is difficult to walk through
   3 = Most of it is difficult to walk through
   4 = All or nearly all of it is difficult to walk through

19 **How upset or distressed do you feel about your acquiring habits?**
   0 = Not at all upset
   1 = Mildly upset
   2 = Moderately upset
   3 = Severely upset
   4 = Extreme embarrassment

20 **To what extent does the clutter in your home prevent you from using parts of your home for their intended purpose? For example, cooking, using furniture, washing dishes, cleaning.**
   0 = Never
   1 = Rarely
   2 = Sometimes
   3 = Frequently
   4 = Very frequently or almost all the time

21 **To what extent do you feel unable to control the clutter in your home?**
   0 = Not at all
   1 = To a mild extent
   2 = To a moderate extent
   3 = To a considerable extent
   4 = Very much so

22 **To what extent has your saving or compulsive buying resulted in financial difficulties for you?**
   0 = Not at all
   1 = A little financial difficulty
   2 = Some financial difficulty
   3 = Quite a lot of financial difficulty
   4 = An extreme amount of financial difficultly

23 **How often are you unable to discard a possession you would like to get rid of?**
   0 = Never have a problem discarding possessions
   1 = Rarely
   2 = Occasionally
   3 = Frequently
   4 = Almost always unable to discard possession

Appendix 4

Scoring Instructions

The Saving Inventory Revised contains 23 items and 3 sub-scales. Items are summed to produce a total score and three sub-scale scores. The higher the score the more severe the problem.

Factor 1 (Excessive Clutter)	Factor 2 (Difficulty Discarding)	Factor 3 (Excessive acquisition)
Item 3	Item 1	Item 5
Item 6	Item 2	Item 8
Item 7	Item 4	Item 9
Item 12	Item 11	Item 10
Item 13	Item 16	Item 15
Item 14	Item 17	Item 19
Item 18	Item 23	Item 22
Item 20	Item 21	

Appendix 4

Yale–Brown Obsessive Compulsive Symptoms Checklist

Reproduced with permission from W. K. Goodman, L. H. Price, S. A. Rasmussen, et al., 'The Yale–Brown Obsessive Compulsive Scale: I. Development, Use, and Reliability', *Archives of General Psychiatry*, 46, (1989), 1006–11.

Obsessions

An obsession is defined as a frequent and persistent thought, image, or urge that is unwanted and just pops into your mind and provokes distress, and that you cannot easily dismiss. Tick those obsessions that are most distressing and handicapping as the basis for listing your target obsessions for rating.

1 *Aggression or injurious obsessions*

I fear harming myself (e.g. from a knife or piece of glass)	
I fear harming other people (e.g. poisoning or hitting a baby, pushing someone in front of a train, hurting someone's feelings)	
I have violent or horrific images in my mind (e.g. murder, carnage)	
I fear blurting out or writing obscenities or insults (especially in a public situation)	
I fear doing something else embarrassing or appearing foolish in a social situation	
I fear I will act upon on an unwanted impulse (e.g. drive a car into a bicyclist or stab a friend)	
I fear that I will harm others by not being careful enough (e.g. hitting someone in a car accident without realizing it)	
I fear I will steal things (or 'cheat' a cashier at a cash register)	
I fear I will be responsible for something else terrible happening by not being careful enough (e.g. fire, burglary, gas explosion)	

2 *Contamination obsessions*

I am concerned or disgusted with my own or others' bodily waste or secretions (e.g. urine, excrement, saliva, semen, vaginal fluids)	
I am concerned with dirt or germs (e.g. from shaking hands, touching door handles or sitting in a certain chair)	
I am excessively concerned with environmental contaminants (e.g. asbestos, radiation, toxic waste sites)	
I am excessively concerned with household chemicals or cleansers (e.g. kitchen or bathroom cleansers or solvents, or insect sprays)	
I am excessively concerned with contamination from touching animals (e.g. dog, cat, or other animal or insects)	
I am bothered by sticky substances or residues (e.g. tape that might trap contaminants)	
I am concerned that I will get ill following contamination	
I am concerned that I will get others ill by spreading contaminants	
I am concerned with disease (e.g. AIDS, hepatitis, STDs)	
I have no concern with consequences of contamination other than how it might feel	

3 *Sexual obsessions*

I have forbidden or perverse sexual thoughts, images, or impulses	
I have sexual thoughts or impulses involving children or incest	
I have sexual thoughts or impulses involving homosexuality	
I have thoughts of inappropriate or aggressive sexual behavior towards others	

4 *Hoarding/saving obsessions*

I have urges to hoard or save things (e.g. magazines, papers, household waste)	

5 *Religious obsessions (scrupulosity)*

I am concerned with sacrilege and blasphemy or sinfulness	
I am excessively concerned with right and wrong or morality	
I have other religious images or thoughts about the devil	
I have other religious obsessions	

6 *Obsession with need for symmetry*

I feel I have to have objects placed symmetrically or 'just so'	

7 *Miscellaneous obsessions*

I feel I need to know or remember certain things	
I fear saying certain words	
I fear not saying just the right thing	
I fear losing things	
I am bothered by intrusive (neutral) mental images	
I am bothered by intrusive nonsense sounds, words, or music	
I am bothered by certain sounds or noises	
I have lucky and unlucky numbers	
Certain colours have special significance for me	
I have superstitious fears	
I fear making mistakes	

8 *Somatic (body) obsessions*

I am excessively concerned with illness or disease	
I am excessively concerned with a part of my body or an aspect of my appearance which I consider defective or ugly	

Compulsions

Compulsions (or rituals) are defined as acts that are repeated with the aim of reducing harm and that a person feels driven to perform. Tick those compulsions that are the most distressing and handicapping as the basis for listing your target compulsions for rating on the following scale.

9 Cleaning/washing compulsions

I wash my hands excessively or in a ritualized way	
I have excessive or ritualized showering or bathing	
I excessively brush my teeth	
I excessively groom or shave	
I have an excessive toilet routine	
I excessively clean household items or other objects	
I do other things like use special cleansers to remove contact from 'contaminants'	
I use other measures to prevent or remove contact with 'contaminants'	

10 Checking compulsions

I excessively check that electricity switches/appliances are turned off	
I excessively check that gas taps are turned off	
I excessively check that doors and windows are locked	
I excessively check that water taps are off	
I excessively check that I did not or will not harm others	
I excessively check that I did not or will not harm myself	
I excessively check that nothing terrible happened	
I excessively check that I did not make a mistake	
I excessively check some aspect of my body because of my physical condition	

11 Repeating rituals

I have to reread or rewrite things	
I need to repeat routine activities (e.g. crossing thresholds, going in/out, up/down from chair, tying shoes, dressing/undressing)	

12 *Counting compulsions*

I have to count a number of times	

13 *Ordering*

I have to have objects in order or arranged 'just so'	

14 *Hoarding/collecting compulsions*

I hoard newspapers or useless objects or sort through waste (this does not include hobbies or collections of objects for monetary or sentimental value)	

15 *Miscellaneous compulsions*

I have mental rituals (other than checking or counting)	
I make excessive lists	
I need to tell, ask, or confess things	
I need to touch, tap, or rub	
I use measures (other than checking) to prevent harm to myself	
I use measures (other than checking) to prevent harm to others	
I use measures to prevent terrible consequences	
I have rituals involving blinking or staring	
I have ritualized eating behaviors (which are not part of OCD)	
I have superstitious behaviors	
I pull my hairs out (from scalp, eyebrows, eyelashes, pubic hair) (trichotillomania)	
I damage or mutilate myself (such as picking my face)	
I seek repeated reassurance from others	

Target Symptom List for Rating on the YBOCS

OBSESSIONS

1
_____

2
_____

3
_____

4
_____

5
_____

COMPULSIONS

1
_____

2
_____

3
_____

4
_____

5
_____

AVOIDANCE

1
_____

2
_____

3
_____

4
_____

5
_____

Yale–Brown Obsessive Compulsive Scale (Self-Report)

This is a self-report version of the YBOCS Scale originally devised by W. K. Goodman, L. H. Price, S. A. Rasmussen et al., 'The Yale–Brown Obsessive Compulsive Scale: I. Development, Use, and Reliability', *Archives of General Psychiatry*, 46, (1989), 1006–11.

The self-report version was developed by R. Rosenfeld, R. Dar, D. Anderson, K. A. Kobak, and J. H. Greist, 'A Computer-Administered Version of the Yale–Brown Obsessive-Compulsive Scale', *Psychological Assessment*, 4, (1992), 329–32.

Make a list of the main obsessions you checked on the YBOCS Symptom Checklist to help you answer the first five questions. Please think about the last seven days (including today), and check one answer for each question.

1 How much of your time is preoccupied by obsessional thoughts? How frequently do the obsessive thoughts occur?

__0 = None*

__1 = Less than 1 hour per day, or occasional intrusions (occur no more than 8 times a day)

__2 = 1 to 3 hours per day, or frequent intrusions (occur more than 8 times a day, but most hours of the day are free of obsessions)

__3 = More than 3 hours and up to 8 hours per day, or very frequent intrusions (occur more than 8 times a day during most hours of the day)

__4 = More than 8 hours per day, or near-constant intrusions (too numerous to count, and an hour rarely passes without several obsessions occurring)

If you checked this answer, also check 0 for questions 2, 3, 4, and 5, and proceed to question 6.

2 How much do your obsessive thoughts interfere with your social or work functioning? (If you are currently not working, please think about how much the obsessions interfere with your everyday activities.) (In answering the question, please consider whether there is anything that you don't do, or that you do less, because of the obsessions.)

__0 = No interference

__1 = Mild, slight interference with social and or occupational activities, but overall performance not impaired

__2 = Moderate, definite interference with social or occupational performance, but still manageable

__3 = Severe interference, causes substantial impairment in social and occupational performance

__4 = Extreme, incapacitating interference

3 How much distress do your obsessional thoughts cause you?

__0 = None

__1 = Mild, infrequent, and not too disturbing distress

__2 = Moderate, frequent, and disturbing distress, but still manageable

__3 = Severe, very frequent, and very disturbing distress

__4 = Extreme, near-constant, and disabling distress

4 How often do you try to disregard these thoughts and let them pass naturally through your mind? (Here we are not interested in knowing how successful you are in disregarding your thoughts, but only in how much or how often you try to do so.)

__0 = I always let the obsessions pass naturally through my mind

__1 = I disregard them most of time (i.e. more than half the time)

__2 = I make some effort to disregard the obsessions

__3 = I rarely disregard the obsessions

__4 = I never try to disregard the obsessions

5 How *successful* are you in disregarding your obsessive thinking? (*Note:* Do not include here obsessions stopped by doing compulsions.)

__0 = Always successful in disregarding obsessions
__1 = Usually successful in disregarding obsessions
__2 = Sometimes successful in disregarding obsessions
__3 = Rarely successful in disregarding obsessions
__4 = I am rarely able to disregard the obsessions even momentarily

Compulsions

Compulsions are behaviors or acts that you feel driven to perform although you may recognize them as senseless or excessive. At times, you may try to resist doing them, but this may prove difficult. You may experience anxiety that does not diminish until the behavior is completed.

List the main compulsions you checked on the YBOCS Symptoms Checklist to help you answer these five questions. Please think about the last seven days (including today), and check one answer for each question.

6 How much time do you spend performing compulsive behavior? How frequently do you perform compulsions? (If your rituals involve daily living activities, please consider how much longer it takes you to complete routine activities because of your rituals.)

__0 = None*
__1 = Less than 1 hour per day is spent performing compulsions or occasional performance of compulsive behaviors (no more than 8 times a day)
__2 = 1 to 3 hours per day are spent performing compulsions, or frequent performance of compulsive behaviors (more than 8 times a day and during most hours of the day)

__3 = More than 3 hours and up to 8 hours per day are spent performing compulsions, or very frequent intrusions (occur more than 8 times a day during most hours of the day)

__4 = More than 8 hours per day, or near-constant intrusions (too numerous to count, and an hour rarely passes without several obsessions occurring)

If you checked this answer, also check 0 for questions 7, 8, 9, and 10.

7 How much do your compulsive behaviors interfere with your social or work functioning? (If you are not currently working, please think about your everyday activities.)

__0 = No interference

__1 = Mild, slight interference with social or occupational activities, but overall performance not impaired

__2 = Moderate, definite interference with social or occupational performance, but still manageable

__3 = Severe interference, substantial impairment in social or occupational performance

__4 = Extreme, incapacitating interference

8 How would you feel if prevented from performing your compulsion(s)? How anxious would you become?

__0 = Not at all anxious if compulsions prevented

__1 = Only slightly anxious if compulsions prevented

__2 = Anxiety would mount but remain manageable if compulsions prevented

__3 = Prominent and very disturbing increase in anxiety if compulsions interrupted

__4 = Extreme, incapacitating anxiety from any intervention aimed at reducing the compulsions

9 How much of an effort do you make to resist the compulsions? Or how often do you try to stop the compulsions? (Rate only how often or how much you try to resist your compulsions, not how successful you actually are in stopping them.)

__0 = I make an effort always to resist (or the symptoms are so minimal that there is no need to actively resist them)

__1 = I try to resist most of the time (i.e. more than half the time)

__2 = I make some effort to resist

__3 = I yield to almost all compulsions without attempting to control them, but I do so with some reluctance

__4 = I completely and willingly yield to all compulsions

10 How much control do you have over the compulsive behavior? How successful are you in stopping the ritual(s)? (If you rarely try to resist, please think about those rare occasions in which you did *try* to stop the compulsions, in order to answer this question.)

__0 = I have complete control

__1 = Usually I can stop compulsions or rituals with some effort and willpower

__2 = Sometimes I can stop compulsive behavior but only with difficulty

__3 = I can only delay the compulsive behavior, but eventually it must be carried to completion

__4 = I am rarely able to delay performing the compulsive behavior even momentarily

Scoring Instructions
Add up your scores for questions 1 to 10, using the numbers next to the answer you checked for each question.

Appendix 4

Interpreting the Results

YBOCS Score	Severity Range
Less than 10	Very mild OCD
10–15	Mild OCD Symptoms
16–25	Moderate OCD symptoms
More than 25	Severe OCD symptoms

Responsibility Interpretations Scale (RIS)

Adapted with permission from P. M. Salkovskis, A. L. Wroe, A. Gledhill, N. Morrison, E. Forrester, C. Richards, M. Reynolds, and S. Thorpe (2000), 'Responsibility Attitudes and Interpretations are Characteristic of Obsessive Compulsive Disorder', *Behaviour Research and Therapy*, 38(4), (2002), 347–72.

We are interested in your reaction to intrusive thoughts that you have had in the *last two weeks*.

Intrusive thoughts are thoughts that suddenly enter your mind, may interrupt what you are thinking or doing, and tend to recur on separate occasions. They may occur in the form of words, a mental image, or an impulse (a sudden urge to carry out some action). We are interested in those intrusive thoughts that are unacceptable. Research has shown that most people have experienced such thoughts, which they find unacceptable in some way, at some time in their lives to a greater or lesser degree, so there is nothing unusual about this.

Some examples of unpleasant intrusive thoughts are:

- Repeated image of attacking someone.
- Suddenly thinking that your hands are dirty and you may cause contamination.
- Suddenly thinking you might not have turned off the gas, or that you left the door unlocked.
- Repeated senseless images of harm coming to someone you love.
- Repeated urge to attack or harm somebody (even though you would never do this).

These are just a few examples of intrusions to give you some idea of what we are looking at; people vary tremendously in the type of thoughts that they have.

IMPORTANT: Think of intrusions of the type described above that you have had in the last two weeks, and answer the following questions with these intrusions in mind. The questions do NOT relate to all thoughts but specifically to your negative intrusions.

Please write down intrusive thoughts that you have had in the last two weeks.

This questionnaire has two parts.

Below are some ideas that may go through your mind *when you are bothered by worrying intrusive thoughts which you know are probably senseless or unrealistic*. Think of times when you were bothered by intrusive thoughts, impulses, and images *in the last two weeks*.

A. Frequency

Indicate *how often* each of the ideas listed below occurred *when you were bothered by these intrusive thoughts, impulses or images*; circle the digit that most accurately describes the frequency of the occurrence of the ideas using the following scale:

Over the LAST TWO WEEKS:

0 Idea never occurred
1 Idea rarely occurred
2 Idea occurred during about half of the times when I had worrying intrusive thoughts
3 Idea usually occurred
4 Idea always occurred when I had worrying intrusive thoughts

Section F1

If I don't resist these thoughts it means I am being irresponsible	0	1	2	3	4
I could be responsible for serious harm	0	1	2	3	4
I cannot take the risk of this thought coming true	0	1	2	3	4

If I don't act now then something terrible will happen and it will be my fault	0 1 2 3 4
I need to be certain something awful won't happen	0 1 2 3 4
I shouldn't be thinking this type of thing	0 1 2 3 4
It would be irresponsible to ignore these thoughts	0 1 2 3 4
I'll feel awful unless I do something about this thought	0 1 2 3 4
Because I've thought of bad things happening then I must act to prevent them	0 1 2 3 4
Since I've thought of this I must want it to happen	0 1 2 3 4
Now I've thought of things which could go wrong I have a responsibility to make sure I don't let them happen	0 1 2 3 4
Thinking this could make it happen	0 1 2 3 4
I must regain control of my thoughts	0 1 2 3 4
This could be an omen	0 1 2 3 4
It's wrong to ignore these thoughts	0 1 2 3 4
Because these thoughts come from my own mind, I must want to have them	0 1 2 3 4

Now rate these items:

Section F2

Thoughts can NOT make things happen	0 1 2 3 4
This is just a thought so it doesn't matter	0 1 2 3 4
Thinking of something happening doesn't make me responsible for whether it happens	0 1 2 3 4

There's nothing wrong with letting such thoughts come and go naturally	0	1	2	3	4
Everybody has horrible thoughts sometimes, so I don't need to worry about this one	0	1	2	3	4
Having this thought doesn't mean I have to do anything about it	0	1	2	3	4

B. Belief

Over the last two weeks, when you were bothered by these worrying intrusive thoughts, how much did you believe each of these ideas to be true? Rate the belief you had of these ideas *when you had the intrusions*, using the following scale; mark the point on the line that most accurately applies to your belief at the time of the intrusion.

Section B1

I did not believe this idea at all

I was completely convinced this idea was true

If I don't resist these thoughts it means I am being irresponsible

0	10	20	30	40	50	60	70	80	90	100

I could be responsible for serious harm

0	10	20	30	40	50	60	70	80	90	100

I cannot take the risk of this thought coming true

0	10	20	30	40	50	60	70	80	90	100

If I don't act now then something terrible will happen and it will be my fault

0	10	20	30	40	50	60	70	80	90	100

I need to be certain something awful won't happen

0	10	20	30	40	50	60	70	80	90	100

I should not be thinking this kind of thing

0	10	20	30	40	50	60	70	80	90	100

It would be irresponsible to ignore these thoughts

0	10	20	30	40	50	60	70	80	90	100

I'll feel awful unless I do something about this thought

0	10	20	30	40	50	60	70	80	90	100

Because I've thought about bad things happening then I must act to prevent them

0	10	20	30	40	50	60	70	80	90	100

Since I've had this thought I must want it to happen

0	10	20	30	40	50	60	70	80	90	100

Now I've thought of bad things which could go wrong I have a responsibility to make sure I don't let them happen

0	10	20	30	40	50	60	70	80	90	100

Thinking this could make it happen

0	10	20	30	40	50	60	70	80	90	100

I must regain control of these thoughts

0	10	20	30	40	50	60	70	80	90	100

This could be an omen

0	10	20	30	40	50	60	70	80	90	100

It's wrong to ignore these thoughts

0	10	20	30	40	50	60	70	80	90	100

Because these thoughts come from my mind, I must want to have them

0	10	20	30	40	50	60	70	80	90	100

Section B2

Now rate these items:

I did not believe this idea at all								I was completely convinced this idea was true

Thoughts can NOT make things happen

0	10	20	30	40	50	60	70	80	90	100

This is just a thought so it doesn't matter

0	10	20	30	40	50	60	70	80	90	100

Thinking of something happening doesn't make me responsible for whether it happens

0	10	20	30	40	50	60	70	80	90	100

There's nothing wrong with letting thoughts like this come and go naturally

0	10	20	30	40	50	60	70	80	90	100

Everybody has horrible thoughts sometimes, so I don't need to worry about this one

0	10	20	30	40	50	60	70	80	90	100

Having this thought doesn't mean I have to do anything about it

0	10	20	30	40	50	60	70	80	90	100

Appendix 4

Scoring the RIS

Four scores are derived from the RIS:

- Section F1 provides a frequency score relating to high-responsibility items. This is obtained by calculating the average for these 16 statements (where *never occurred* = 0 and *always occurred* = 4).
- Section F2 provides a frequency score relating to low-responsibility items. Calculate the average for these six statements.
- Section B1 provides a percentage belief rating for each high-responsibility idea (where 0 = *I did not believe this idea at all* and 100 = *I was completely convinced this idea was true*). The score is obtained by calculating the average rating for these 16 statements.
- Section B2 provides a percentage belief rating scale for each low-responsibility idea. The score is obtained by calculating the average rating for these six statements.

Scores

F1	F2	B1	B2

RESPONSIBILITY ATTITUDES SCALE (RAS)

(Reproduced with permission from P. M. Salkovskis, A. L. Wroe, A. Gledhill, N. Morrison, E. Forrester, C. Richards, M. Reynolds, S. Thorpe. 'Responsibility attitudes and interpretations are characteristic of obsessive compulsive disorder', *Behavior Research and Therapy*, 38(4), (2000), 347–372.

This questionnaire lists different attitudes or beliefs which people sometimes hold. Read each statement carefully and decide how much you agree or disagree with it. For each of the attitudes, show your answer by putting a circle round the words which BEST DESCRIBE HOW YOU THINK. Be sure to choose only one answer for each attitude. Because people are different, there is no right or wrong answer to these statements.

To decide whether a given attitude is typical of your way of looking at things, simply keep in mind what you are like MOST OF THE TIME.

1. I often feel responsible for things which go wrong.

| TOTALLY AGREE | AGREE VERY MUCH | AGREE SLIGHTLY | NEUTRAL | DISAGREE SLIGHTLY | DISAGREE VERY MUCH | TOTALLY DISAGREE |

2. If I don't act when I can foresee danger, then I am to blame for any consequences if it happens.

| TOTALLY AGREE | AGREE VERY MUCH | AGREE SLIGHTLY | NEUTRAL | DISAGREE SLIGHTLY | DISAGREE VERY MUCH | TOTALLY DISAGREE |

3. I am too sensitive to feeling responsible for things going wrong.

| TOTALLY AGREE | AGREE VERY MUCH | AGREE SLIGHTLY | NEUTRAL | DISAGREE SLIGHTLY | DISAGREE VERY MUCH | TOTALLY DISAGREE |

4. If I think bad things, this is as bad as *doing* bad things.

| TOTALLY AGREE | AGREE VERY MUCH | AGREE SLIGHTLY | NEUTRAL | DISAGREE SLIGHTLY | DISAGREE VERY MUCH | TOTALLY DISAGREE |

5. I worry a great deal about the effects of things which I do or don't do.

TOTALLY AGREE	AGREE VERY MUCH	AGREE SLIGHTLY	NEUTRAL	DISAGREE SLIGHTLY	DISAGREE VERY MUCH	TOTALLY DISAGREE

6. To me, not acting to prevent danger is as bad as causing a disaster.

TOTALLY AGREE	AGREE VERY MUCH	AGREE SLIGHTLY	NEUTRAL	DISAGREE SLIGHTLY	DISAGREE VERY MUCH	TOTALLY DISAGREE

7. If I know that harm is possible, I should always try to prevent it; however unlikely it seems.

TOTALLY AGREE	AGREE VERY MUCH	AGREE SLIGHTLY	NEUTRAL	DISAGREE SLIGHTLY	DISAGREE VERY MUCH	TOTALLY DISAGREE

8. I must always think through the consequences of even the smallest actions.

TOTALLY AGREE	AGREE VERY MUCH	AGREE SLIGHTLY	NEUTRAL	DISAGREE SLIGHTLY	DISAGREE VERY MUCH	TOTALLY DISAGREE

9. I often take responsibility for things which other people don't think are my fault.

TOTALLY AGREE	AGREE VERY MUCH	AGREE SLIGHTLY	NEUTRAL	DISAGREE SLIGHTLY	DISAGREE VERY MUCH	TOTALLY DISAGREE

10. Everything I do can cause serious problems.

TOTALLY AGREE	AGREE VERY MUCH	AGREE SLIGHTLY	NEUTRAL	DISAGREE SLIGHTLY	DISAGREE VERY MUCH	TOTALLY DISAGREE

11. I am often close to causing harm.

TOTALLY AGREE	AGREE VERY MUCH	AGREE SLIGHTLY	NEUTRAL	DISAGREE SLIGHTLY	DISAGREE VERY MUCH	TOTALLY DISAGREE

12. I must protect others from harm.

TOTALLY AGREE	AGREE VERY MUCH	AGREE SLIGHTLY	NEUTRAL	DISAGREE SLIGHTLY	DISAGREE VERY MUCH	TOTALLY DISAGREE

13. I should never cause even the slightest harm to others.

TOTALLY AGREE	AGREE VERY MUCH	AGREE SLIGHTLY	NEUTRAL	DISAGREE SLIGHTLY	DISAGREE VERY MUCH	TOTALLY DISAGREE

14. I will be condemned for my actions.

TOTALLY AGREE	AGREE VERY MUCH	AGREE SLIGHTLY	NEUTRAL	DISAGREE SLIGHTLY	DISAGREE VERY MUCH	TOTALLY DISAGREE

15. If I can have even a slight influence on things going wrong, then I must act to prevent it.

TOTALLY AGREE	AGREE VERY MUCH	AGREE SLIGHTLY	NEUTRAL	DISAGREE SLIGHTLY	DISAGREE VERY MUCH	TOTALLY DISAGREE

16. To me, not acting where disaster is a slight possibility, is as bad as making that disaster happen.

TOTALLY AGREE	AGREE VERY MUCH	AGREE SLIGHTLY	NEUTRAL	DISAGREE SLIGHTLY	DISAGREE VERY MUCH	TOTALLY DISAGREE

17. For me, even slight carelessness is inexcusable when it might affect other people.

TOTALLY AGREE	AGREE VERY MUCH	AGREE SLIGHTLY	NEUTRAL	DISAGREE SLIGHTLY	DISAGREE VERY MUCH	TOTALLY DISAGREE

18. In all kinds of daily situations, my inactivity can cause as much harm as deliberately bad intentions.

TOTALLY AGREE	AGREE VERY MUCH	AGREE SLIGHTLY	NEUTRAL	DISAGREE SLIGHTLY	DISAGREE VERY MUCH	TOTALLY DISAGREE

19. Even if harm is a very unlikely possibility, I should always try to prevent it at any cost.

TOTALLY AGREE	AGREE VERY MUCH	AGREE SLIGHTLY	NEUTRAL	DISAGREE SLIGHTLY	DISAGREE VERY MUCH	TOTALLY DISAGREE

20. Once I think it is possible that I have caused harm, I can't forgive myself.

TOTALLY AGREE	AGREE VERY MUCH	AGREE SLIGHTLY	NEUTRAL	DISAGREE SLIGHTLY	DISAGREE VERY MUCH	TOTALLY DISAGREE

21. Many of my past actions have been intended to prevent harm to others.

TOTALLY AGREE	AGREE VERY MUCH	AGREE SLIGHTLY	NEUTRAL	DISAGREE SLIGHTLY	DISAGREE VERY MUCH	TOTALLY DISAGREE

22. I have to make sure other people are protected from all the consequences of my actions.

TOTALLY AGREE	AGREE VERY MUCH	AGREE SLIGHTLY	NEUTRAL	DISAGREE SLIGHTLY	DISAGREE VERY MUCH	TOTALLY DISAGREE

23. Other people should not rely on my judgement.

TOTALLY AGREE	AGREE VERY MUCH	AGREE SLIGHTLY	NEUTRAL	DISAGREE SLIGHTLY	DISAGREE VERY MUCH	TOTALLY DISAGREE

24. If I cannot be *certain* I am blameless, I feel that I am to blame.

TOTALLY AGREE	AGREE VERY MUCH	AGREE SLIGHTLY	NEUTRAL	DISAGREE SLIGHTLY	DISAGREE VERY MUCH	TOTALLY DISAGREE

25. If I take sufficient care then I can prevent harmful accidents.

TOTALLY AGREE	AGREE VERY MUCH	AGREE SLIGHTLY	NEUTRAL	DISAGREE SLIGHTLY	DISAGREE VERY MUCH	TOTALLY DISAGREE

26. I often think that bad things will happen if I am not careful enough.

TOTALLY AGREE	AGREE VERY MUCH	AGREE SLIGHTLY	NEUTRAL	DISAGREE SLIGHTLY	DISAGREE VERY MUCH	TOTALLY DISAGREE

Scoring the RAS

For each item score:

1 for '*Totally agree*'
2 for '*Agree very much*'
3 for '*Agree slightly*'
4 for '*Neutral*'
5 for '*Disagree slightly*'
6 for '*Disagree very much*'
7 for '*Totally disagree*'

The total score is the sum of all the items.

Problem and Goal Sheet

Problem	Date	Date	Date	Date
	Rating	Rating	Rating	Rating
	Date	Date	Date	Date
	Rating	Rating	Rating	Rating

Rate the severity of your emotional problem 0–10, where 0 = no distress/no impairment in ability to function and 10 = extreme distress/virtually unable to function in any area of life.

Goal	Date	Date	Date	Date
	Rating	Rating	Rating	Rating
	Date	Date	Date	Date
	Rating	Rating	Rating	Rating

Rate how close you are to achieving your goal 0–10, where 0 = no progress whatsoever and 10 = goal achieved and sustained constantly.

Appendix 4

Self-Ratings for Obsessions and Rituals

1 Description
Brief description of the most troublesome intrusive thought, image, or urge, and the most troublesome compulsions and rituals being rated:

Thought, image, or urge _____

_____

Compulsions and rituals _____

_____

2 Specific ratings
Please rate the above thought and compulsions/rituals on each of the following scales, according to how they have been *in the past week.*

(a) Distress experienced:

0	1	2	3	4	5	6	7	8	THOUGHT	☐
Absent		Slight		Moderate		Marked		Extreme	RITUAL	☐

(b) Interference caused in your life:

0	1	2	3	4	5	6	7	8	THOUGHT	☐
Absent		Slight		Moderate		Marked		Extreme	RITUAL	☐

(c) Please estimate, on average, how long each day you are troubled by the intrusive thoughts and compulsions:

THOUGHT _____ hours _____ minutes

RITUAL _____ hours _____ minutes

3 Avoidance
Please estimate the overall severity of avoidance.

0	1	2	3	4	5	6	7	8	☐
Not at all		Slight		Moderate		Marked		Extreme	

The Hospital Anxiety and Depression Scale (HADS)

The depression subscale has been reproduced by kind permission of Dr Snaith. The scale was first published in Zigmond, A. and Snaith, R.P. 'The Hospital Anxiety and Depression Scale', *Acta Psychiatrica Scandinavica*, 67, (1983), 361–70.

Answer each question as described below, and add up your scores.

Please read each group of statements carefully, and then pick *one* statement (by circling the number beside it) that comes closest to how you have been feeling in the past week. Don't take too long over your replies: your immediate reaction to each item will probably be more accurate than a lengthy thought-out response.

1 I still enjoy the things I used to enjoy:
   0   Definitely as much
   1   Not quite so much
   2   Only a little
   3   Hardly at all

2 I can laugh and see the funny side of things:
   0   As much as I always could
   1   Not quite so much now
   2   Definitely not so much now
   3   Not at all

3 I feel cheerful:
   3   Not at all
   2   Not often
   1   Sometimes
   0   Most of the time

4 I feel as if I am slowed down:
   3   Nearly all the time
   2   Very often

1   Sometimes
0   Not at all

5 I have lost interest in my appearance:
    3   Definitely
    2   I don't take so much care as I should
    1   I may not take quite as much care
    0   I take just as much care as ever

6 I look forward to things:
    0   As much as I ever did
    1   Somewhat less than I used to
    2   Definitely less than I used to
    3   Hardly at all

7 I can enjoy a good book, radio or TV program:
    0   Often
    1   Sometimes
    2   Not often
    3   Very seldom

TOTAL SCORE ___

Scoring Instructions

Statements are summed to produce the total score for the depression subscale. The range of scores for the depression subscale is 0–21.

  0–7 = normal

  8–10 = mild disorder

11–14 = moderate disorder

15–21 = severe disorder

Appendix 5

Progress Charts

Hierarchy of exposure to feared triggers

Trigger (object, word, place, person, situation, substance)	Estimated anxiety or distress (0–100%)	Actual anxiety at end (0–100%)

Appendix 5

Obsessions and Compulsions Record Sheet

Trigger	Intrusive thought (words, image, doubt, impulse)	Interpretation – What the intrusive thought meant to me	Response – What I did (compulsions or safety behaviors)	Alternative response or behavioral experiment

Theory A or Theory B?

Write out your two theories below to explain your problems:

Theory A _____

_____

_____

_____

Theory B _____

_____

_____

_____

Behavioral Experiment

Prediction	Experiment	Result	Conclusion from results of the experiment

Appendix 5

Cost–Benefit Analysis Form

Option 1 _____

Short-term cost	Short-term benefit
To myself	To myself
To others	To others

Long-term cost	Long-term benefit
To myself	To myself
To others	To others

Appendix 5

Option 2 _____

Short-term cost	Short-term benefit
To myself	To myself
To others	To others
Long-term cost	Long-term benefit
To myself	To myself
To others	To others

Appendix 5

My Formulation

Factors that increased my vulnerability to OCD: for example, early life experiences, a family history of OCD or mental health problems, or aspects of my personality

The attitudes, beliefs, and rules that drive my OCD

Triggers that set off my OCD or make it worse

Appendix 5

A Model of OCD: The 'Vicious Flower' Diagram

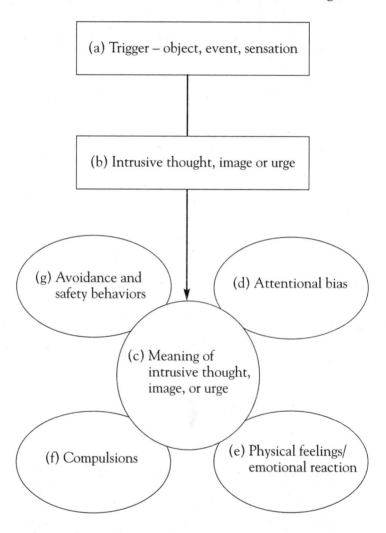

Frequency Record

Day/Date: _____ DAILY FREQUENCY RECORD OF _____ (RITUAL)

R = Urge to ritualize resisted, E = Ritual followed by exposure, U = Unable to resist ritual

		Total frequency for the day
Midnight–6 a.m.		R ☐
6–7 a.m.		
7–8 a.m.		
8–9 a.m.		
9–10 a.m.		E ☐
10–11 a.m.		
11–noon		
Noon–1 p.m.		
1–2 p.m.		U ☐
2–3 p.m.		
3–4 p.m.		
4–5 p.m.		
5–6 p.m.		
6–7 p.m.		
7–8 p.m.		
8–9 p.m.		
9–10 p.m.		
10 p.m.–Midnight		

Relapse Prevention Worksheet

What have been the most helpful things you've learned that have helped you overcome your OCD?

_____

_____

_____

_____

_____

What have been the most helpful techniques you've applied in overcoming your OCD?

_____

_____

_____

_____

_____

What do you think are events or situations that might trigger a setback?

_____

_____

_____

_____

_____

How could you plan to tackle these events or situations to minimize their impact?

_____

_____

_____

_____

_____

What could you do to practise coping with them?

_____

_____

_____

_____

_____

In order for you to maintain your gains what are the main things you need to work on?

_____

_____

_____

_____

Index

Numbers in bold indicate tables; those in italics indicate figures.

Index

Index

Index

Index

Index

Index

Index

About the Authors

DAVID VEALE, FRCPsych, MD, BSc, MPhil, Dip CACP is a consultant psychiatrist at The Priory Hospital, North London, and an Honorary Senior Lecturer in the Department of Mental Health Sciences at the Royal Free and University College Medical School, University College, London. He is an accredited cognitive behavior therapist and his main research and clinical interests are in obsessive compulsive disorder (OCD) and body dysmorphic disorder (BDD). He has written approximately forty publications and has sat on the National Institute for Clinical Excellence (NICE) group, which provides national guidelines for treating OCD in the UK. A former chair of the charity OCD Action (www.ocdaction.org. uk), he remains on their committee and is involved in organizing an annual conference for individuals with OCD and anxiety disorders (www.anxiety conference.org.uk).

ROB WILLSON BSc is a cognitive behavior therapist in private practice. He also works at the Priory Hospital, North London and is a visiting tutor at Goldsmiths College, University of London. He holds an honours degree in psychology, an MSc in rational emotive behavior therapy, and a postgraduate diploma in social and behavioral health studies. He has been involved in treating individuals with OCD for the past eleven years and his main clinical interests are in OCD and BDD, the application of cognitive behavior therapy in groups, and the value of acceptance in helping to achieve change.

Order further books in the *Overcoming* series

No. of copies	Title	Price	Total
	Anger and Irritability	£7.99	
	Anorexia Nervosa	£7.99	
	Anxiety	£7.99	
	Bulimia Nervosa and Binge-Eating	£7.99	
	Childhood Trauma	£7.99	
	Chronic Fatigue	£9.99	
	Depression	£7.99	
	Low Self-Esteem	£7.99	
	Mood Swings	£7.99	
	Panic	£7.99	
	Relationship Problems	£9.99	
	Sexual Problems	£9.99	
	Social Anxiety and Shyness	£7.99	
	Traumatic Stress	£7.99	
	Weight Problems	£9.99	
	Your Smoking Habit	£9.99	
	P&P & Insurance		£2.50
	Grand Total		£

Name: _____

Address: _____

_____ Postcode: _____

Daytime Tel. No. / Email _____
(in case of query)

Three ways to pay:
1. **For express service telephone the TBS order line on 01206 255 800 and quote 'CRBK1'. Order lines are open Monday–Friday 8:30a.m. – 5:30p.m.**

2. I enclose a cheque made payable to **TBS Ltd** for £_____

3. Please charge my ❏ Visa ❏ Mastercard ❏ Amex ❏ Switch (switch issue no. ....) £_____

   Card number: _____

   Expiry date: _____ Signature _____
   (your signature is essential when paying by credit card)

Please return forms (*no stamp required*) to, Constable & Robinson Ltd, FREEPOST NAT6619, 3 The Lanchesters, 162 Fulham Palace Road, London W6 9BR. All books subject to availability.

Enquiries to readers@constablerobinson.com
www.constablerobinson.com

Constable & Robinson Ltd (directly or via its agents) may mail or phone you about promotions or products. Tick box if you do not want these from us ❏ or our subsidiaries.